SUSTAINABLE
CONCRETE
ARCHITECTURE

David Bennett

RIBA ✳ **Publishing**

© David Bennett, 2010

Published by RIBA Publishing, 15 Bonhill Street, London EC2P 2EA

ISBN 978 1 85946 352 9

Stock code 69976

The right of David Bennett to be identified as the Author of this Work has been asserted in accordance with the Copyright, Design and Patents Act 1988.

All rights reserved. No part of this publication may be reproduced, stored in a retrieval system, or transmitted, in any form or by any means, electronic, mechanical, photocopying, recording or otherwise, without prior permission of the copyright owner.

British Library Cataloguing in Publications Data
A catalogue record for this book is available from the British Library.

Publisher: Steven Cross
Commissioning Editor: Matthew Thompson
Project editor: Alasdair Deas
Designed and typeset by Kneath Associates
Printed and bound by Polestar Wheatons, Exeter

While every effort has been made to check the accuracy and quality of the information given in this publication, neither the Author nor the Publisher accept any responsibility for the subsequent use of this information, for any errors or omissions that it may contain, or for any misunderstandings arising from it.

RIBA Publishing is part of RIBA Enterprises Ltd.

www.ribaenterprises.com

Cover image: Photo © Sarah Blee

CONTENTS

PREFACE

This book illustrates the 'state of the art' in sustainable construction using concrete to create visually exciting, energy-efficient buildings fit for adaptation to climate change.

The wide range of case studies is supported by in-depth technical analysis and explanation of the benefits of using this versatile but complex building material to deliver sustainable projects.

Many of the raw materials may be familiar to the reader, but derivation of their embodied CO_2 may not be. For example, there are low-carbon cements available, masonry blocks that are carbon neutral, aggregates that are low carbon and formwork that can be reused in the permanent architecture to sequester CO_2. These materials, their details and their descriptions, and many more, are comprehensively covered in the book.

As designers we have a responsibility to specify buildings that have low CO_2 emissions, both in their construction and in their long-term energy performance. This book provides the guidance to make it possible, whether it's concrete, steel, timber or plastic, and will help you to make informed decisions on CO_2 and low-energy systems with reasonable accuracy and confidence.

It would have been ideal to have all the CO_2 data for construction materials validated and checked. The data included is the best fit average from the sources available at the time of writing. It will only get better if all manufacturers throughout the supply chain are required to audit their products responsibly for CO_2 emissions.

I would like to thank The Concrete Centre for their technical support in the production of this publication; the manufacturers Castle Cement, Aggregate Industries, Civil and Marine, UKQAA, London Concrete, BRC, Celsa, UPM Kymmene, Lignacite and RockTron, for providing detailed product information; Cundall, for supplying the services data; Mansell Construction, for providing plant and labour data for the construction CO_2 audit; and finally the architects who provided the case study material and the building energy data, which have made this book come alive.

David Bennett

June 2010

INTRODUCTION

GLOBAL WARMING AND CARBON DIOXIDE

Turn over the sheet of a newspaper today, or the glossy pages of a topical magazine, and you will find reference to greenhouse gases, global warming, rising sea levels and the rapidly receding polar ice caps somewhere on the page. These are not freak events due to transient or seasonal phenomena, such as solar flares, a meteorite shower, a tsunami, an earthquake or a volcanic eruption, after which the climate returns to normality. The increase in greenhouse gases is permanent, and has been building up over the past 500 years as a result of the burning of fossil fuels and the deforestation of vast tracts of land. Significant sources of greenhouse gases include the extraction of oil and gas, the excavation of mineral ore and precious stones, gas emissions of the internal combustion engine, discharges from the manufacture of industrial and household goods and the building of houses and offices.

As responsible designers and builders of the future, we all wish to find ways to sustain our planet and to reduce global warming by designing buildings that are energy efficient and by constructing buildings that have a small carbon footprint. It really is that simple, but getting to the core of the issue has been clouded by misconceptions, and the rather short-term outlook advocated in some published guidance notes may generate no real long-term benefits.

If we simply assess a raw material's embodied carbon dioxide (CO_2) and use that figure to find a green building solution, we may be ignoring many other major factors. This is true for all building materials, whether concrete, steel, timber or masonry. Timber, for example, may be carbon neutral, but it has to be felled, logged, cut, processed, treated, transported, assembled on site, supported on a foundation, framed with glass, pinned, glued, clad, roofed and lined to be useful. A building may contain miles of electrical cabling, plastic conduits and metal ducting for heating and ventilation, insulation, carpets, lighting, painted walls and ceilings, plaster and plasterboard linings, a sprinkler system, switches, plugs, boilers for heating water, and so forth. We need to measure the CO_2 emissions from all of these components as well.

And how are the components assembled during the construction of a building? It requires people, vehicles, scaffolding, machines and mechanical plant. People have to journey to and from their workplace every day, often by car, so how much CO_2 is contained in those car emissions? Materials are delivered to the site by road transport, and we may hire mechanical plant for excavation and for lifting and placing materials; this all requires fuel and creates CO_2 emissions. This is the bigger picture during the construction phase.

But the argument prevails that, because these components are common for buildings of the same height and plan area, why bother to measure all these items when there is a direct benefit from using a carbon-neutral material in the frame! It is the same argument put forward about the food we eat if we want to keep slim. It's the calorie count that's important, not the fact that the food is organic. Therefore, we must measure and assess all the CO_2 emissions in the construction phase, not just those of a few materials in isolation.

We also know that up to 95 per cent of the CO_2 emissions from a building are generated by the energy consumed during the life of the building and not by the materials used in its construction. This energy consumption is created by the need for heating, lighting and running electrical appliances, which will continue for 30 years or more for a typical building. It makes sense to also focus our green building design on the long-term reductions, such as by using thermal mass. In the future, as we specify more energy-efficient buildings and reduce our dependence on fossil fuels, CO_2 emissions in the construction phase will become just as critical.

A certain amount of greenhouse gas in the atmosphere, principally CO_2, is not at all bad for the planet, and in fact is essential for life – it is responsible for sustaining an average year-round temperature of 14 °C. This is due to the absorption by greenhouse gases of infrared radiation from the earth's surface. If there were no greenhouse gases in the atmosphere, the earth's temperature would plummet by 33 °C and we would not be able to survive. The greenhouse blanket has been created by the presence of methane, water vapour and CO_2 in the atmosphere, discharged by living creatures and microorganisms and from the decay of forests and greenery many thousands of years ago. But now, with the exponential rise in man-made greenhouse gases over the past decades, these gases can no longer be limited by natural reabsorption by algae, plants and plankton, and their levels are escalating out of control.

By and large, chlorofluorocarbons (CFCs) and hydrochlorofluorocarbons (HCFCs) have been banned as coolants for refrigeration and replaced by ecofriendly substitutes, and nitrous oxide emissions have been curbed by legislation and electrostatic screening. However, emissions of CO_2 are still far too high, so we must find simple yet effective ways of reducing them.

The long-term goal is to return to the levels of CO_2 emissions of, say, 1,000 years ago. It may take the next 50 to 100 years, and will require a worldwide agreement on the measures to be taken and a drastic change in Western lifestyles. The present target is a CO_2 concentration in the atmosphere of 300 parts per million (ppm) by volume. If we project forward using current emission levels, but including renewable energy sources and assuming that present policies prevail, we can expect a concentration of around 700 ppm of CO_2 by the year 2100. However, that would rise to 2,000 ppm if we assume the same population growth as in the past decade but we do nothing.

Put another way, that makes everyone in the world responsible on average for 4,200 kg of CO_2 per year at current emissions rates. However, in the USA, each person produces 20,000 kg of CO_2 per year on average – that is a huge deficit to make up. In India, the average is 800 kg per person, so they are in carbon credit, while in the UK the figure is 9,600 kg per person, so we are in deficit. In the Gulf States the average has risen to 90,000 kg per person.

So what are the biggest sources of CO_2 emissions, and how can designers and builders make a telling contribution to their reduction? Of the total CO_2 produced, 32 per cent comes from transport (mainly cars and commercial vehicles); 28 per cent from housing (mainly consumption of gas and electricity); 19 per cent from commerce (consuming mainly gas and electricity); and industrial processes and manufacturing account for 20 per cent. We can say from these figures that the building market is a major contributor to global CO_2 emissions.

Therefore, it is clear that the most significant improvement we can make is to design buildings that consume less energy. The section of this book on heating and cooling (in Chapter 2) will consider the long-term benefits of using passive cooling in summer and utilising concrete's thermal mass to reduce heating and cooling loads. Where economically viable, renewable energy sources could be considered, although they currently show a poor return on investment at today's energy prices. Terms such as admittance, fabric energy storage, embodied CO_2, thermal mass and many more will be fully explained.

Currently, *The Green Guide to Specification* (BRE Press, 2009) and other Building Research Establishment publications that focus on recommendations for sustainable construction consider, in the main, the embodied CO_2 of raw materials and largely ignore the transportation, process and construction CO_2. For example, the green rating of materials is given as A to E rankings, without any indication of the CO_2 per m^3 of the completed building. As a direct result of this, many specifications and designs for sustainable construction, particularly in housing, are written with a bias towards timber-frame construction. The whole CO_2 picture needs to be evaluated; otherwise, there may be no reduction, and even an increase, in CO_2 emissions in the long term.

In the section on assessing CO_2 emissions in construction (in Chapter 2), a simple yet robust approach has been developed to show how to map the carbon footprint of a project, accounting for material delivery mileage, factory production and assembly on site, as well as the embodied CO_2 of the raw and composite materials. There are cements with low embodied CO_2 that can be specified, as well as lightweight aggregates that reduce the thermal conductivity of concrete (so that no insulation is needed) and various other concrete options to help reduce and control CO_2 output. The key to this approach is the willingness and openness of the supply chain and the construction industry to provide data on a project-by-project basis.

The small but important group of companies that have assisted in providing the construction data for this book have shown how useful this can be in revealing which components are the most critical and what is the best way to manage CO_2 emissions. It is a balance between designing buildings with lower embodied CO_2, reducing material wastage and ensuring the lowest long-term energy consumption.

The contributions from the architects and engineers whose projects are detailed and illustrated in the case studies provide the hard evidence and practical information on how to deliver elegant, low-carbon, concrete building designs with success and at an affordable price.

HOW TO USE THIS BOOK

This book is divided into two parts. Part I covers in detail the materials and technology issues affecting the embodied CO_2 of buildings, while Part II presents real-world examples of sustainable concrete architecture.

Chapter 1 describes the various materials and products (and their manufacture and processing) that are common in reinforced concrete and concrete masonry construction. At the end of each descriptive section, the embodied CO_2 of the material is given. If a CO_2 material audit has been undertaken by the manufacturer the CO_2 figure quoted will be accurate for that product or process. In all other cases, the CO_2 figures shown are based on the published data summarised in Table A.1 (see the Appendix to Part I), based on desk research. The CO_2 values are not product-specific for a particular supplier – a steel fabricator or brick manufacturer, for

example – nor are they validated for transport or production CO_2; rather, they are generalised best-fit approximations from published data and therefore contain some degree of inaccuracy. Table A.2 (see the Appendix to Part I) presents validated CO_2 data for specific manufacturers' products.

The Construction CO_2 Audit shows how to calculate a building's total CO_2 emission at the end of the construction phase. This will give valuable insight and better understanding about which building elements bump up CO_2 and which frame materials offer better CO_2 management in both the short term and the long term.

Chapter 2 covers heating and cooling of buildings, and how to use concrete's thermal mass to reduce long-term energy consumption in residential and office building. Various forms of concrete construction are reviewed, along with different ways to heat and cool office buildings, from using passive and naturally ventilated systems to chilled beams and forced ventilation systems, including ducted air, radiant cooling and ground source heat pumps.

Part II contains twenty-four superbly illustrated and detailed case studies, from private houses to apartment buildings, from schools to universities, galleries to museums, visitor centres to office buildings. Each case study has a statement on the building's energy efficiency, energy rating and CO_2 emmisions. This is the compelling evidence that sustainable concrete architecture is the future for low-energy, green building design and why architects and designers should turn to concrete for their solutions.

ESTIMATING
CONSTRUCTION
CO_2

01

CEMENT AND CEMENT REPLACEMENTS

CEMENT MANUFACTURE

A number of different types of cement are available, but the most common is Portland cement. This was named by its inventor, Joseph Aspdin, after its supposed resemblance to Portland stone when set. Portland cement has been produced for over 150 years and is available worldwide. It is important to know how cement is manufactured in order to understand why the production CO_2 emissions are so large and how cement makers try to reduce them.

The manufacture of Portland cement is a closely controlled process, akin to large-scale chemical engineering. The principal ingredients are a source of calcareous material, typically limestone or chalk, which makes up about 80 per cent of the raw material, and a source of silica – either clay or shale. A pinch of sand and iron oxide are added to optimise the chemistry.

Chalk-based cements are produced in the southern half of the UK, from Lincolnshire and the Wash down to the south coast, where chalk is available. Limestone-based cements are produced in the rocky regions of the South West, Wales, central and northern England and Scotland.

The energy consumption and energy efficiency of cement production vary between different manufacturing plants. The 'dry process' of manufacture is the most energy-efficient method and the one that most plants use.

During the calcing process, all the CO_2 trapped in the raw ingredients is released, allowing the remaining elements to fuse together and form cement. This produces a far harder, stronger and more durable material than lime or lime mortar, which is essentially a weak bonding material for stonework and brickwork.

In the dry process, the raw materials are introduced without additional water. The ingredients are finely ground and blended (homogenised) in the optimum proportions. The homogenised materials may then be preheated in a flow of hot kiln exhaust gases prior to being placed into the cement kiln. This preheating dries the materials, and in the similar but more efficient process known as precalcining it also decarbonates the majority of the calcium carbonate in the limestone or chalk. The dry materials are then heated in a rotating kiln to a temperature of around 1,500 °C. At this temperature the homogenised raw materials are partially melted, but there is a complete transformation of the mineral assemblage. The partial melting combined with the rotation of the kiln produces a granular material known as cement clinker. The raw materials remain in the kiln for about half an hour in a precalcined, dry process system.

Below
Locations of UK cement works

● **Lafarge Cement UK**
1   Dunbar
2   Hope
3   Cauldon
4   Aberthaw
5   Westbury
6   Northfleet
7   Cookstown
8   Barnstone

▲ **Cemex**
9   South Ferriby
10 Rugby
11 Barrington

■ **Castle Cement**
12 Ketton
13 Padeswood
14 Ribblesdale

☀ **Buxton Lime Industries**
15 Tunstead

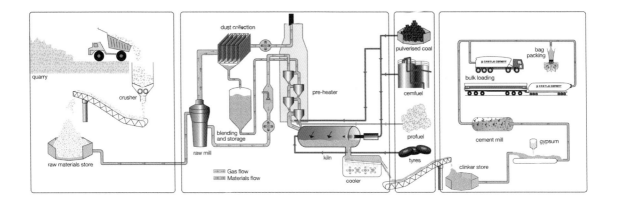

TYPES OF CEMENT

Although Portland cement is by far the most widely used cement, the European standard for common cements, BS EN 197-1, lists a total of 11 different groups of factory-produced cement in common use in Europe. All these cements contain a proportion of Portland cement clinker, but not all of them are available in the UK. Cements produced commercially throughout the UK are:

— Portland cement (CEM I), sometimes also known as PC or ordinary Portland cement (OPC); this group also includes white Portland cement

— Portland-flyash cement (CEM II/A-V, CEM II/B-V)

— Portland-limestone cement (CEM II/A-LL, CEM II/B-LL).

The following cement types are also produced in some areas of the UK:

— blastfurnace cement (CEM III/A, CEM III/B, CEM III/C)

— Portland-slag cement (CEM II/A-S, CEM II/B-S).

In addition to these groups, there are also sulphate-resisting Portland cement (SRPC), which is still covered by a residual British Standard (BS 4027), and masonry cement, covered by BS EN 413-1.

Embodied CO_2
Portland cement CEM I, general ex works
930 kg CO_2/tonne

CASE STUDY :
SUSTAINABLE CEMENT PRODUCTION AT RIBBLESDALE WORKS

Iain Wallpole, Castle Cement

Introduction

Ribblesdale Works commenced cement production in the 1930s using limestone quarried locally from Lanehead Quarry. The works presently produce around 800,000 tonnes of cement using a single in-line calciner kiln. The clinker produced by this kiln is ground in closed-circuit ball mills to make cement.

Cement is made to a precise recipe. At Ribblesdale the raw materials are mainly limestone and shale together with sandstone, pulverised fuel ash (PFA) and iron oxide. The limestone and shale, which make up around 90 per cent of the raw materials, are quarried on site at Ribblesdale, and sandstone is supplied from local quarries within a few miles of the works. The other minor component, PFA, is sourced from power stations within 50 miles of the works.

Where possible, Ribblesdale Works utilises wastes in place of the natural raw materials. MRM (Mineral Resource Management), a sister company of Castle Cement, is responsible for identifying and sourcing waste streams that have the correct chemical composition for use in cement making. The materials currently used include waste foundry sands, sea shells and water treatment sludge.

Above
Cement
manufacturing
process

Manufacturing process

Cement manufacture is energy intensive and therefore an environmentally sensitive process. Cement kilns are, however, capable of using a wide range of fuels, from gas and flammable liquids to solid fuels such as coal.

Following quarrying, the constituent raw materials are crushed and blended, then ground together to a fine powder (raw meal). The raw meal is transported to the top of the preheater and then descends through the preheater tower, where it is heated by the hot gases rising from the rotary kiln. The meal passes though a series of cyclone furnaces, raising the temperature to 900 °C, causing combustion of the carbon present in the raw materials, principally the quarried shale and PFA. At this point the meal enters the calciner, where the calcium carbonate in the limestone is calcined, releasing CO_2; this represents around 500 kg CO_2 per tonne of cement and is essentially irreducible.

The calcined material then enters the rotary kiln and is heated to about 1,450 °C by direct heating. At this temperature complex chemical reactions take place and calcium silicates are formed. The heated material balls up into nodules, which vary in size from 50 mm diameter down to dust. This is called clinker. The clinker is cooled, then ground with about 5 per cent gypsum to make the familiar grey powder that is cement.

The principal active components of cement are calcium silicates, such as $3CaO \cdot SiO_2$ and $2CaO \cdot SiO_2$. These components react with water to form calcium silicate hydrates, which harden. Cement is used to bind together sand particles to make mortar, or sand and aggregate particles to make concrete. The presence of water is essential to the proper setting of cement in concrete or mortar. The basic product, known as ordinary Portland cement (OPC), takes upwards of 28 days to achieve its full strength potential.

Fuels

Ribblesdale Works utilises coal, Cemfuel – a highly specified liquid fuel manufactured from industrial wastes such as paint, ink residues, waste solvents and resins – shredded tyres and meat and bonemeal. The Ribblesdale kiln uses approximately 60 per cent of the fuel in the

Left
Pro-Fuel

Left
Shredded tyres
used as fuel

calciner and 40 per cent in the main kiln burner. Coal represents around 50 per cent of the total fuel consumption; it is sourced on the world market and delivered by rail. The waste-derived fuels are all supplied by road from within a 100-mile radius of the works. The use of waste as a fuel is essentially carbon neutral as it replaces a fossil fuel and prevents the production of methane that would occur if the organic waste were disposed to landfill. Ribblesdale Works uses over 100,000 tonnes of fossil fuel per year and the net CO_2 emissions from the fuel amount to 136 kg CO_2 per tonne of cement, excluding biomass and organic waste.

This level of emissions from the combustion of fuel and from the raw materials means the net direct emission of CO_2 is 705 kg per tonne of cement (CEM I) produced.

Indirect CO_2 emissions

The main indirect CO_2 emission from the production of cement is that resulting from the consumption of electricity. This is mainly used in the crushing and grinding of raw materials and the cement, and by the fans used to transport the gases through the kiln system. Ribblesdale Works uses over 100,000 MWh of electricity per year. Assuming UK grid electricity average emission factors, the CO_2 from electrical power consumption is equivalent to 80 kg per tonne of cement.

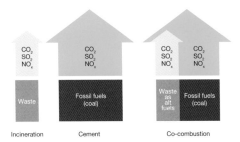

Incineration   Cement   Co-combustion

Other indirect CO_2 emissions, such as the transportation of fuels and raw materials to the works (2.5 kg/tonne cement) and employees' travelling (less than 0.1 kg/tonne cement), are negligible when compared with the direct emissions from the manufacturing process.

Embodied CO_2 – Ribblesdale Works

Cement CEM I, delivered to ready-mixed plants: 782 kg CO_2/tonne.

This is inclusive of factory, plant, employee travel and delivery mileage.

CO_2 reabsorption factor: remember that when mixed in concrete, cement will absorb CO_2 from the atmosphere. The estimated absorption is around 20–30 per cent after 60 years for a dense concrete, and will continue even when it is crushed during and after demolition. Therefore, the net CO_2 embodied in cement is actually 70 per cent of the calculated figure. This applies to all Portland cements but not PFA or GGBS cements.

(See Appendix: Table A.6, Ribblesdale Works CO_2 audit, for further details.)

CEMENT REPLACEMENTS, AKA THE 'ECO-CEMENTS'

Forty years ago, ground granulated blastfurnace slag (GGBS) was virtually unheard of in the UK construction industry. It was only available from a single source at Scunthorpe, with production and sales reaching a meagre 25,000 tonnes per year. Today, the situation is very different and now nearly 50 per cent of all ready-mixed concrete supplied to sites contains GGBS. GGBS is readily available throughout Great Britain.

Pulverised fuel ash (PFA), produced from coal-burning power stations, has also been used in concrete for many years. The basic properties of PFA are pozzolanic; that is, it reacts with lime to form a hardened paste. In modern times, the use of PFA in concrete was pioneered in the 1930s in the USA. PFA was first used in the UK in the 1940s, in dam construction in Scotland, following successful research work carried out by the University of Glasgow. The variability of fly ash in terms of its fineness, carbon content and lack of quality control proved problematic until the 1970s, so its uptake was spasmodic. PFA is now used in about 20 per cent of ready-mixed concrete consumed in the UK, where it is used as binder at 30 per cent replacement. Currently, around 500,000 tonnes of PFA per annum is used in ready-mixed and precast concrete production.

This expanding use of both PFA and GGBS in concrete has been driven by their low cost, reduced early-age temperature rise and greater resistance to alkali–silica reaction, chloride ingress and sulphate attack; and, more recently, by the significant reduction in embodied CO_2 they offer.

There are reserves of both PFA and GGBS to satisfy future demand for cement replacements, but there is always the opportunity to develop new cements with low embodied CO_2 using other waste materials and non-carbonate materials. The good news is that there is considerable optimism that more cements with

Glasgow

Teeside

Belfast

Scunthorpe

Port Talbot
Llanwern   Purfleet

low CO_2 emissions, and even carbon-neutral concretes, will be available in the next few years. For example, ConGlassCrete, which contains recycled crushed glass – beer bottles, wine bottles, car windscreens and windows – has proven its effectiveness as a cement replacement through exhaustive and rigorous testing. RockTron, a new cement company, recovers PFA from landfill sites at a coal-burning power station. Its product has just come onto the market. Pioneering new cements with great promise, based on magnesium oxide or geopolymers extracted from oil-based residues, all of which are low embodied CO_2 cements, may become commercially viable in the next few years, making 'green' concrete very competitive on price.

The main concern in this section is how we can reduce the embodied CO_2 of concrete right now using the cements that are currently available, but we must also be aware of new cements that will soon be available.

Ground granulated blastfurnace slag (GGBS)

Manufacture

Blastfurnace slag is a waste product from the manufacture of pig iron for steel making. It consists of lime, silica and alumina, and has

a similar chemical composition to Portland cement. The raw materials going into a blastfurnace are iron ore, limestone and coke; the products emerging are iron and blastfurnace slag. These two products separate naturally at a temperature of approximately 1,500 °C, the heavier iron sinks to the bottom of the furnace and the molten slag is taken off from the top.

To be used as a cement replacement, the slag has to be quenched with water so that it solidifies as a glass, preventing it crystallising. The rapid cooling of the slag results in its fragmentation into a granulated material, which is then finely ground and sold as a bulk material, just like cement.

Although GGBS has the same fineness as Portland cement, it has a much lower early strength gain. GGBS cement will reach the same long-term strength as Portland cement provided the GGBS content is no more than 50 per cent. Some guidance documents suggest GGBS can be as much as 70 per cent

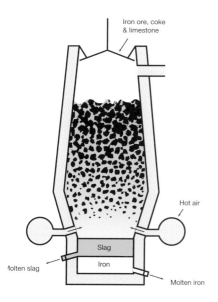

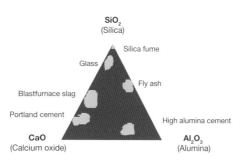

replacement. That is ideal for use in deep foundations, to reduce temperature rise, but there are other restrictions and secondary effects which need to be fully addressed at this level of replacement. Above 70 per cent replacement, GGBS cement may take a considerable time to harden, and when GGBS reaches 100 per cent it is unlikely to set at all.

Cement chemistry

GGBS will not set by itself if mixed with water, it has to be activated by the hydration products of Portland cement to kick-start its hydration. Once started, the further hydration of GGBS does not need the liberation of calcium hydroxide compounds from Portland cement to keep the reaction going.

GGBS blended with Portland cement at 50 per cent replacement has similar properties to Portland cement as regards fineness and soundness. It will have lower heat gain during hydration compared with a pure Portland cement, which is useful in mass concrete pours or thick wall sections, where temperature rise has to be restricted. In cold temperatures, the low heat gain coupled with a moderate rate of early strength gain can lead to frost damage, and therefore extended curing times will be necessary before formwork can be removed. The high sulphate resistance and lower permeability of GGBS cement make it ideal in seawall construction.

Blastfurnace slag is very consistent in chemical composition because iron blast furnaces are very sensitive and need to be fed with a very consistent mix of raw materials. The blast furnace engineers analyse the slag rather than the iron to control the process. The iron content of GGBS is very low (generally less than 1 per cent, measured as iron oxide) so virtually no iron is incorporated in the chemical structure.

The consistent chemical composition of blastfurnace slag means its colour is also uniform. The granulated slag is a pale yellow colour, and in common with other materials it becomes lighter after grinding. A finer powder creates a more closely packed surface area, increasing the amount of light reflected, and affects how light is scattered and absorbed, creating a lighter colour.

Left
GGBS (left) and
Portland cement

Bleed water and finishing

The setting time for a GGBS concrete is slightly slower than for a Portland cement mix, and often excess bleed water can rise to the surface after compaction, which can hinder surface finishing, trowelling and floating. If left unchecked it may discolour the top level of the concrete permanently. To overcome this risk, the top layer of the concrete may require reworking one to two hours after placement, when it begins to firm up. For this reason GGBS blended mixes are not generally recommended for power-trowelled industrial floors.

Formwork pressure

The slower setting rate of GGBS mixes will increase the hydrostatic pressure gradients on vertical formwork, and this must be considered at the temporary works design stage in line with recommendations of CIRIA Report 108.

Sustainability of GGBS

GGBS cement is probably one of the few 'green' cements available. In comparison with Portland cement, GGBS requires less than 20 per cent of the energy to process and produces less than 10 per cent of the CO_2 emissions. Further 'green' benefits are that no quarrying of virgin materials is required, and if the slag were not used as cement it might have to be disposed of to landfill.

Embodied CO_2
GGBS, ex works: 52 kg CO_2/tonne
This is the energy used in rapidly cooling and then grinding the clinker into fines

Pulverised fuel ash (PFA)

Around 40 per cent of the UK's electricity is derived from coal. The well-publicised issues of security of supply relating to natural gas, the gradual decline of the existing nuclear power station capacity, the timescales involved in building new nuclear power stations and the slow development of renewable forms of electricity generation would appear to mean that coal-fired power generation will be necessary for some years to come. And as there is estimated to be in excess of 200 years' reserves of coal around the world, such an energy resource cannot simply be ignored. The development of clean coal power stations with carbon-capture technology means that coal will continue to be a viable option in the future.

PFA is produced by the burning of powdered (pulverised) coal at power stations. The combustion of pulverised coal at high temperatures produces different types of ash residue. The fine ash fraction is carried upwards with the flue gases but is captured before reaching the atmosphere by highly efficient electrostatic precipitators. This material is PFA or 'fly ash'. It is composed of extremely fine, glassy spheres and looks similar to cement. The coarse ash fraction falls through grates below the boilers, where it is mixed with water and pumped to lagoons. This material, known as furnace bottom ash (FBA), has a gritty, sand-like texture and is not suitable for use in concrete. It is used as a simple fill material.

PFA is a pozzolanic material high in silica, but it differs from GGBS in that it contains little calcium and needs the lime set free from the hydration of Portland cement to form compounds of calcium silicate. For this reason, the levels of PFA replacement in cement are much lower than for GGBS, generally not more than 30 per cent.

PFA will slow the hydration process and the rate of early strength gain, and at the same time beneficially reduce the heat gain of concrete. Its inclusion can reduce the permeability of concrete and increases sulphate resistance. It is ideal for mass concrete, thick wall sections and deep foundations.

The fineness and carbon content of PFA has to be strictly controlled to make it a suitable cement replacement, and only those materials that conform to BS EN 450-1, S and N, Category B carbon content are suitable. (The S designation denotes that the PFA is finer and has water-reducing properties; the N denotes it does not necessarily have water-reducing properties.) Such PFAs can be used as cement replacements provided that the loss on ignition value of the carbon content does not exceed 7.0 per cent and the sulphate content expressed as SO_3 is below 3.0 per cent. The limit of 7.0 per cent is a UK limit, and does not apply in other EU countries, which mostly have a 5.0 per cent limit.

PFA is dark grey in colour; the shade varies depending on the source of the coal and the process plant. The dark colour is due to a combination of the iron compounds present in the coal and carbon residues left after combustion. Colour control is generally not important for sales of PFA, but the product is suitable for architectural concrete mixes when special measures are used to control colour. For example, the requisite amount of product can be blended and stored to ensure colour consistency.

Above
Conditioned PFA – dark grey in colour

Left
PFA under the microscope

There are 18 power stations in the UK from which a number of companies – CEMEX, ScotAsh, Ash Solutions, Castle Cement and Lafarge – are processing and marketing PFA. At the current rate of utilisation, existing stockpiles alone would last for at least 100 years.

Embodied CO_2
PFA: 4 kg CO_2/tonne
This is the factory gate environmental figure

RockTron – superior PFA cement
Philip Michael, RockTron

After two decades of research and development, RockTron has produced an innovative recycling technology that transforms coal-fired power station waste (fly ash) into valuable eco-cements and aggregates on an industrial scale. The new process plant at Fiddler's Ferry in Cheshire can recycle up to 800,000 tonnes of fly ash a year. It is designed to process both fresh and stockpiled fly ash, effectively solving the problems of large scale waste storage and removal, site remediation and conservation of natural resources. Slowly and surely, the unsightly slag heaps of the Welsh and English countryside will disappear, turned into cement replacement, concrete aggregate and inert fill.

The processed PFA, branded RockTron, has superior properties and performance values to a conventional PFA and should enable replacement levels of up to 60 per cent for structural-grade concrete. RockTron's competitive price and low embodied CO_2 will dramatically reduce concrete's carbon footprint and give concrete the 'environmentally friendly' tag it has long sought.

Sustainability impact
Cement and concrete manufacturing accounts for more than 5 per cent of the world's CO_2 emissions, greater even than aviation. Substituting RockTron cement for 50 per cent of Portland cement in ready-mixed concrete and precast concrete products would reduce the industry's impact on global warming. Using 500,000 tonnes of RockTron instead of Portland cement would save over 400,000 tonnes of CO_2 per year in the UK alone.

One of the other major benefits of the RockTron process is its environmental remediation capability. Currently, over 2 billion tonnes of coal-fired power station fly ash waste is dumped in landfill sites worldwide, with over 100 million tonnes dumped in the UK alone. This waste can be taken directly from the power station as it is produced, or more significantly from the 50-year-old stockpiles of fly ash waste, and transformed into valuable, environmentally friendly cement and concrete products.

The RockTron process
Essentially, RockTron uses a traditional mining technology called froth flotation. This process separates and washes the components that make up fly ash to produce new minerals. The overall objective is to process power station fly ash waste from tips, lagoons and fresh arisings to produce economically viable products with no waste or effluent. Historically, BS 3892 and BS EN 450-1 – the British and European standards stipulating the use of fly ash as a cement substitute – emphasise the key measures of particle size and carbon content. Power stations producing fly ash with a high carbon content (due to a high percentage of unburnt coal residues) did not meet this standard and had no alternative but to stockpile and dump this waste. The RockTron process removes the carbon content in these stockpiles to produce an economically viable cementitious alternative that meets the standard, with typically less than 5 per cent loss on ignition (LOI).

The four-stage process is as follows:

— *Conditioning* – Fly ash, either from stockpiled lagoon tailings or direct from power station precipitators, is mixed with water and the slurry pumped into receiving vessels, where gentle agitation and physical separation takes place. Fly ash recovered from tips or lagoons is re-pulped to its original particle size and any extraneous material is removed, so the material has a similar size distribution to a fresh ash. Any soluble salts are removed, thereby improving the surface reactivity.

— *Flotation* – The slurry is mixed with reagents to float off the carbon fraction.

The carbon is dewatered and, if required, flash dried. In filter cake form, the carbon is ideal for mechanical handling and reuse by the power station, ensuring full carbon utilisation. As a high-grade powder product, it has many applications in the metallurgical and chemical industries as well as liquid and gas filtration.

— *Magnetite removal* – Following carbon removal, the remaining alumino-silicate product also contains spherical magnetic particles. The magnetite can be left in, or can be recovered by powerful magnets, creating a new supply of spherical magnetite for applications such as conductive polymers.

— *Classification* – The remaining alumino-silicates are classified into two particle size groups: alpha particles (fine: $d_{50} = 5$–$10 \ \mu$m) and delta particles (coarse: $d_{50} = 60$–$80 \ \mu$m). The product is then dewatered and stored.

Alpha and Delta cements

Conventional fly ash has chemical and physical characteristics that limit its substitution levels due to its relatively low cementitious properties when compared with OPC (CEM I). The RockTron beneficiated Alpha cement is finer and more reactive, thus increasing the cementitious contribution when used with OPC. So, when blends of OPC and Alpha cements are used in concrete for structural applications, the range of strength obtainable with substitution of up to 50 per cent will remain essentially the same. For a given design strength at 28 days, the early strength gains may be slower than a 100 per cent OPC mix, but the longer term strength gain at, say, 56 days will be greater.

For the first time, a fly ash product for use in concrete can be produced with controlled LOI value, high degree of fineness and consistent light colour (rivalling GGBS for colour). Conventional PFAs are dark in colour, and the tint can vary from power station to power station depending on the type of coal being burnt and the nitrous oxide emissions – this is not the case with RockTron.

Thus the construction industry will have a homogenised product of low variability and light colour, available throughout the year, derived from fresh or stored fly ash. The improved characteristics will allow higher levels of cement substitution when compared with normal PFA cement.

The Alpha product, which meets all of the criteria specified in BS EN 450-1:2005+A1: 2007, Class A and Class S, is now undergoing trials at independent test laboratories using substitution levels up to 60 per cent.

The Delta product also has a consistent colour, reliable year-round supply, guaranteed LOI and fineness. This lower density product is targeted at concrete products, including lightweight bricks and precast lightweight panels.

Alpha and Delta cements can be used as CEM II combinations as defined by BS 8500:

— CEM II/A-V:
  substitution of CEM I up to 20 per cent
— CEM II/B-V:
  substitution of CEM I up to 35 per cent
— CEM IV/B-V:
  substitution of CEM I up to 55 per cent.

Despite the proven and established technical benefits of using fly ash in concrete and the fact that fly ash concretes are now recognised as superior in all aspects of durability and long-term strength, some in the industry remain sceptical about the link between LOI and increased strength. However, a correlation between high LOI and high strength has been established. The strength development obtained using 50 per cent CEM I substitution with 1 per cent LOI is the same as for 30 per cent substitution with 7 per cent LOI. The economics and environmental benefits of using low-LOI Alpha cement are self-evident.

Energy data
RockTron recovers three times as much energy as it consumes in the form of carbon for reuse in the power stations.

The embodied carbon for RockTron products is still work in progress, but the indications are that the averaged embodied CO_2 value for RockTron material produced is approx 50 kg CO_2/tonne (cradle to gate calculation).

ConGlassCrete – crushed waste glass as cement replacement

The following section is extracted from a WRAP Research report written by the late Dr Ewan Byers, Centre for Cement and Concrete (CCC), University of Sheffield, and reproduced with permission. The full report is available from WRAP.

This research project, completed in 2002, assesses the chemical properties of waste glass from all waste sources – flat, lighting, bottle glass and fibres – and its suitability as a cement replacement. Borosilicate and cathode-ray tube (CRT) waste glass were specifically excluded from this work. The results have shown that the chemistry of the glass in the waste streams tested had essentially similar major oxide contents. In addition, it was found that the chemistry did not vary significantly between waste glass types or between clean and contaminated sources of a single waste glass.

A comprehensive study of the pozzolanic reaction (which allows normally inert materials to contribute to a concrete's physical and chemical properties) between ground glass and cement was undertaken. Thirty-three recovered glasses from various sources were ground to a range of finesses and used as replacement cement in mortar mixes and the fresh and hardened properties measured. The important findings from this work were as follows:

— Waste glass reactivity in cementitious systems is more related to fineness than the waste glass itself, or the source or the degree of contamination.

— Waste glass ground to a fineness of greater than 300 m²/kg (surface area), irrespective of source, has a strength activity index equivalent to PFA to BS EN 450. A specification for glass as a pozzolana in concrete has been proposed, based on the results obtained on near enough 250 concrete mixes that were tested.

— BRE certification has confirmed the work by overseeing duplicate testing at a UKAS-accredited laboratory and by publishing an independent pre-certification report on glass pozzolanic properties developed from the work at Sheffield.

The information generated in this study has been widely disseminated by a 100-page website (up to 1,000 hits per day), six newsletters, two seminars and two papers.

Waste glass volumes

Tables 1.1 and 1.2 show the 2002 published data on UK production, importation, exportation, consumptions and recovery of container glass. The importation and exportation percentages have been estimated from the assumption that most imports are green wine and beer bottles and most of the exports are clear whisky bottles.

In Table 1.2, the potential arisings for container glass have been estimated from a sorting study carried out on bottle bank samples. The recovery figures were obtained from literature.

Table 1.3 shows the consumptions, arisings and recovery data for flat glass. The automotive glass arisings have been estimated assuming that each of the 1.9 million vehicles scrapped annually has approximately 33 kg of glass. In addition, it has been estimated that car window replacement generates another 15,000 tonnes/year of waste glass. Arisings from building demolition were calculated from the estimation that the glass content of construction and demolition waste is 0.7 per cent. Arisings from other sources (furniture and interior decoration) were estimated assuming that this stream generates arisings similar to those observed for plate and automotive streams (65 per cent).

Certification

Third party pre-certification was sought for glass as a pozzolana and for concrete products containing glass pozzolana and glass aggregates. The first step in the process was to review existing specifications for similar materials (BS EN 450, BS 3892 and ASTM C 311) to develop a working specification for glass pozzolana. BS EN 450, which addresses the physical, chemical and strength performance criteria for fly ash for use in concrete, was selected as the most appropriate model for glass pozzolana.

Based on this, Table 1.4 gives the proposed parameters, criteria and test methods to ensure the quality and performance of glass pozzolana in concrete. Values for chloride content, SO_3, strength activity index, soundness and initial setting times given in BS EN 450 have been retained for glass pozzolana, but others, such as the SiO$_2$ and LOI, have been modified to values typically found in post-consumer glass samples that perform at an appropriate level in concrete. New criteria, such as fineness (surface area) and lead content, have been adopted to ensure the material reaches the BS EN 450 criteria for strength activity index and prohibits contamination by CRTs.

Pre-certification of glass pozzolana was conducted in partnership with BRE, which supervised the UKAS-accredited testing on selected samples of ground glass pozzolana

to corroborate the CCC results. BRE has now produced a pre-certification report stating that ground glass pozzolana is suitable for use as a pozzolanic cement replacement material at levels up to 25 per cent by weight of cementitious material.

Market forces

CCC contacted every local authority in the UK in an attempt to gain intelligence about a potential collaborative glass recycling scheme between the concrete industry and the glass collection sectors. The responses were not encouraging and the majority indicated that collection contracts were already in place. One

Table 1.1.
UK production, importation and exportation of container glass in 2001

Glass colour	Production 10³ tonnes/year	%	Importation 10³ tonnes/year	%	Exportation 10³ tonnes/year	%	Consumption 10³ tonnes/year
Green	323	19	1039	90	−53	10	1335
Amber	272	16					303
Flint	1105	65	115	10	−472	90	691
Total	+1700		+1154		−525		2329

Table 1.2.
UK consumption, arisings and recovery of container glass

Glass colour	Consumption 2001 10³ tonnes/year	%	Arisings 2002 10³ tonnes/year	%	Recovery 2002 10³ tonnes/year	%	Recycling rate
Green	1335	57	1320	60	388	52	29.4
Amber	303	13	286	13	105	14	36.7
Flint	691	30	528	24	254	34	48.8
Other	–	–	66	3	No data	No data	No data
Total	2329		2200		747		38.3

Table 1.3.
UK consumptions, arisings and recovery data for flat glass

Flat type	Consumption 2001 10³ tonnes/year	%	Arisings 2002 10³ tonnes/year	Recovery 2002 10³ tonnes/year	Recycling rate %
Automotive	115	10	78	No data	No data
Plate	805	70	508	No data	No data
Other*	230	20	50	No data	No data
Total	1150		736	180	24.5

*Including furniture and interior applications.

of the major precast concrete partners to the project followed up some of the more positive responses, but concluded that it would not be feasible to progress due to diverse availability and high prices being charged for collection.

That was in 2002; trends have changed since and the market conditions could be opportune for exploitation by the concrete supply industry. The Government and local authorities should offer incentives to encourage the take-up of glass cement in bulk as the embodied CO_2 will be less than that of GGBS cement – around 30 kg/tonne – as it just needs to be crushed.

Embodied CO_2
Estimated to be less than 30 kg CO_2/tonne (cradle to grave)

Magnesium oxide cements

Magnesium oxide cements are claimed to provide a sustainable alternative to Portland cement. They are produced by low-temperature heating or calcination (approx. 650 °C) of naturally occurring minerals, such as magnesite and brucite, precipitated from seawater and brines. When used in porous or semi-

porous materials, such as blocks and pavers, the magnesium oxide in the cement forms carbonates, thus reabsorbing most of the CO_2 emitted during calcining. These are therefore near carbon-neutral cements – but how long must we wait for them to reach the market?

To date, magnesium oxide cements have not been produced in sufficient quantities to allow comparison of manufacturing cost and performance against Portland cement. At Massachusetts Institute of Technology (MIT) researchers found that the calcium-silicate-hydrate nanoparticles of ordinary cement were arranged either in a manner similar to oranges randomly jam-packed in a box or like the pyramidal arrangement of oranges in a grocery store. With these two arrangements, the particles fill approximately 70 per cent of the volume of the cement paste, the rest being water and air. The relative volumes that the nanoparticles occupy in the paste controls the mechanical properties of the cement. MIT researchers are now planning to change the components in cement by substituting magnesium oxide for calcium carbonate so that it takes less heat to make cement but the resulting nanoparticles still have the same packing arrangement as the calcium-silicate-hydrate nanoparticles in Portland cement. They also plan to study

Table 1.4.
Parameters, criteria and methods to guarantee the pozzolanic reactivity of waste glass for use in concrete

Parameters	Criteria	Methods
SiO_2, min %	68	BS 196-2
Fe_2O_3, Al_2O_3, Na_2O, K_2O, CaO and MgO	To be provided	BS 196-2
Chloride, max %	0.1	BS 196-21
Sulfur trioxide (SO_3), max %	3	BS 196-2
Loss on ignition, max %	1.5	BS 196-2
Surface area, min m²/kg	300	BS 196-6
Activity index, min	75% at 28 days	
	85% at 90 days	BS 196-1
Soundness, max expansion	10 mm	BS 196-3
Initial setting time, max	2 h more than control	BS 196-3
Lead, max %	0.1	BS 6748

cement nanoparticles until they understand them at atomic level. This will give them even more freedom to nanoengineer cement in order to make further reductions in CO_2 emissions, allow use of less cement, or give a higher strength for the same volume of cement.

The contribution below on Novacem gives further encouragement that carbon-neutral cement may well be on the market in five years' time. It is sincerely hoped that the raw material deposits of magnesium oxide are not limited nor localised, and that as a binder it outperforms hydraulic lime and asphalt.

Novacem – magnesium oxide cement

Stuart Evans, Chairman Novacem

Novacem is a trade name for a magnesium oxide cement developed in the labs in the basement of Imperial College London's Bessemer Building. Novacem uses magnesium oxide, which together with other mineral additives hardens by rapidly absorbing CO_2 from the atmosphere. There is a plentiful supply of the raw material worldwide; it is not just confined to deposits in a few foreign fields.

The carbon footprint of Novacem production is between a third and a half of that of a typical Portland cement because producing a tonne of Novacem creates about 200–400 kg of CO_2. By comparison, Portland cement releases 700–900 kg of CO_2 per tonne, as the kiln temperature is around 1,600 °C.

In addition, the setting process of Novacem gives an even larger environmental benefit as the cement can reabsorb most of the CO_2 that has been calcined and driven out during manufacture, provided the surface is open to

the atmosphere. This may create carbon-neutral cement, or very near zero emissions.

The cost of production has the potential to be about the same as traditional cement. The mixing process is similar to that for Portland cement, so contractors and concrete suppliers will not need to change the way they work. The new cement product must be and will be competitive with ordinary cement. It is likely that low-grade Novacem will be available in the next few years for block making, roadbase construction and flooring products.

Novacem is still far from proving itself commercially. Imperial College has created a test plant in its labs and plans to build a small industrial plant in Britain next year. Imperial Innovations is providing half of the funding for this task, but needs to raise a further £3 million to continue its development – they are actively seeking sponsors. The Royal Society Enterprise Fund and the London Technology Fund invested in Novacem in August 2009. The company is also working with construction industry partners – including Laing O'Rourke, WSP Group and Rio Tinto – to help establish the first factory and evaluate the cement technology. It is hoped that by 2015 or soon after there will be several plants producing Novacem in the UK.

Embodied CO_2
Expected to be 400 kg CO_2/tonne, with a reabsorption potential of about 80 per cent of all the CO_2 released in the calcining process. It is a direct replacement for Portland cement. The net CO_2 embodied is estimated to be around 200 kg/tonne.

Table 1.5
Cement comparison at a glance

	Portland cement	Novacem
Materials	Carbonate, abundant reserves of raw materials	Non-carbonate, abundant reserves of raw materials
Thermal process: °C	1500	650
CO_2 emissions: kg/tonne cement	850–950	300–400
Construction	Low capital cost and operational costs	Cost parity with Portland cement
CO_2 reabsorption: %	20–30	60–80

Geopolymer cements

In recent years a new generation of alkali-activated cements has been researched. One example, Pyrament, was produced by cement-makers Lone Star Industries for making rapid repairs to runways and bridge decks.

Geopolymer cement is a form of inorganic alumino-silicate material based on carbunculus (K, Ca)-poly(sialate-siloxo) and kandoxi (K, Ca)-poly(sialate-disiloxo) cements, which are derived as by-products from the oil industry.

The production of 1 tonne of geopolymer cement generates only 180 kg of CO_2. This comes solely from the combustion of fossil fuel used to heat the mixture to 800 °C as the cement does not generate CO_2 in its chemistry.

Embodied CO_2

Geopolymer cements have great potential as low CO_2 cements at 180 kg CO_2/tonne (net CO_2 after reabsorption is 125 kg CO_2/tonne), but they cost a lot more to produce than Portland cement and may therefore only be suitable for specialised applications.

AGGREGATES AND CONCRETE BLOCKS

There is a wide variety of naturally occurring aggregates suitable for the production of concrete and concrete products. There are also many manufactured secondary aggregates – lightweight and recycled waste aggregates – that are suitable for structural, decorative and block-making concrete.

In this section, the commonly available natural aggregates, manufactured lightweight aggregates, recycled waste aggregates and even organic aggregates are described and reviewed for their applications and embodied CO_2.

NATURAL AGGREGATES

Natural aggregates can be divided into three main types:

— land-based sands and gravels
— marine aggregates
— crushed rock.

When selecting what aggregates to use on a project, it is not simply a matter of choosing between a crushed rock and a natural gravel, but will instead depend on what aggregates are locally available.

Land-based sands and gravels

The most widely used and economic aggregates are land-based sands and gravels. Sand and gravel deposits occur as superficial drifts laid down by rivers or as glacial spread left behind when the last ice sheets melted.

Sands and gravels were formed by the erosion, transportation and deposition of rock by wind, water or ice. Sand quarries are usually shallow, sometimes only 5–6 metres deep, and their operation is likely to be shorter term than for a rock quarry, with progressive restoration normally following closely behind extraction.

River deposits are generally the most satisfactory for concrete production as they have a consistent grading and are fairly clean. The main deposits occur in the Thames and Trent valleys and their tributary valleys, such as the Stort and the Lea.

Glacial deposits are widely spread across the country, but are not always economically viable. Major extraction of glacial sands and gravels can be found in the Vale of St Albans, East Anglia, the Midlands and parts of the north-east of England. The Lancashire and Cheshire deposits are manly sands, while in Clwyd it is mainly gravel.

Embodied CO_2

Low, at 8–10 kg CO_2/tonne

Marine aggregates

Marine aggregates are aggregates sourced from the seabed or from rivers or estuaries. These aggregates are generally well rounded and smooth, just like land-based sand and gravel, but have a much higher chloride content. The sands tend to be a bit on the coarse side as all marine aggregates have to be thoroughly washed and cleaned to ensure they are free of chlorides, dust, and clay and silt particles.

Embodied CO$_2$
Negligible

Extraction and processing of natural sands and gravels

Land-based sand and gravels are excavated from gravel and sand pits, while coastal gravel and sands are extracted by dredging from river estuaries or from coastal regions adjacent to the mouths of major rivers.

The extracted material is first split into sand and gravel by a separating screen. The gravel is then fed to a refined screening plant, which separates it into single-size stockpiles (20 mm, 10 mm and 5 mm). Oversized aggregates are sometimes reduced at a crusher plant and then returned for screening. The sand is washed and sieved using classifiers, to meet grading standards for building sand and concreting sands.

Crushed rock aggregates

Crushed rock aggregates are sourced from inland quarries. Three main types of rock are used to produce crushed rock aggregates. Their classification, petrographic examination and prehistory will be critical in determining whether or nor they are suitable for concrete.

— *Igneous* – formed by molten lava flow. This group includes the granites, basalts, dolerites and gabbros. The granites and basalts are hard, dense materials and make excellent aggregates.
— *Sedimentary* – created by the settlement and cementing of particles on seabeds and in lakes millions of years ago. These include limestones, sandstones and gritstones. The hard, dense carboniferous limestone found in the Mendips and Derbyshire is suitable for concrete. Ferruginous and siliceous sandstones are also hard and dense and are suitable as aggregates.
— *Metamorphic* – formed by the transformation of an existing rock material by heat and pressure. These rocks are very variable in character. In this group, marble and quartzite are usually adequately dense and tough for use as aggregates.

Quarries supplying crushed rock aggregates grade and classify the materials as suitable or unsuitable for concrete aggregates in accordance with British Standard specifications.

Embodied CO$_2$
Low, around 20–27 kg CO$_2$/tonne

Production of crushed rock aggregates

Material is extracted from the quarry face by blasting, the shattered stone then being conveyed to the crushing plant by large tipper trucks. The primary crushing plant reduces the material into pieces of 75 mm diameter or less. These pieces are fed to jaw crushers and disc crushers for further reduction, and then graded by passing over a vibrating screen into 20 mm, 10 mm and 5 mm stockpiles.

Sand is produced by rod mills or roll crushers, where the crushed coarse aggregate material is fed between toothed and serrated rollers and crushed to a sand consistency. The material is then graded by screening and separated into building and concrete sands.

LIGHTWEIGHT AGGREGATES

There are a number of different lightweight aggregates – a few are suitable for structural concrete, but most are used in the production of lightweight concrete building blocks. The materials range from volcanic rocks that are naturally air entrained – such as pumice, pozzolanas and volcanic slag – to materials manufactured from clay, shale, slate, fly ash and even wood.

The material properties that benefit construction are a low bulk density, low thermal conductivity, low coefficient of expansion and high tensile strain capacity. The major disadvantage for most of the manufactured materials is that they have a high embodied CO$_2$ because they need to be heated to create the expansion for air entrainment. The exceptions are wood-based lightweight aggregates made from graded wood, hemp or sawdust. As wood and hemp sequester CO$_2$ in their growing stage, these aggregates come with a carbon credit. However, they have to be conditioned by mixing with lime or other chemical pretreatments, otherwise residues from the organic material may affect the hydration of the cement binder.

Structural lightweight aggregates

Sintered PFA (Lytag)

Sintered PFA is produced by heat treatment of fly ash collected from power station flue gases. PFA, which consists of minute spherical glass particles as fine as cement, is damped down with water and mixed with coal slurry then fed onto rotating pans to form spherical pellets. These pellets are then sintered at a temperature of 1,400 °C, which causes the ash particles to coalesce without fully melting, forming a lightweight aggregate. Sintered PFA is commercially known as Lytag in the UK.

It is currently not manufactured in the UK but is imported from Poland. The process is sensitive to the loss on ignition value of the fly ash. An unburnt coal dust content of around 6 per cent is acceptable for production. However, this value can be much higher, depending on the type of coal and the control of toxic nitrogen oxide and sulphur dioxides emissions, so not all coal-burning power stations in the UK produce fly ash suitable for Lytag.

Lytag aggregates are available in two natural sizes: 5–8 mm and 8–13 mm. For fine aggregates the particles have to be crushed.

Properties of Lytag

— Bulk density: typically 825–1,100 kg/m³

— Lightweight concrete density: 1,550–2,000 kg/m³

— Coefficient of thermal expansion: typically 7×10^{-6}/K

— Thermal conductivity, with a density between 1,750 and 1,880 kg/m³: 0.81 W/mK.

Embodied CO_2
14 kg CO_2/m³ or 15 kg CO_2/tonne ex works, plus transport CO_2 from Poland to UK is 65 kg CO_2/tonne

Liapor

When certain types of clay and shale are heated to about 1,200 °C they reach a point where the gases generated in the mass rapidly expand, forming a honeycomb of small cells separated by walls of vitrified material. This property is exploited to produce Liapor, a lightweight aggregate with an aerated core and high compressive strength.

Quarried shale is transferred by tipper truck to a processing plant, where it is crushed, dried and milled into a powder less than 70–90 μm. The shale powder is conditioned, mixed with water, and pelletised into small round granules and then coated with a fine limestone dust. The pellets are then graded into sizes and then conveyed to a three-stage rotary kiln and heated to 1,200 °C. This heating causes the pellets to expand and harden.

The technique used allows the amount of expansion of the pellets to be controlled and the density and size of the granules to be engineered and graded precisely. The coating of lime powder increases the amount of surface vitrification that occurs, forming a dense, impermeable coating.

Liapor is available as 4–8 mm and 8–16 mm diameter aggregates as well as crushed sands (0–4 mm), and the density can be varied from 325 to 800 kg/m³ according to the application and usage. It has an ideal spherical shape, with a closed surface and a slightly roughened texture. It is completely frost resistant and can be stored in the open under any weather conditions.

Concrete containing a Liapor 8 graded aggregate, comprising 4–12 mm aggregates with a Liapor bulk density of 800 kg/m³ and combined with natural sand, has achieved compressive strengths of 80 MPa at a design density of 1,800 kg/m³. For a lower density concrete, the natural sand is replaced with a Liapor sand. A concrete density of 1,400 kg/m³ can be achieved with a Liapor grade 6 coarse aggregate and a Liapor sand, to give a compressive strength of 40 MPa. Clearly, Liapor allows the strength and density of concrete to be fine tuned and engineered to suit the structural characteristics of a particular project.

The principal properties of Liapor are:

— bulk density: 225–950 kg/m^3
— thermal conductivity (of the aggregates – Liapor grade 3; 325 kg/m^3): 0.85 W/mK.

The different Liapor plants produce different levels of CO_2 emissions. The Austrian plant replaces almost 90 per cent of the primary burning media with CO_2-neutral ones; in Tuningen (in the Black Forest) about 15 per cent of the primary fuel is replaced with biogas from a waste depot; and in the Czech Republic, different CO_2-neutral materials are mixed with gas.

Embodied CO_2
7 kg CO_2/m^3 or 5 kg CO_2/tonne ex works
Includes all sources: burning media, limestone powder and the raw shale

Lightweight block-making aggregates

Generally, a much lower grade of lightweight aggregate is required in block manufacture as the compressive strength of blocks needs only to be 2–14 MPa. There is therefore scope to use a wider range of raw materials. Some blockwork products are air cured while others are heat treated or autoclaved for a faster set and a quicker production cycle.

The following paragraphs list materials that have been used in block manufacture, although they are not all currently in production. This may change under future 'green' legislation.

Foamed slag
Molten slag from iron blast furnaces is treated with a controlled amount of water so that steam is trapped in the mass. This gives the slag a porous structure, very similar to natural pumice. As the material is relatively inert, the relevant British Standard only specifies that sulphates do not exceed 1 per cent.

Foamed slag is available in three sizes: 16–10 mm, 10–3 mm and 3 mm to dust.

Expanded clay
Expanded clays have been produced in the UK using the trade names Aglite and Leca. Like

Liapor, they exploit the property of certain types of clay to expand on heating to high temperatures.

Leca is produced from a special clay that is pelletised and passed through a rotary kiln to form spherical pellets with a glazed but porous skin. Aglite is produced by passing pellets containing a mixture of clay and coke over a sintering hearth and then through crushers to control the particle size.

Aglite is angular in appearance because it is crushed, whereas Leca is smooth and rounded. Both are available in three sizes: 16–10 mm, 10–5 mm and 4 mm to dust.

Aerated concrete, aka 'Aircrete'
Lightweight aerated concrete blocks are made using cement, lime and silaceous materials (e.g. sand), which are expanded by the addition of controlled quantities of aluminium powder. The aluminium admixture reacts with the lime to give off hydrogen, which causes the mixture to expand, creating a microcellular structure.

The mixture (cake) is cast in large steel moulds, where the hydrogen is quickly replaced by air. The cake is cut into various block sizes, then transported to high-pressure steam autoclaves where it is cured for 18 hours. This stabilises the blocks and improves their strength.

The resulting concrete blocks have densities of between 500 and 1,040 kg/m^3.

Embodied CO_2
Around 380 kg CO_2/tonne

Organic aggregate concrete

Wood particles
Graded wood particles have been used as aggregates for many years. However, some method of pretreatment and conditioning is usually necessary, otherwise the tannins, soluble carbohydrates, waxes and resins contained in the wood may affect the hydration of the cement.

Various patent processes are available, but with most softwoods it is usual to condition the wood particles by mixing with calcium chloride or lime. Another treatment is to boil the particles in water to which ferrous sulphate has been added.

Woodcrete has been used in the manufacture of durable bird boxes, to make them resistant to squirrel or woodpecker damage. The author has one in his garden, made in Germany.

The great advantage of wood-based aggregates is that each cell of wood captures or sequesters CO_2 in its formation. This can help offset the embodied CO_2 of the cement binder, and even makes it theoretically possible to engineer a zero-carbon concrete.

Sawdust concrete

Sawdust concrete has been made for use in non load-bearing walls, to make nailing into concrete easy. Because of the very large moisture movement, sawdust concrete should not be used where it is exposed to moisture.

Sawdust concrete consists of equal parts of cement, sand and pine sawdust, with just enough water to give a low slump (about 50 mm). Such a concrete bonds well to normal concrete and is a good insulator. Other wood wastes, such as splinters and shavings (suitably pretreated), have also been used to make non load-bearing concrete.

Chemical treatment of the sawdust is required to fix the wood residue, which prevents it affecting the hydration of the cement, stops it rotting and reduces its moisture absorption. Best results are obtained with sawdust particle sizes of 6–1 mm, and trial mixes are recommended because of the variable nature of the wood.

Sawdust concrete has a density of between 650 and 1,600 kg/m³.

Embodied CO_2
Effectively carbon neutral

Lignacite blocks (with wood chip)

The Lignacite block is the only block that uses wood chip aggregate, which sequesters CO_2, to make the block the most ecofriendly block in the UK. The recycled pine wood shavings are supplied as a waste product from local joiners and manufacturers of wood products. It is shredded in a mill into 3 mm strands and then soaked to ensure it does not absorb any of the mix water and affect the cement hydration. The wood captures and stores CO_2 in converting carbon to cellulose. The CO_2 can only be released if the wood is burnt or biodegraded; but as the wood fibres in the block are coated and cemented together and kept stable by the cement in the block they will not be able to biodegrade, even when crushed. It is therefore reasonable to offset the CO_2 sequestered by the wood fibres and deduct this from the embodied CO_2 of the other materials. The sequestered CO_2 of the wood is calculated as 1.84 times the density of the wood.

A typical Lignacite block mix contains OPC (9.81%), GGBS (1.09%), recycled pine wood particles (26%), sharp sand (29.1%), crushed recycled Lignacite block waste (30%) and mixing water (4%). The block strength ranges from 7 to 10 N/mm²; and the density from 1,500 to 1,600 kg/m³. Length and height dimensions of the blocks are fixed as 440 × 215 mm, with various widths: 75, 90, 100, 140, 150, 200, 215 mm. The most common sizes are the 100 mm and 140 mm widths.

The embodied CO_2 of the block is the lowest of all blocks, at around 6 kg CO_2/m³ (materials only), assuming the cement in the block has recarbonated by 50 per cent after 20 years. Carbonation of 30 N concrete is assumed to be 1 mm per year. For a block mix this may be higher as it is more porous, so after 20 years the

Left
Lignacite block

CO_2 calculation for Lignacite blocks

Materials embodied CO_2

Material	% volume	Density (kg/m³)	Weight/m³ (kg)	kg CO_2/kg	Embodied CO_2 (kg)
Cement	9.81	3,200	313.9	0.930	291.9
GGBS	1.09	2,900	31.6	0.052	1.6
Sand	29.10	2,200	640.0	0.005	3.2
Crushed block	30.00	1,500	450.0	0.005	2.3
Water	4.00	1,000	40.0	nil	nil
Wood shaving	26	450	117.0	sequestered	nil
Total					299

Sequestered CO_2

Material	Sequestered CO_2 (kg)
Wood shaving: 117 kg × 1.84	215
Carbonated cement 50%, calcining = 0.5 kg CO_2/kg × 0.5 × 313.9	78
Total	293

Net embodied CO_2: = embodied CO_2 – sequestered CO_2 = 6 kg CO_2/m³

total depth is nearer 25 mm from each face. A phenolthalien test can be used to verify this. For a 100 mm block it is around 0.6 kg CO_2/m².

Materials are delivered to the factory in 30-tonne bulk transporters, and then loaded into an automatic batching/weighing system and fed via conveyor belts to a 3 m³ dry batch mixer. Cement is added separately to the mix. After 1 minute of mixing, a moisture sensor calculates the material moisture content and then gauges the water to be added to give the total water content. After thorough mixing, the semi-dry mix is transferred to the block-making machine and then fed into a steel mould via a metering belt. The semi-dry mix fills the 215 mm deep moulds in a few seconds, helped by a high-frequency vibrating table. The vibration gives a clean even face texture to the block and ensures an even density. By using this method of consolidation rather than conventional compaction, good colour consistency and even strength across the depth of the block is ensured.

The blocks are made in an eight-chambered steel mould, forming eight blocks at a time, and then transferred to a curing chamber where they are left to cure for 8 hours. The curing chamber has an innovative low-energy method of warming the air, using heat pumps salvaged from old fridges, rather than burning gas or oil.

When the blocks are cured they are removed from the chamber by an automatic hydraulic robot, and then fed by conveyor to a 'cubing system', which packs them into 72-block units. The units are stacked by forklift and crane in a holding yard, ready for delivery to customers.

Other products made by Lignacite using the same process are the Ashlite block, containing a high percentage of waste recycled aggregates, and a dense, load-bearing Lignacrete block, containing 10 per cent recycled aggregates. The RoofBlock is designed to replace a wood or plastic soffit at the roof overhang of houses. Being made from recycled concrete it is long-lasting and maintenance free, and has a natural void that can be used as a nest site by house martins and bat species.

All products are tested to ISO 9002 (quality systems) and certified to BS EN ISO 14001 (environmental management systems). In addition, Lignacite Ltd has A+ Environmental Accreditation from BRE for the Lignacite block.

Hemcrete

Hemcrete is a lime-based organic aggregate concrete that has been used in France as a material for insulation and wall linings for over 20 years. It has been developed for use in residential and commercial buildings, where high insulation values, high thermal mass and low-carbon concrete are essential.

Hemcrete as a block is made with a blend of hydraulic lime and Portland cement as binder and 'shiv', which is the chopped woody part of hemp. The materials are mixed together with just the right amount of water to form a biocomposite concrete with a very low water content.

Hemcrete can be sprayed in place, but does not have the workability or the flowing characteristics to allow it to be poured or cast in place. The Portland cement addition is important as it sets much faster than the lime binder, and prevents the shiv from disintegrating due to the moisture in the mix.

The density of the mix can range between 200 and 500 kg/m^3, depending on the application required – the higher the density, the greater the compressive strength and thermal mass. Besides good thermal insulation, it also has good sound absorption properties because of the air trapped in the fibres.

The main reason for specifying Hemcrete is as a carbon-neutral concrete for construction. Before harvest, the hemp sequesters a large amount of CO_2 in the production of cellulose. The amount of CO_2 that hemp sequesters as it grows is equivalent to 1.84 times the density of the woody material. The high CO_2 accredited to the shiv offsets the embodied CO_2 of the cement and the lime binder. The resulting biocomposite material is carbon-neutral as the embodied CO_2 of the Portland cement and lime is just about equal to the sequestered CO_2 of shiv.

Hemcrete load-bearing blocks can be designed using the current code of practice for cavity blockwork construction – the design values for Hemcrete blocks are derived from extensive test work carried out at Bath University. Hemcrete walls have to be rendered to make them watertight. Although construction costs may be slightly higher than for conventional blockwork, the lower ongoing energy costs may make it worthwhile in the long term.

Embodied CO$_2$
Hemcrete mix is carbon neutral

Manufacture of concrete aggregate blocks

The concrete mixtures used for making different types of blocks will vary according to the material properties and load capacity required. The cement to aggregate ratio by volume may vary from as rich as 1:2 for structural blocks to as lean as 1:10 for lightweight, non load-bearing insulating blocks.

The manufacturer must provide the mix design information in order for the embodied CO_2 and the production CO_2 to be estimated, but many manufacturers seem reluctant to divulge these figures. If that is the case for a project, the designer should use the general CO_2 tables in this book as a guide to estimate these values (Tables A.1 and A.2, see Appendix to Part I).

The manufacture of lightweight and dense concrete blocks is usually carried out in highly automated factories located near to the source of the aggregate materials. The blocks are made using semi-dry mixes that are moulded by vibration and pressure into the required shapes. Blocks may be left to cure naturally, or may be steam cured to 80 °C to reduce the curing time.

— *Solid blocks* – are voidless, but can have end groves or small cavities to reduce weight proved they do not exceed more than 25 per cent of the gross volume.

— *Hollow blocks* – have central cavities that pass through the block, comprising up to 50 per cent of the gross volume.

Embodied CO$_2$

8 MPa (1,500 kg/m³)	60 kg/t or 90 kg/m³
10 MPa (1,800 kg/m³)	75 kg/t or 135 kg/m³
2 MPa (2,000 kg/m³)	80 kg/t or 160 kg/m³

For specific products contact the manufacturer for concrete mix data to estimate embodied CO$_2$.

AGGREGATES FROM WASTES

Recycled aggregate concrete

(with reference to BRE Digest 433)

Recycled aggregates – crushed concrete and brick masonry – have been used in the UK for many years as general hardcore and fill material, usually for making temporary site roads or hardstanding platforms for piling rigs or other heavy machinery. They have not been used as a replacement material for natural aggregates in concrete or for road sub-bases because there has been little quality control and testing carried out to show that the materials comply with the required performance standards. However, recent improvements in the grading, assessment and specification of recycled aggregates allow designers to specify with confidence such materials for use in structural concrete and roadbase construction.

Quality control

Any recycled aggregate to be used in concrete must meet the requirement of BS 882. The maximum permitted levels of impurities (by weight) present in a Class (11) material are:

— wood: 1 per cent

— foreign matter, such as metal, plastic, asphalt, glass: 1 per cent

— sulphates (as acid-soluble SO$_3$): 1 per cent.

The chloride content should be checked if the concrete is to be reinforced or contain embedded metal.

Each batch of unprocessed material arriving at the crushing plant should be inspected and placed in a stockpile designated by the quality of the aggregate to be produced. Although waste transfer notes and input inspection may suffice for preliminary quality control, better quality materials benefit from inspection of the demolition sites and preparation of deconstruction plans for their recovery. The frequency of testing of crushed concrete aggregate will depend on the information available on the waste material at input.

Although a large proportion of natural aggregates used in concrete and construction are classed as 'normally reactive', some are not. Therefore, it is prudent to be cautious and to classify recycled concrete aggregate (RCA) as 'highly reactive' until long-term test data become available. A calculation can be made according to BRE Digest 330, taking into account the measured alkali content of the RCA.

RCA as a fine aggregate is not recommended for general use in concrete because of its adverse effect on water demand and increased levels of contamination.

Properties of RCA concrete

Frost resistance is not a problem with RCA concrete unless the source of crushed concrete has suffered frost damage due to use of non-durable aggregates. But will the supplier know this, and will they pass this information on to the customer? If in doubt, and where RCA concrete is specified for fairly severe exposure conditions, it is best to carry out freeze/thaw tests.

RCA concrete mixes require a higher cement content than concrete containing natural aggregates, which reduces the elastic modulus and slightly increases the shrinkage, creep and coefficient of thermal expansion. For concrete in which RCA replaces not more than 20 per cent of the natural aggregates, the effects of this change are marginal and can be ignored, but for any high proportion of RCA, the effects may need to be accounted for in the design.

Sustainability

The environmental arguments for the greater use of recycled aggregates are not conclusive, apart from the obvious benefits of limiting the excavation and quarrying of natural aggregates from greenfield sites. Where natural aggregates are locally available, the use of recycled aggregate concrete does not appear to reduce net CO_2 emissions. There is, however, a clear advantage to using recycled aggregate concrete when natural materials have to be transported some distance. In the long term, as extraction of land-based natural materials is restricted, recycled aggregate concrete will become more established.

To make precise embodied CO_2 comparisons between different recycled aggregates, accurate values would be needed for each. This may cause problems for designers if such a comparison is required. Additionally, and unfortunately, the use of secondary aggregates does not provide any additional BREEAM points under the current material rating criteria.

> **Embodied CO$_2$**
> Around 20–27 kg CO_2/tonne, as for crushed rock

China clay stent

China clay is extracted using high-pressure water jets to wash the kaolinised granite (china clay) from quarry faces. The clay-laden water flows to the bottom of the quarry and is pumped to treatment plants, where the china clay settles out and is dried. Most of the china clay is exported by sea from the port of Par, close to St Austell, Cornwall, where the UK china clay industry is mainly based.

The extraction process also washes out a larger, unkaolinised granite rock fraction – approximately 9 tonnes of waste is generated for each tonne of china clay produced. The composition of this waste varies between locations, depending on the quality and age of the deposit, but typically it comprises 4.5 tonnes of 'stent' (the largest fraction, which can range in size from less than 100 mm to over 2 m in diameter), approximately 3.5 tonnes of sand and 1 tonne of micaceous waste.

China clay stent is classed as a natural secondary aggregate because it is a by-product of an industrial process and has not previously been used in construction. As a secondary aggregate it is exempt from the aggregates levy imposed by the UK government, but it appears to have been largely ignored by many studies of secondary materials for use in concrete.

Previous experience

China clay stent has a long history of satisfactory use as a coarse aggregate in ready-mixed concrete in much of Cornwall and parts of Devon, driven not so much by sustainability considerations as by its local availability and the lack of suitable alternatives. Indeed, china clay sand (see below) is also used widely in ready-mixed concrete in these areas for the same reasons, despite its unfavourable properties in terms of high water demand and the consequent need for a high cement content.

Stent is currently being supplied as the coarse aggregate for the London 2012 Olympic Park, where London Concrete is incorporating it in most of the concrete being supplied for the structures and roadways. The Aquatic Centre alone, by the time it is completed, will have used over 15,000 m³ of stent aggregate concrete.

Source and supply

Stent of a quality suitable for use as a concrete aggregate is available from at least two sources in the St Austell area. Atlantic Aggregates is able to supply material from the Gunheath Quarry by ship from Par, but as only relatively small ships are able to use the harbour, transportation by rail is preferred. The transport costs for stent aggregate are believed to account for the greatest part of the overall supply cost.

> **Embodied CO$_2$**
> Around 20–27 kg CO_2/tonne, as for crushed rock

China clay sand

China clay sand is available in large quantities from the same source as stent, as well as from other outlets in Cornwall and Devon. The production of this waste material far outweighs its demand, making it exempt from the aggregates levy. It is suitable for use as concreting sand and is in common use in ready-mixed concrete near its sources. Nevertheless, it is far from an ideal fine aggregate due to its high water demand, which necessitates a higher cement content to achieve the required level of workability and strength.

The need for increased cement content, the cost of transport and the ready availability of cheaper concreting sands make china clay sand an unrealistic proposition for most of the UK.

Waste glass

Concrete using waste glass as a fine aggregate has been shown to have great potential. However, it is not currently available on a commercial scale, or with the required level of technical experience needed for a large project. There is a perceived risk of alkali–silica reaction from using waste glass as a fine aggregate – Sheffield University has assessed this risk and given recommendations on safeguards to prevent this problem.

However, until it is recognised as a common concreting sand within a British Standard, the technical concerns over the use of waste glass aggregate in structural concrete are likely to remain a barrier to its universal acceptance.

Embodied CO_2
Approx 20–27 kg CO_2/tonne

Blastfurnace slag aggregate

In the UK many tens of millions of tonnes of blastfurnace slag (BFS) have been used as aggregates in construction. BFS is a by-product in the manufacture of iron, with approximately one-third of a tonne being produced for every tonne of iron. It makes sense to utilise it fully where possible, not only to avoid the creation of unsightly slag heaps, but also to reduce the need to extract natural aggregates.

It is important to distinguish between BFS, which chemically is relatively consistent, and 'old bank' slags, which can present difficulties due to their inherent variability. Measures need to be taken to guard against the risk of potential volumetric expansion if there is contamination.

Approximately 3 million tonnes of BFS is produced annually. The majority is rapidly quenched, granulated and ground to make GGBS cement. The remainder is processed into aggregates for construction. European and British standards apply to all applications.

BFS is a mineral and comprises primarily the silicates and aluminosilicates of calcium and magnesium, with other compounds of sulfur, iron, manganese and other trace elements.

Air-cooled BFS is excavated from the open-air pits and transported to the crushing and screening plant, where it is initially processed prior to being naturally weathered in controlled stockpiles. After completing an appropriate period of weathering, BFS is processed further by crushing and screening, where it is converted into the standard range of aggregate sizes. The physical properties of BFS make it ideally suited for use as an aggregate, demonstrating good shape with a rough surface texture providing good frictional properties and good adhesion to cementitious binders.

Air-cooled BFS provides quality controlled aggregates for use in construction. At present the principal applications include aggregates for use in asphalts and surface dressings in accordance with BS EN 13043 and aggregates for use in unbound mixtures, BS EN 13242, covering sub-bases, cappings and fills.

Embodied CO_2
53 kg CO_2/tonne, as for GGBS

REINFORCEMENT

This section assesses the embodied CO_2 of bar and wire mesh reinforcement arising from CO_2 emissions in its manufacture and factory production. The data produced here are specific to materials supplied by Celsa UK Ltd and BRC Ltd. In all other cases, the CO_2 for reinforcement may be estimated (in the absence of detailed energy data) using the data in Table A.1 (see Appendix to Part I) and factored for delivery CO_2 and factory production CO_2.

Reinforcing steel is produced from recovered ferrous scrap. Structural steel, however, is produced from pig iron imported into the UK, which is smelted at a much higher temperature and then combined with carbon and other metal alloys, before being heated again for rolling and processing into steel sections and steel plate. It has far greater embodied CO_2 per tonne than reinforcing steel, which uses locally sourced material and only requires a low energy electric arc furnace.

STEEL DUCTILITY AND GRADE

Use of the correct grade of reinforcing steel is important as greater ductility assists in ensuring the structure's robustness. Ductility class B reinforcement is required as a minimum if there is more than 20 per cent moment redistribution in the design to BS EN 1992-1-1. For common building structures, i.e. those designed to BS 8110, use of steel bars of ductility class A is acceptable for 12 mm bar and below, as it is unlikely that in flexure the members concerned will be structurally significant.

Key concrete specifications, such as the National Structural Concrete Specification and the Specification for Highway Works, are clear in their approach in specifying steel with a particular ductility.

Despite what might seem to be an orderly situation in design terms, concern has been expressed that reinforcing steel of the wrong ductility grade is being received on site. Standards and specifications for the manufacture and processing of reinforcing steel are well established, although they have gone through a series of changes over recent years. The specifications that cover the design of concrete structures are also well established, including those parts which refer to the manufacture and use of reinforcing steel and associated processed reinforcement.

The following three grades of reinforcing steel are specified by BS 4449:2005:

— Grade B500A
— Grade B500B
— Grade B500C.

These designations describe steel with a yield strength of 500 MPa. Within this description of grade, the capital letter B preceding the yield strength denotes reinforcing steel. The capital letters A, B and C following the yield strength denote the ductility class, with A being the lowest. With the exception of BS 4449 grade B500A in sizes below 8 mm diameter, these conform to the three ductility classes of BS EN 1992-1-1:2004, Annex C.

To ensure that the correct grade of reinforcement is supplied, the designer should specify on the bending schedule prepared for the reinforcement supplier the grade to be supplied, giving the specific ductility class required.

REINFORCEMENT MANUFACTURE

Richard Howells, Celsa Steel UK

Celsa Steel UK is the largest manufacturer of bar and rod reinforcement in the UK, and one of the largest manufacturers of other long steel products. From its facilities in Cardiff, Celsa produces and delivers around 1.2 million tonnes of finished product each year, mainly to the UK and Irish markets.

Sustainability

Celsa is dedicated to being a sustainable producer. It operates quality, environmental and health and safety management systems to ISO 9001:2000, ISO 14001:2004 and OHSAS 18001:2007 respectively. All of the steel produced in the melt shop is manufactured from scrap metal, using the electric arc furnace (EAF) process. The EAF process uses 100 per cent locally sourced and recovered ferrous scrap metal as the primary raw material, which is melted down in the furnace and cast in moulds to produce steel billet, from which the finished bar and rod products are manufactured. The recycled content of the finished product is about 95 per cent. Around 4 per cent of the total raw material is lime, which is used in the production process to remove impurities from the steel. All scrap metal and lime is sourced from the UK.

Steel production using the EAF method consumes only one-third of the energy and emits only one-sixth of the CO_2 when compared with other steel-making processes. In other words, Celsa produces steel in the most sustainable manner available.

Celsa adopts a holistic approach to sustainability. Central to this approach is the examination and assessment of environmental impact throughout its entire supply chain; from constituent material procurement through to end-product delivery to customers. This sustainability philosophy is further consolidated by participation in the Eco-Reinforcement responsible sourcing scheme. Eco-Reinforcement is a third-party certification scheme developed by the UK reinforcing steel sector to comply with BRE's global BES 6001:2008 framework standards for the responsible sourcing of construction products.

Production

Celsa Steel UK has two facilities for the production of reinforcing bars and coils: a melt shop for producing crude steel in the form of steel billet (ingots of steel), which is located at its Tremorfa site, and a rolling mill for processing the billet into finished product, located two miles away at the Castle Works site.

The melt shop

In December 2006 a new state-of-the-art melt shop was opened, increasing crude steel production capacity at the site to 1.2 million tonnes per year.

- *Scrap* – Scrap arrives by rail and road for delivery to the melt shop. Each product has a different recipe for scrap type utilised, depending on its final use.
- *Electric arc furnace* – The prepared scrap is charged into the furnace and heated to around 1,600 °C. Alloying elements are added to the molten steel, which combine with impurities and prevent them from affecting the steel's properties.
- *Secondary steel making* – The molten steel is moved to the ladle arc station, where the temperature and composition of the steel are adjusted to tightly controlled limits. Alloying elements such as manganese or vanadium may be added to produce the necessary strength or ductility in the final steel.
- *Continuous casting* – Once the ladle of molten steel is of the required temperature

and chemical composition, it is moved to the continuous caster. The molten steel is run into a tundish, from which it flows into six water-cooled square moulds. Once the molten steel comes into contact with the mould, it starts to solidify from the outside. The strand of steel is continuously withdrawn from the mould, as molten steel is fed from the tundish above.

- *Billets* – The solidifying strand is straightened, and then cut to the required length by gas torches. This produces billets up to 15 m in length, which will then be rolled into finished products. The cast billets of steel are transferred by rail to the rod and bar mill.

The rod and bar mill

The rod and bar mill has a production capacity of 0.89 million tonnes of reinforcing and wire rod products per year. Where possible, Celsa tries to hot charge billets in order to save energy. This means that the melt shop and mill rolling programmes are coordinated so that billets arriving from the melt shop are immediately placed in the mill's reheat furnace, reducing the time and energy required to reheat the steel to rolling temperature. Once in the mill furnace, billets are reheated to around 1,150 °C, making the steel softer and more ductile, so that the

final shape can be produced more efficiently. When the correct temperature is reached, billets are pushed into the rolling stands, each of which has a pair of grooved cylindrical steel rollers. As the steel is forced through the grooves, the area of the cross-section is reduced. This process is repeated continually over several stands, with the cross-section reducing each time until the required dimensions are achieved. Notches are cut into the grooves of the final rolling stand and the steel that fills these notches forms the ribs on the bar surface.

Celsa Steel UK only produces the highest grade of reinforcing steel that can be specified in current British Standards: grade B500C to BS4449:2005. To achieve the strength and ductility required by this high ductility grade, the steel is cooled by high-pressure water jets. This results in a hard, strong surface with a soft, ductile central core. This process is known as quench and self-temper (QST). Once cooled, the bars are sheared to a length of around 80 m and transferred to a cooling bed, where they cool further in still air. The bars are then sheared to the required customer lengths, bundled, labelled and moved into storage, awaiting despatch.

Embodied CO$_2$

422 kg CO$_2$/tonne reinforcement

See also Table A.4 (Appendix to Part I) for Celsa's CO$_2$ emission calculations

---

Despatch

Following the rolling process, reinforcing steel products are stored prior to sale. Celsa supplies its products to customers throughout the UK and Ireland, aiming to despatch within 24 hours for the former and 48 hours for the latter. Where possible, Celsa aims to utilise the most efficient methods of transport.

REINFORCEMENT FABRICATION

Jamie Holling, BRC Ltd

BRC is the largest supplier of steel reinforcement in the UK. Its commercial activities focus on the processing and distribution of steel for the reinforcement of concrete. BRC supplies reinforcing bar, fabric, mesh, prefabricated elements, including carpet rolls of bar, and specialist accessories.

The company is committed to being a sustainable manufacturer and supplier. It also operates quality, environmental and health and safety management systems to ISO 9001:2000, ISO 14001:2004 and OHSAS 18001:2007 respectively, and sources its steel from mills that use the EAF method of steel production.

BRC provides innovative reinforcement solutions that optimise the amount of reinforcement required and reduce assembly and fixing time on site. Adopting a just-in-time approach to delivery minimises the amount of reinforcement required to be held on site and reduces manual handling. This in turn accelerates productivity and site efficiency, reducing construction waste associated with traditional fixing of cut and bent reinforcement.

BRC's commitment to being a sustainable manufacturer and supplier is also demonstrated by its participation in the Eco-Reinforcement sourcing scheme, the third-party certification scheme designed to encourage compliance with BES 6001:2008.

Production

Steel reinforcement is divided into two groups:

— *Fabric* (or mesh) sheets, which are pre-welded using combinations of wire between 5 mm and 12 mm diameter. A variety of sheet sizes and diameters are stocked for direct delivery to the customer, while non-standard sheet sizes and diameters are tailored to the customer's specific requirements.

— *Loose bar*, cut and bent to shape and tied together with wire on the construction site, with diameters between 8 mm and 50 mm.

Production operations at BRC sites include cutting, bending and welding of steel reinforcement. These use power and ancillary products, such as lubricants, but their impact on the environment is considered to be minimal.

Prefabrication is best carried out at one of BRC's seven reinforcement depots – supplemented where necessary by on-site assembly at ground level. Simpler reinforcement cages and mats and welded fabric panels may be delivered to site ready for installation. Units that may be too large for practical road transport are better assembled on site from a combination of smaller fabricated units. In general, prefabricated panels, mats or cages for delivery by road should not exceed 12 m in length and 3.2 m in width. To maximise construction efficiency, the location of both the vehicle off-loading and the site assembly areas should enable prefabricated units to be crane-handled directly into position.

Most preassembled arrangements of reinforcement may require a modification to the traditional reinforcement detailing in order to simplify and standardise the prefabrication process. Prefabrication of reinforcement requires a commitment at the design stage, if the benefits of faster construction and earlier completion are to be fully exploited.

Distribution

Each BRC depot is strategically positioned to service the requirements of customers located within a 75-mile radius. Finished reinforcement products and accessories are delivered to construction sites and other customer facilities in line with client requirements and delivery schedules. Reinforcement products are not 'packaged' but are generally tied or bundled using steel wire, which is also recyclable.

BRC uses specialist contract hauliers rather than operating a vehicle fleet of its own. These hauliers work closely with their respective depots and are responsible for the development of distribution strategies and schedules that reflect their local constraints and optimise delivery route efficiency.

CO_2 emissions

The following energy consumption figures are based on kWh readings for gas and electricity supplied from the national grid, and for diesel and other fuels, then multiplied by the Defra converter constants to arrive at the CO_2 totals (see Table A.7 in the Appendix to Part I).

Mansfield depot – bar reinforcement factory

Mansfield depot is typical for the delivery mileage and reinforcement bar tonnage of all BRC depots. The delivery vehicles are flatbed articulated lorries. The lorry emissions figures in CO_2/km have been used to calculate the total CO_2. Figures are for 2008.

Above left
Reinforcement mesh

Above
Loading mesh for delivery

— Bar reinforcement supplied = 40,000 tonnes

— Gas – estimated usage for propane welding bottles, not used for heating so not metered

— Electricity = 881,942 kWh × 0.537 kg CO_2/kWh = 473.60 tonnes CO_2

— Transport (total delivery miles, goods out) = 650,000 miles

— Diesel (forklift trucks) = 22,800 litres × 2.63 kg CO_2/litre = 59.96 tonnes CO_2

Embodied CO_2 = 63.35 kg CO_2/tonne of bar reinforcement

Barnsley depot – typical welded-mesh reinforcement factory

— Mesh reinforcement supplied = 73,000 tonnes

— Gas = 2,343,592 kWh × 0.185 kg CO_2/kWh = 433.56 tonnes CO_2

— Electricity = 5,185,340 kWh × 0.537 kg CO_2/kWh = 2,784.52 tonnes CO_2

— Transport (total delivery miles, goods out) = 1,000,000 miles

— Diesel (forklift trucks) = 46,600 litres × 2.63 kg CO_2/litre = 122.56 tonnes CO_2

Embodied CO_2 = 88.20 kg CO_2/tonne of mesh reinforcement

FORMWORK

Timber is the material most often selected for use as formwork because it is relatively inexpensive, can be cut and shaped easily and does not rust. In terms of embodied CO_2, wood-based material is carbon positive – due to the sequestration (or trapping) of CO_2 in the making of cellulose – so it is better than all other construction forming materials. When wood decomposes aerobically (not buried) or is burnt, the entrapped CO_2 is released, and so we can say that timber is totally carbon neutral right to the end of its useful life.

According to Robert Matthews of the Forestry Commission, the quantity of CO_2 sequestered in wood fibres is equivalent to 1.84 times the density of the wood (whatever the species). If the wood is protected and not allowed to biodegrade during the life of the building, the CO_2 sequestered in the wood can be used to offset the construction CO_2 emissions. It is best to burn timber at the end of use, rather than let it break down anaerobically (without the presence of oxygen), such as if buried in a landfill site. Burning releases carbon as CO_2, making the timber carbon neutral, but if the wood breaks down anaerobically it will release methane rather than CO_2, which is twenty times more polluting to the environment.

When timber is processed to produce plywood, the embodied CO_2 will be increased – heat is needed to dry out the ply veneers, and energy is required to manufacture the glues that bond the

Table 1.6
Mansfield depot – bar reinforcement

Source	tonnes CO_2/year
Gas	100.00
Electricity	473.60
Deliveries	1,841.00
Cars (home to work)	66.39
Forklift trucks (goods yard)	59.96
Total	2,540.95

Table 1.7
Barnsley depot – mesh reinforcement

Source	tonnes CO_2/year
Gas	433.56
Electricity	2,784.52
Deliveries	3,078.00
Cars (home to work)	20.07
Forklift truck (goods yard)	122.56
Total	6,438.71

veneers and the resin coating on the surface to make it impermeable to moisture. However, it is still the most sustainable material to use for cast in-situ concrete, especially if the wood has been certified as coming from a renewable source. In precast concrete production, especially flat-bed casting, metal formwork is often preferred as it can be reused over a hundred times before it needs replacing – in this instance, metal can be said to be carbon neutral for each casting.

The formwork support systems – props, walers, soldiers, ties, bolts, washer plates, sole plates, channel sections, beam sections, scaffold tubes, anchors etc. – may be prefabricated from steel, aluminium or timber and are used hundreds of times over, so they are also deemed to be carbon neutral. Conversely, disposable column formers, custom-made metal forms for casting columns and walls for one-off projects, latex rubber form liners, and chipboard and glass-reinforced plastic (GRP) formers must be assessed for their embodied CO_2 as it will be high. Such data must come from the manufacturer, otherwise only a very crude estimate from the materials CO_2 table can be made (Table A.1, see Appendix to Part I), which ignores the source of energy used and the transport and factory CO_2 emissions, which may be significant if items are imported.

For these reasons this section looks more closely at natural timbers and film-faced, reusable and recyclable plywood from sustainable sources. The selection of the correct form face is critical both for the visual appearance of the cast concrete and for minimising the CO_2 released from biodegradation (and methane production from anaerobic decomposition). This can be controlled by reusing the formwork many times to reduce the volume of waste, and by recycling the formwork into the permanent architecture so that there is no waste.

As the designer, you must make the key decisions on formwork selection – whether you want to use FSC-grade timber, recycle the timber or detail the panels to reduce wastage – to control and manage the embodied CO_2 of the construction. It is unreasonable to leave all these decisions to the contractor, whose prime objective is to reduce costs by simplifying the construction and then assembling it economically. The designer should have a clear understanding of the finish required and

the material that will achieve that finish, and should provide the contractor with a statement giving guidance on the products to be used and procedures to be followed.

TYPICAL FORMWORK MATERIALS

Sawn board timber

A wide range of finishes can be obtained from sawn board timber, varying from smooth to deeply grained. The deeper the grain, the more likely it is that some of the grain will be lost after each use. In all cases it is best to seal the face with an acrylic water repellent that has a durable hard film, which will minimise grain loss after casting and allow the board to be used four or more times.

If the board is *locally sourced*, from home grown forests, the importation CO_2 will be zero.

Timber density

Douglas fir	710 kg/m³
Hem-Fir	410 kg/m³
Oak	730 kg/m³

Embodied CO_2

Production: take as zero
Allow for CO_2 from transport and machining for end use

Coating: waterproof coating, polyurethane equivalent to PVC = 11,060 kg CO_2/m³ (Table A.1, see Appendix to Part I), coating = 2 × 10 μm; embodied CO_2 = 11,060 × thickness = 0.2 kg CO_2/m²

Plywood

The plywood imported from Canada is Douglas fir and redwood, while plywood from Finland, Sweden and Latvia, for example, is spruce, whitewood, redwood and birch, in combinations of hardwood and softwood veneers. Plywood from Brazil, Chile, Indonesia, Malaysia and China is tropical hardwood. The common types are considered here.

Natural birch

The long-established timber yards of northern Europe produce FSC grade material or the equivalent – FSC stands for Forest Stewardship Council, which promotes responsible management of the world's forests. Local timber merchants may have stocks of birch ply panels, both 'combi' (birch faced) and 'through birch' (completely birch), that are suitable for small projects.

For fine finishes it is best to use a B, S or possibly BB grade. When the birch ply is to be recycled into the permanent architecture, choose a B or S grade and ensure that no nails or screws are used to fix the panels to the formwork.

The glue bonding the ply veneers should be weather resistant and boil proof (WBP for short), so that it is suitable for external use and meets the requirements of BS 6566 parts 3 to 8 as appropriate.

Panel thickness for construction should be between 18 and 25 mm for site handling and rigidity, and there should be about seven to thirteen veneers. For forming curved walls and similar constructions, individual ply sheets of around 4 mm, which allow bending, should be used and built up to make the 20 mm thickness.

Clear, fast-drying acrylic urethane and polyurethane and wax emulsions that are recommended for waterproofing untreated timber should be applied to the face in controlled conditions, under cover where possible. For site application, always ensure that the timber has been stored in the dry before treating, as the moisture content can be critical to the performance of the coating.

Film-faced plywoods

Special surface coatings have been developed for plywoods to enhance the appearance of the concrete finish and to maximise the potential number of reuses of the formwork, thereby reducing costs. In addition, these coating films have the benefit of masking the wood grain or any defects, and prevent wood sugars and resins impregnating the concrete. Many panels are coated on two sides to balance the panel and prevent warping; however, some plywood manufacturers have developed technology that produces a stable panel coated on one side only, thereby reducing costs.

Phenolic film faced (PFF)

PFF is the generic term for high resin content (64 per cent) surface coating with a film density from 120 to 800 g/m². Colours available are black or brown. PFF is a fully cured and impervious coating made by mixing phenolic resin with paper. Most commonly used PFFs have a film density of 120 g/m² and 240 g/m². A higher film density improves the wear and tear of the coating, but increases the cost and does not alter the surface finish. The higher density coatings are used in slip-forming and climbing formwork applications.

Medium density overlay (MDO)

To overcome the problems of veneer imperfections, absorbency, grade quality and

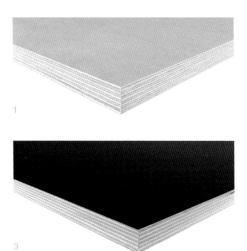

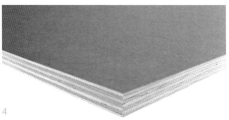

release of tannins, the top ply is commonly faced with a film of paper that is impregnated with resin – the reverse of the phenolic film face.

For the MDO film, the resin saturation levels vary between 30 and 60 per cent. The ply can often be seen behind the overlay (with some brands), especially when the resin impregnation is as low as 30 per cent saturation.

If the backing ply is visible behind the MDO then the film is quite porous and will allow moisture migration. This can cause tannins to be drawn out of the backing ply as the concrete hydrates, especially if it is in contact with the overlay for a long period, which in turn causes light brown staining to the concrete surface. This can be a problem when casting suspended floors and beams, but does not happen for walls and columns using the same product, provided the forms are struck after a day or two.

> **Embodied CO$_2$**
>
> Ex works: 676 kg CO$_2$/m^3 is typical (Table A.1, see Appendix to Part I)

Plywoods summary

Formwork plywoods are produced with either a resin paper or phenolic film face to create an engineered panel that can be reused for casting and forming concrete many times.

Typical uncoated panels

WISA – Birch.

Typical PFF panels

WISA – Betofilm, Fepcoplex, Kronoply FF Spezial, Syktyvkar, Riga Form.

Typical paper-faced panels

MDO: Thomasi Plastform MDO-333, WISA-Form Duo, WISA MDO, Ainsworth Pourform 107.

Sizes available

Dimensions: 2,440 × 1,220 mm; thickness: 12–25 mm plus. Other sheet sizes are available but they need to ordered in advance in quantities of 50 plus. Check with suppliers.

Applicable standards

BS EN 313/314 – plywood classification, terminology and bonding quality.

BS EN 635/636 – plywood classification by surface appearance and specification.

BS 5268 – structural specification.

CASE STUDY/
WISA PLYWOOD

Peter Stewart, UPM Kymmene

Wood remains ever popular in concrete construction, combining strength, durability, lightness and outstanding visual appearance. The excellent physical properties of plywood as well as the accurate dimensional tolerances are important selection criteria.

But, in addition to the technical requirements, one criterion is being valued more and more by today's environmentally conscious end-users: its sustainability. The fact that wood is a renewable raw material is just one of the many benefits of plywood. So how is plywood processed, and what is its manufactured carbon footprint?

Climate change

Forests are often referred to as the lungs of the planet. However, unlike human lungs, growing forests absorb CO$_2$, and release nearly the same amount of oxygen. For this reason, forests play a prominent role as a carbon sink.

Wood that is processed has carbon stored in its fibres. This carbon remains within the plywood throughout its lifetime, provided the plywood is fully protected. If it is burnt or left to biodegrade it will release that carbon. The coatings on film-faced WISA plywood help to prevent the early breakdown of the wood fibres when boards are exposed to moisture and wet concrete, allowing concrete shuttering to be used several times.

Disposing of plywood to landfill will cause the fibres to decompose under anaerobic conditions, releasing methane gas into the atmosphere. Methane is twenty times worse as a greenhouse gas than CO$_2$. Therefore, careful disposal by burning or as biomass for energy generation are preferred options.

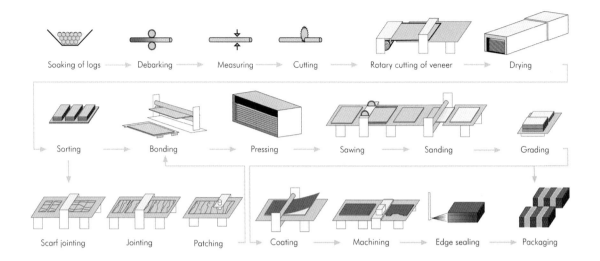

Soaking of logs → Debarking → Measuring → Cutting → Rotary cutting of veneer → Drying

Sorting → Bonding → Pressing → Sawing → Sanding → Grading

Scarf jointing ← Jointing ← Patching ← Coating → Machining → Edge sealing → Packaging

Acting responsibly

Renewable raw materials and recyclable products are the core of UPM's business. And eco-responsibility is seen as a core part of all its operations and activities. The company constantly strives to reduce the impact on the environment by taking into account the whole supply chain, from the sourcing of raw materials to the reuse and disposal of the end products.

UPM continuously measures and assesses the environmental loads and impacts of its operations and strives to manage these systematically in accordance with the principle of continuous improvement. All plywood mills have environmental permits in accordance with the legislation of the country in question and ISO 14001 certified environmental management systems.

The manufacturing of plywood does not create large quantities of CO_2. The CO_2 emissions are due to thermal energy generation, for gluing ply together and heat treating the phenolic resin, and transportation of ply from Finland to the UK by ship.

About 20 per cent of the overall energy consumed in plywood production is electricity, the rest is heat. However, the thermal energy used in manufacturing is generated using biofuels, which are obtained from the by-products of harvesting and production, such as bark, chips and sawdust.

Veneer drying consumes the highest amount of thermal energy (70–75 per cent) in plywood manufacturing, and pressing and air conditioning of the production premises bring the total up to 90 per cent of the heat energy required. To further increase energy efficiency, a significant amount of heat energy can be recovered from exhaust air and from condensate from the veneer drying lines. That secondary energy is mostly used for heating the logs in soaking basins before the peeling process.

The transportation of raw materials and finished products generates the highest CO_2 emissions. These can be minimised by sensible routing, by favouring rail and ship transport and use of low-emission fuels and by transporting full loads.

Sustainability

UPM is committed to sustainable forest management and recognises that the sustainable use of natural resources is a requisite for responsible business operations. The company aims at increasing the use of certified wood

in its products and supports all credible forest certification schemes. FSC and PEFC labels guarantee that the wood used in these products is legally sourced and originates from well-managed FSC/PEFC certified forests.

The FSC chain of custody (CoC) system is a tool for tracing and verifying the amounts of wood coming from certified forests. A company with a certified CoC system may use the PEFC/FSC label. All of UPM's plywood mills have the right to use PEFC, or in some cases FSC, labelling. UPM always ensures that the wood it receives is legally sourced, and requires its wood suppliers to operate within a framework that is responsible and financially, socially and environmentally sustainable.

The objective of forest certification is to promote ecologically, economically and socially sustainable forest management. A forest certificate is issued by an impartial third party, based on an audit.

FSC/PEFC certification ensures that the wood raw material used for WISA plywood:

— comes from properly managed certified forests

— was harvested legally

— does not come from a nature conservation area.

Embodied CO_2

Processed plywood: 676 kg CO_2/tonne

WISA birch, 18 mm with resin film face both sides:

Plywood = density 680 kg/m^3 = 993 kg CO_2/m^3 × 0.018 = 17.9 kg CO_2/m^2

Phenolic resin (use PVC from Table A.1) = 2 × 0.5 mm × 11,060 kg CO_2/m^3 = 11.1 kg CO_2/m^2

Total = 29.00 kg CO_2/m^2

OTHER FORMWORK MATERIALS

Formliners

Formliners can be constructed from plasticised PVC, polyurethane, fibreglass and other synthetic materials that are flexible and easily mouldable, and give good definition of finished concrete and have a high reuse factor. They can be imprinted with a wide variety of surface textures and patterns, and can even replicate board marking. Formliners are very expensive and will require plywood backing panels to support them, but they can become economical if used more than 20 times with the same liner. They are most suited to precast production.

Embodied CO$_2$

Very high. Seek manufacturer's advice on material thickness

Estimate:

Typical 50 mm thick elastomeric liner

From Table A.1 select PVC = 11,060 kg CO$_2$/m^3

Embodied CO$_2$ of liner = 553 kg CO$_2$/m^2 for single use

Precast manufacture often uses liners 10 to 20 times. Net CO$_2$ if used 10 times is 55 kg CO$_2$/m^2

Disposable column formers

A number of manufacturers offer disposable circular column formwork, made from spirally wound rigid paper tube that is impermeable and resistant to water absorption. The tube is internally lined with a smooth-faced plastic release sheet for good surface finish and appearance, so there is no need to apply release agent to the inside of the tube. The tubes must, however, be protected from rain during storage and when in use. A tarpaulin that totally covers the tubes in storage would usually be sufficient for short-term protection, provided they are stacked off the ground on pallets.

The disposable tubes are supplied to the required length and diameter. If tubes need to be shortened on site, they should be cut from the bottom using a fine-tooth blade. This will ensure that the tear-off strip action is not impaired. The cut rim of the liner should then be resealed with a suitable formwork tape.

Embodied CO$_2$

Typical 500 mm diameter column

Unlined:

5 mm industrial cardboard with wire reinforcement = 6 kg CO$_2$/m^2 (equivalent to fibreglass: 115 kg CO$_2$/m^3, Table A.1)

Lined:

5 mm industrial cardboard wth wire reinforcement = 6 kg CO$_2$/m^2

3 mm GRP liner (plastic: 20,000 kg/m^3, Table A.1) = 102 kg CO$_2$/m^2

Total for lined = 108 kg CO$_2$/m^2

READY-MIXED CONCRETE PRODUCTION

READY-MIXED CONCRETE

Ready-mixed concrete is the universal way that concrete is delivered to construction sites today. It is a fast, efficient, quality assured, same-day, doorstep delivery service. It can provide a bespoke blend or a standardised mix of liquid rock to satisfy a customer's every requirements, and can match a wide variety of material specifications.

We are forever in the debt of Kjeld Ammentorp from Denmark, who in 1931 erected the first ready-mixed plant in the UK, at Bedfont near Heathrow Airport. Today, the annual production figure for ready-mixed concrete is approximately 25 million cubic metres, produced by around 1,200 ready-mixed plants spread across the UK.

The type of plant and equipment that a ready-mixed company uses to batch concrete is dictated by the size of the local market, peak volume demand within the catchment it serves and when the plant was built. A concrete plant can supply sites within a radius of 5–8 miles, but there are exceptions. In a major city, for example, the radial distance could be as short as 3 miles due to traffic congestion and journey times. In areas with lower population and less congested roads that could increase to 20 miles.

Most modern batching plants supplying large volumes of concrete in and around city-centre sites will have sophisticated computer-controlled wet mix or wet batch production systems, with enclosed cement silos and aggregates hoppers to minimise dust nuisance and noise levels. For smaller and perhaps older plants, a dry batch process may be in operation, with open storage areas for stockpiled aggregates. It is important to understand the differences between these two operations, and the control and influence they have on the quality and consistency of the concrete supplied to a project. Wet mix systems premix the concrete before it is discharged into the truck mixer. In dry batching the materials are placed dry into the truck mixer drum, where it is mixed by rotation of the tilting drum as the required water and admixture dosages are added to the dry mix.

Wet mix or wet batch plants

The raw materials are stored in separate bins and silos. Cement and cement replacement products are kept in silos – there will be at least two silos, with one for an ordinary cement (OPC, for example) and one for a cement replacement, such as GGBS or PFA. The cement is fed from the silos to the wet mixing chamber when required in pre-measured quantities using an internal screw pump and weighing flume.

The sand and coarse aggregates are stored in bins. The sand may be a crushed rock that has been brought in by rail, or a natural estuarine sand from nearby sand pit, which will have been washed and graded. The coarse aggregate may also be a crushed rock or gravel won from a nearby pit. It is more usual to find gravel and natural sands combinations or all crushed rock materials at a batching plant. If a lightweight concrete is being supplied then a bin carrying pelletised PFA (Lytag) will be available.

At a typical plant there will be a bin for the sand, a bin for a graded 5–20 mm coarse aggregate and perhaps one for a lightweight aggregate. In London, for example, a modern wet mix plant may store the coarse aggregates in single-size bins – 20 mm, 10 mm and 5 mm – for better quality control and consistency of the concrete. The advantages of doing this are that it can help reduce the cement content of a mix and so the cost of the concrete, and reduce the quality variation of the concrete batched at the plant.

Put simply, better control by wet batching in mixing and proportioning the concrete reduces the design margin of the concrete required to achieve its characteristic compressive strength. The target mean strength of the mix is the specified characteristic strength of the concrete plus the design margin. The design margin ensures that the actual strength of the concrete is within the 95 per cent confidence limit that the actual strength will be greater than the characteristic strength.

Dry batch plant

The materials are stored in bins and silos as in a wet batch plant, but are discharged dry into the drum of the truck mixer. The sand is loaded first, then half the cement and cement replacement, then all the coarse aggregates, then the rest of the cement and cement replacement.

The concrete truck has a tilting drum mixer which can mix up to 8 m³ of concrete at a time. The water and admixture are added directly from the batching plant to the dry materials and the drum rotated at 80–100 revolutions a minute for 8–10 minutes to ensure the materials are thoroughly mixed and that the concrete is uniform throughout the load. If the concrete is not thoroughly mixed there is the risk that the first batch discharged may be drier than the latter part of the load. This can have an impact on the final concrete colour as there may be marked differences in the water to cement ratio.

The consistency, flow and uniformity of the concrete throughout the tilting drum are crucially important in architectural concrete. It is for these reasons that wet mixing is the preferred method of ready-mixed production, but this type of plant is not always available.

SELF-COMPACTING CONCRETE

This is special type of concrete that can be placed into formwork using a tremie pipe or flat hose without the need for compaction. It is not readily available at many ready-mixed plants in the country. It requires a wet batch plant, very careful control and monitoring of the mix ingredients, a concrete technician to test its fresh properties and a local source of sand with a high percentage of very fine or powder material. It is also more expensive than ordinary concrete as the cement content can be as high as 400–500 kg/m³.

There is compelling evidence that self-compacting concrete can be produced satisfactorily from many combinations of materials. The extra cost of the high cement content and the special admixtures can be justified by the better finish and the labour cost savings. Value engineering exercises at present will probably discount its use on all but the largest projects. The elimination of compaction opens up the possibility of greater automation in the concrete construction process. At present, the general adoption of self-compacting concrete is hindered by the lack of user-friendly guidance or standard test methods and the need for specialists to interpret the results from site testing.

ADMIXTURES

The admixtures most commonly used in ready-mixed concrete are water reducers, high-range water reducers (also known as superplasticisers), retarders, air entrainers and accelerators. In concrete mixes for fine finishes, water-reducing admixtures and superplasticisers are those most often incorporated in the mix.

— *Water-reducing admixtures* – The active components are surface active agents, derived from either lignosulphonic acids, a by-product of the wood pulp industry, or hydroxylated carboxylic acids.

— *Superplasticisers* – These are also water-reducing admixtures but they have a much greater effect on the workability of concrete so are defined as high-range water reducers. Chemically, they are sulphonated melamine formaldehyde condensates and sulphonated napthalene formaldehyde condensates. The only real disadvantage of a superplasticiser is its relatively high cost compared with a water-reducing admixture. Superplasticisers are essential for high-strength and self-compacting concretes and for flowing self-levelling concrete.

CASE STUDY/
LONDON CONCRETE READY-MIXED CONCRETE PRODUCTION

Jack Sindhu, London Concrete

London Concrete Ltd supplies the full range of concrete mixes to EN206/BS 8500, from blinding, over-site, foundation and structural-grade concretes to heavyweight, lightweight, air-entrained, high-strength, low-heat, foamed and coloured concretes.

The company's batching plants are fully computerised in weighing and gauging materials. Throughout the batching process, the moisture contents of the aggregates, especially the fine aggregates, are continuously monitored

via the moisture probes fitted to the aggregate bins. Allowances are made automatically by an 'ALKON' batch computer for water adjustment. All materials are discharged uniformly into the mixer and without loss. To ensure homogenous mixing, the cement and aggregates are fed into the drum simultaneously at a uniform rate and the mixing time is sufficient to achieve an even mix. Slump and workability control is achieved in the mixing process with the aid of a calibrated ammeter (slump meter).

Quality control

London Concrete carries out inspection, monitoring and testing of all incoming materials at batching plants, including cement and aggregates, plus sampling and testing of the fresh mixed concrete by standard cubes taken and crushed at 7, 14 and 28 days.

Test data are analysed on a continuous basis and small adjustments to concrete mixes are made to maintain the quality needed to meet the required standards. London Concrete is a member of the Quality Scheme For Ready Mixed Concrete and has third party accreditation.

The boxed examples on page 41 consider the carbon footprint of ready-mixed production and delivery by comparing the CO_2 outputs from a typical town-based plant and a sophisticated city-centre plant.

Left
A London Concrete wet-mixed batching plant

Typical city-centre plant – Bow

There are two batching plants within the site: Plant One is a wet batch system with a 2 m³ pan, Plant Two has a 9 m³ Erie Strayer drum mixer for dry batching.

Trucks

A fleet of fifteen 8 m³ trucks is based at the plant. Additional trucks can be transferred when the demand exceeds the fleet capacity.

Materials

Cement :

Plant One – cement is stored in four 50 tonne silos, two of which hold Portland cement and two hold cement replacement, such as GGBS or PFA.

Plant Two – cement is stored in two 125 tonne silos, one of which holds Portland cement and the other PFA. There is an additional 250 tonne Portland cement silo.

Aggregates:

Plant One – five 60 tonne overhead aggregates bins.

Plant Two – five 80 tonne overhead aggregates bins.

The aggregates include 4–10 mm and 4–20 mm crushed limestone to 0–4 mm land-based sand. All aggregates are delivered to the plant by rail. Additional secondary aggregates are available if required, including Lytag.

Capacity

Plant One has the capacity to weigh a full 8 m³ batch.

Plant Two has the capacity to weigh a full 9 m³ batch.

Output

Plant One can produce 120 m³ per hour of concrete.

Plant Two can produce 150 m³ per hour of concrete.

Embodied CO_2

Assumes rail-delivered aggregates are zero carbon rated.

Plant
= 0.44 kWh per tonne of concrete batched
= 0.44 × 0.537 (grid electricity)
= 0.24 kg CO_2 per tonne

Truck = 0.35 kg CO_2 per tonne of concrete delivered

Total = 0.59 kg CO_2 per tonne delivered concrete

Typical town-based plant – Purley

The plant uses a Steelfields Major 90 wet batch system with a 2 m³ mixing pan that can also dry batch concrete. A dedicated fleet of four 8 m³ truck mixers is based at the plant. Additional trucks can be brought in when the demand exceeds the static fleet's capacity.

Materials

Cement:

Cement is stored in four 50 tonne silos, two of which hold Portland cement and two hold cement replacement material, such as GGBS or PFA.

Aggregates:

There are five 60 tonne storage bins. Two bins contain 4–20 mm crushed limestone, one holds 4–10 mm crushed limestone and one 0–4 mm land-based sand. All the aggregates are delivered by rail. Additional secondary aggregates are available if required, including Lytag (lightweight aggregate). There is ground storage for in excess of 3,000 tonnes of aggregates.

Admixtures:

Various admixtures are stocked, including plasticisers, superplasticisers, air entrainers, retarders, water reducers, pore blockers and accelerators. They are introduced into the mix through automatic dispensers.

Capacity/output

The plant has the capacity to weigh a full 8 m³ batch.

The plant's maximum output is 120 m³ of concrete per hour.

Embodied CO_2

Assumes rail-delivered aggregates are zero carbon rated.

Plant = 0.31 kWh per tonne of concrete batched

= 0.31 × 0.537 (grid electricity) = 0.17 kg CO_2 per tonne

Truck = 0.46 kg CO_2 per tonne of concrete delivered

Total = 0.63 kg CO_2 per tonne delivered concrete

Sustainability

London Concrete is dedicated to being a sustainable producer and as such complies with the requirements of ISO 9001:2000 and ISO 14001:2004. The company promotes the use of secondary and recycled materials, such as china clay stent aggregate, and replacement cements to reduce the embodied CO_2 of concrete.

All aggregates are delivered into London by rail. Cement arrives by overnight road transport from the cement works, when there is the minimum of road traffic or delays and with the vehicles working at peak efficiency.

Additionally, as part of Aggregate Industries we are the first company in the UK to obtain a BRE Global BES 6001:2008 Certificate for Responsible Sourcing. Responsible sourcing is an ethos of supply chain management and product stewardship and encompasses the social, economic and environmental impacts of construction products over their whole life. (See Table A.3 in Appendix to Part I for a CO_2 audit.)

PRECAST CONCRETE MANUFACTURE

OVERVIEW

Precast concrete is a factory-made, off-site product. Precast elements available range from beam and block flooring, hollow core slabs and beams, and composite slabs, to structural frames and cladding panels. It has not been possible to assess the embodied CO_2 of all these elements as each will depend on the concrete mixes that the manufacturer chooses to use, the type of product, the energy consumed in running the factory and the transport CO_2. Much of the data will be project specific, of course, but quite a lot will not, such as cement type and cement content, and this can be usefully generalised for estimating the embodied CO_2 of precast products on a building project using Tables A.1 and A.2 (see Appendix to Part I).

Quite soon all precast manufacturers will be required to produce this information, to comply with legislation and to satisfy the specification for environmentally responsible architecture. Some companies, such as Charcon Precast

Solutions Ltd, have completed an independent CO_2 audit of their factories and been given a high green rating by BRE for transporting their aggregate products by rail and using recycled materials and cement replacements. The data on their precast products given in Table A.2 shows the total embodied CO_2 for production, heating and delivery of units to site.

Precast concrete offers opportunities to express the intrinsic qualities of concrete through varying the cement, the aggregates and the pigment. There is also the potential to reduce embodied CO_2, through the use of replacement cements, renewable energy sources and perhaps even organic aggregates, to create carbon-neutral products in the future. The energy required to run the factory can be generated from renewable sources and biomass, and if transportation of products is by hybrid fuelled vehicles then the production of precast elements could indeed be carbon neutral. There is the green future for the precast industry to aspire to.

> **Embodied CO_2**
> CO_2 can be estimated for any precast element using the values in Tables A.1 and A.2 (see Appendix to Part I) if the section sizes are known and the concrete mix and rebar content are given

PRECAST FLOORING OPTIONS

Precast beam and block

Beam and block flooring systems are popular
for domestic buildings. They can be installed
in suspended ground and upper floors with
minimum fuss and maximum effectiveness.
Quick to install, they provide an immediate
safe working platform and eliminate problems
associated with backfill, clay heave and
shrinkage. The slabs with an in-situ topping
are generally 150–300 mm deep. The beams
or joists are either reinforced or prestressed
concrete inverted T sections that can span 4–7 m.

Hollow core slabs

Hollow core slabs are quick to install. They
also have a wide range of spans and loading
capabilities and can be used with masonry, steel,
precast and in-situ forms of construction. They
are sound insulating, highly load-bearing, fire
resistant and allow the easy accommodation
of services. With the option of prestressing or
reinforcement, they offer a span capability of up
to 12 m and a depth range of 150–400 mm.

COMPOSITE PRECAST FLOORS

Soffit slabs/lattice girder floors

Soffit slabs comprise precast prestressed units
that are 60–100 mm thick and 0.6–2.4 m wide
and which have an in-situ topping.

Lattice girder floors are made up of a permanent
precast concrete formwork acting compositely
with an in-situ concrete structural topping. The
lattice girder provides stability, good connection
with the in-situ concrete and self-supporting
properties during construction. Typically, the
slab is 40–100 mm thick, 2.4 m wide and up to
12 m long. The dimensions of the lattice girders
are determined by the overall depth of the slab,
cover and the temporary condition requirements
during construction.

Double T-beams – Scandinavia

Double T floor units in prestressed concrete
have a ribbed cross-section and a smooth under
face. The units are mainly used for long spans
and for high imposed loadings. The units are
manufactured with two standard widths – 2.4 m

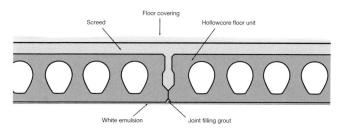

Screed   Floor covering   Hollowcore floor unit

White emulsion   Joint filling grout

and 3.0 m – and the standard cross-sections
are given in the manufacturers' brochures.
Beam depths vary from 0.5 to 0.8 m. The
ends of the units can be notched to reduce the
overall structural depth. A structural topping
can be used to ensure both vertical shear
transfer between adjacent units and horizontal
diaphragm action in the floor plate. The
standard double T-beam units have a minimum
fire resistance of 60–120 minutes. Anchor rails
can be cast into the soffits of the webs.

Versatile and expressive, prestressed long-
span beam units with a 2.4 m-wide top flange
section have been used extensively for car park
structures in the UK. They are often used in
office building construction in Europe, with
exposed soffits for thermal efficiency, such
as in the Katsan Building, Stockholm (White
Architects) and the Tuborg Nord Building,
Copenhagen (Arkitema). The beam depth will
depend on the span and loading conditions
and the available mould sizes from the precast
supplier.

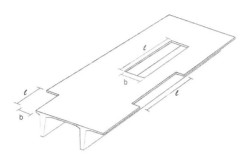

Double T-beams – Tarmac

Typically, for a Tarmac double T-beam, the beam depth is 0.6 m and the top flange is 2.4 m wide and 50 mm thick. A structural topping 75 mm thick of 40 MPa concrete is usually applied. The reinforcement and prestress tendon amount to approximately 2 per cent of the gross section area. The spans can range from 10 to 20 m according to the imposed loading and required fire rating.

The double T-beam creates large areas of uninterrupted floor space, free from column obstructions, and allows flexibility in the building for change of use. Its high-strength concrete requires minimal maintenance and so does not require a false ceiling, especially if its thermal mass is to be used.

Embodied CO_2

Ex works

Concrete:
Cement CEM I: 500 kg/m³
Cement CO_2 = 760 kg CO_2/tonne ÷ 2 = 380 kg CO_2/m³

Aggregates: take as zero

Formwork: reusable

Reinforcement:
Rebar = 8% of concrete volume = 624 kg/m³
Rebar CO_2 = 480 kg CO_2/tonne × 0.624 = 300 kg CO_2/m³ (Table A.2)

Total material CO_2 only = 680 kg CO_2/m³

PRECAST WALL SYSTEMS

Crosswall

Crosswall is a generic system of building that uses a series of precast dividing walls to transfer the floor loads through the building to the foundation. The system uses vertically cast load-bearing walls, which are suitable for direct decoration with only minor treatment. External walls are effectively only cladding panels, supporting their own weight, and do not necessarily contribute to the stability of the building. The system allows either concrete perimeter wall infills or lightweight cladding alternatives for a variety of elevation treatments.

The Crosswall system generally utilises stair cores and lift cores for overall stability, using the floors as stiff diaphragms for the transmittal of horizontal forces into shear walls located at staircase and lift shaft positions. The floors are made up of precast hollow core slabs, in-situ slab or precast composite construction.

Left
Double T-beam element

Above
Double T-beams used to create an open entrance and reception space

Twin-Wall

Twin-Wall is a permanent shuttering system comprising two external factory-produced precast concrete panels joined with reinforcement. The panels are erected on site and the cavity is filled with in-situ concrete. This produces walls that are fair faced on both sides and dimensionally accurate. If the surface is simply painted, the Twin-Wall system will provide a high level of thermal mass. Twin-Wall also offers excellent acoustic performance, making it especially useful for separating wall applications. It can also be supplied with integral insulation for external walls.

CASE STUDY/
CHARCON PRECAST SOLUTIONS: BARNSLEY PRECAST FACTORY

The Barnsley precast factory is a relatively new plant, opened in 2008. The factory has a large open-plan area where all steel reinforcement is bent, prepared and fixed, and where precast mould changes take place and the concrete is poured. The factory has the resource of fully automated reinforcement bending machines, two 20-t capacity overhead cranes, a 1.5 m³ automated batching plant, aggregate recycling machines and rainwater collection systems for use in the production of concrete. The factory has a 2 ha stock yard with additional parking for many transport trailers.

The factory can precast Twin-Wall and Crosswall systems, structural frame elements and cladding units, but has initially specialised in producing stair and landing units, parapet walls, ground beams and conduit troughs. All products are precast to minimum tolerances using timber moulds, with the exception of the ground beams, which are cast using steel moulds. As the moulds are used many times over, the forming is carbon neutral.

Where possible, concrete will contain cement replacements, such as GGBS and PFA. A key ingredient when appropriate is China clay waste granite or stent, although the location of the factory will dictate whether this is economic or another locally sourced secondary aggregate such as BFS aggregate can be incorporated. All of these materials have the effect of reducing the embodied CO_2.

There are two general concrete mix designs used at Barnsley: a conventional vibrated mix for the precast stair units, and a self-compacting mix for the other products. Both mixes are a C40 mix.

> **Embodied CO_2**
> Charcon Precast products:
> 773–778 kg CO_2/m³
> (See Table A.2, Appendix to Part I)

MODERN PRECAST FAÇADES

Precast concrete façades will have a higher cement content than in-situ concrete to achieve the necessary early-age strength and surface quality. The cement is usually imported white Portland cement, so the embodied CO_2 will be higher than for locally produced cements. The proportion and combination of sand, coarse aggregates (up to 20 mm), cement and pigments will be selected to give the desired finish. The concrete mix will include water-reducing admixtures and waterproofing agents.

Some manufacturers may prefer to use resin-faced plywood or GRP-lined timber for constructing the moulds. Others will use metal forms for casting standardised products because of their high reuse factor. For surface profiling and embossed decorative features, GRP and synthetic rubber liners are placed in the timber moulds. These synthetic materials may have high embodied CO_2, but as the moulds are capable of being used 100 times – assuming a high degree of design repetition and standardisation – the forming CO_2 is negligible.

For economic production, moulds should have at least 30 uses before being discarded. However, it is rare to find a building that has 30 or more identical units on the façade. To avoid the penalty arising from low repetition, façade panels should be designed as similarly shaped units which can be cast from one master mould. Major economies in production costs and lower embodied CO_2 can be achieved by making small alterations to a master mould.

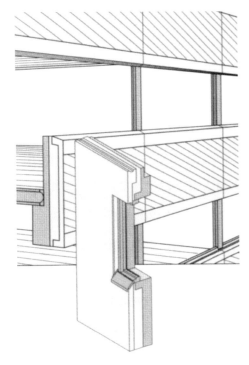

Thermal insulation can either be factory applied to the back of a façade unit or fixed on site after installation. Composite precast sandwich panels, which have thermal insulation in the core, are manufactured in some European countries, where the problem of cold bridging has been overcome by the use of proprietary anchors.

Large precast panels are usually formed with an integral nib, which sits on the supporting floor slab or beam, with the top of the panel pinned to the main structure to allow for differential movement. Joints between panels are sealed using silicone or polysulphide sealants.

SANDWICH PANEL CONSTRUCTION

Sandwich panels are a cost-effective solution for high-quality, multi-storey residential buildings and B1-type medium-rise office buildings. The panels are storey-high units up to 8 m long with an outer façade panel 60–80 mm thick (which can be finished with a wide range of stone-like surfaces), a layer of insulation and then a backing leaf of either load-bearing or self-bearing precast concrete 90–120mm thick. When the inner leaf is load-bearing the panel can support the structural floor and façade above it.

The outer layers of the panel are interconnected by steel ladder reinforcement, which acts as wind and shear connectors. Thermal bridging through the steel connectors is minimal. The system has the advantage of providing structural integrity without placing any reliance on the insulation for load transference. The structural floors are usually precast hollow-core planks that are stitched to the top of the storey-high inner panel.

Load-bearing sandwich panels offer many advantages. They are fast to erect, they eliminate the need for columns and wet trades, they are self-finished and they are the most competitively priced residential building system in northern Europe.

The composite embodied CO_2 of a sandwich panel can be derived from the cement content of the concrete and the type of insulation material. The forming and production CO_2 estimates are negligible, as there is a very high degree of standardisation and reuse of moulds and a fast output of panels through the factory. The U-value and insulation thickness can be designed to meet or surpass all current codes and Building Regulations requirements.

GLASSFIBRE REINFORCED CONCRETE (GRC)

GRC is composed of a mortar mix of cement, selected crushed aggregates, sand, fillers, admixtures and water with the addition of alkali-resistant glass fibre strands. The glass fibres are typically 6–51 mm long and 10–30 μm in diameter and obtain their alkali resistance from a coating applied during manufacturing. Using combinations of fibre lengths will ensure that adequate bond strength develops between the fibres and the cement matrix and encourages a quasi-ductile failure by fracture of the fibres.

GRP panels are produced by spraying, using a mixture with a water to cement ratio lower than 0.4 (low in comparison with most concrete) and a cement content of not less than 800 kg/m³ (high for concrete). A typical hand-sprayed GRC mix produced by Trent Concrete contains around 5 per cent of glass fibre strands. A fully automated spray system for manufacturing GRC façade panels operated by Durapact in Germany uses fibre lengths of 12–50 mm, again at 5 per cent by volume.

Typically, the skin thickness of a GRC panel is 25–50 mm, making its self-weight as much as 80 per cent lower than a corresponding precast unit. Weight reduction of this magnitude offers substantial savings in transportation CO_2 and handling and site erection costs.

ULTRA HIGH PERFORMANCE CONCRETE

Ultra high performance concretes are used increasingly for a range of structural applications, and standards in a number of countries are being revised to accommodate these improved materials. The material properties are far superior to ordinary concrete in every respect. As well as a higher compressive strength, the bond and shear strengths are far greater and Young's modulus is much improved, while the tensile strength and ductility are enhanced by the introduction of steel fibres. Precast ultra materials are structural-grade materials used for precasting slim, lightweight load-bearing façade elements, thin cantilever balcony slabs, elegant staircases and supporting columns and remarkably slender bridge structures.

A special group is the fibre-reinforced high-performance concretes. One example is CRC (Compact Reinforced Composite), developed by Aalborg Portland and marketed by CRC Technology in Denmark, which has a strength range of 150–300 MPa. Another is Ductal, developed by Lafarge and Bouygues in France, which is composed of cement particles, steel fibres, special sand fillers and plasticisers and is able to fully hydrate with little added water.

Embodied CO_2
CRC, ex works:
Cement = 1.2 × 760 = 912 kg CO_2/m³
Sand, assume carbon neutral
Steel fibre = 0.18 × 510 = 91.8 kg CO_2/m³
Total = 1,004 kg CO_2/m³
(See Table A.2)

EMBODIED CO_2 IN BUILDING MATERIALS

The following section presents the results of desk-based research commissioned by The Concrete Centre for this publication.

PART A: DESK-BASED RESEARCH

The CO_2 data that have been published, in general, only assess the amount of embodied CO_2 in materials at the factory gate, after manufacturing but before transport to the building site. Embodied CO_2 in building materials should refer to the total amount of CO_2 emitted during the extraction, refining, manufacture, transport, installation and eventual recycling of the materials. These data have been virtually non-existent. Some embodied energy data are given in kWh/m³, which is not the ideal way to present information, so they have to be converted to CO_2/m³. The conversion factor will depend on the type of energy being used in the production process. Each source of energy has a different conversion factor – it is high, for example, if you use electricity from the grid, less for gas and fuel oil and lowest for wood pellets. The Defra Energy Conversion Factors shown in the Appendix to Part I (Tables A.7 and A.8) were used to convert kWh to CO_2. As there was not the time available to contact every manufacturer to find out what energy source they used; a simple multiplying constant was used based on 30 per cent gas and 70 per cent electricity consumption. Some results will therefore not be as accurate after conversion, but it is far better than no information. Defra also produces a list for converting distance travelled in various vehicles (Table A.9 in the Appendix to Part I), which is useful for calculating the CO_2 emitted in transportation of goods.

The principal source of CO_2 information appears to be the BRE in the UK. However, the data that BRE has been prepared to publish through *The Green Guide to Specification* and online tools such as Envest are based on an 'eco ranking' points scale, used to compare and to rank building materials. The origin and weighting of the data used in the publications and software are not transparent, nor are figures given for the embodied CO_2 of materials or how they were derived. As a design tool it is not precise and makes many assumptions that may not hold true for all conditions. If there were nothing else available then it would be the best data that we have, but that is no longer the case.

The data published in *The Environmental Handbook* by Feilden Clegg Bradley Studios (2007) shows embodied energy in kWh/m³ for a number of common building materials. This is the best reference book that can be found. The sources for these data were the BRE's Approved Environmental Profiles (1994); BSRIA's *Environmental Rules of Thumb* (2000) and *Environmental Code of Practice for Buildings and their Services*; the University of Wellington; the Association of Environmentally Conscious Builders; *The Architects' Journal* (8 June 1997); *Canadian Architect*; and Beyer Plastics. High and low figures are used to show the range of values quoted for individual materials, and kWh figures have been converted to CO_2 using the Defra guidelines.

Another useful publication is *The Green Building Bible*, volume 1 (Hall, 2007), which shows a list of embodied energy values in

kWh/m³ for common building materials. The data sources were the Centre for Alternative Technology; *Environmental Science Handbook*; Pittsburgh Corning; the Timber Trade Federation; CIRIA; and Green Pro.

The University of Bath has compiled a publicly available database called the Inventory of Carbon and Energy, which aims to create an inventory of embodied energy and carbon coefficients for building materials. The compilers have used only sources in the public domain, avoiding subscription-based information to avoid copyright issues. The scope of their study is defined as 'cradle to gate', which means measuring the CO_2 output and energy involved from extraction through to the finished product, ready for delivery from the factory gate. However, these figures cannot be checked or validated so there may be discrepancies. According to a desk study undertaken by Leeds Metropolitan University, there was a rather limited range of materials on the database. So the data captured were only used to corroborate values compiled from the two primary sources.

There is very little else in print regarding CO_2 emissions from the manufacturers of specific building products. This arises from a natural reluctance on the part of some manufacturers to disclose too much information about their commercial processes, and also because of natural variations in techniques which can lead to a wide range of values for similar products. However, some material group organisations – for example the British Cement Association and the Mineral Products Association (via The Concrete Centre) – have been helpful with CO_2 data on a country-wide basis, but the data are not company-specific. If you wish to purchase a bag of groceries, you go to a supermarket. But if you wish to know exactly how much you will have to pay, you go to a specific and trusted supermarket near to your home. It the same with CO_2 data – they have to be product- and manufacturer-specific to be useful.

Table A.1 (see Appendix to Part I) shows all the CO_2 data found in Part A of the desk research and combines them into a best fit average for each material category.

Density of building materials

A list of typical densities for common buildings materials has also been compiled. The data extracted for publication are less contentious and more easily accessible. Some are listed in the BSI British Standards publications or in the Eurocodes. The majority were derived from *The Way We Build Now* (Orton, 1987), *The Green Building Bible*, volume 1 (Hall, 2007) and various publications from The Concrete Centre. These figures are shown in Table A.1 in the Appendix to Part I.

Improvements in data accuracy

As environmental reporting becomes more common, due to legislation and as companies wish to stay ahead of the competition, more solid datasets regarding all aspects of building material properties will be available in the public domain.

During the compilation of these data, many suppliers indicated that they intend to publish data on the embodied CO_2 in their products in the near future. It is hoped that all suppliers will be able to conduct their own CO_2 audits and not have to rely on expensive auditing exercises by government bodies or external consultants. The practicalities of this have been demonstrated by the contributions from the concrete product companies in Part B of this research.

Summary

The Way We Build Now by Andrew Orton (1987) and Feilden Clegg Bradley Studios' *The Environmental Handbook* (2007) were the starting points for this study. There are a number of other useful publications which deal with such data, although none are as complete or as consistent. Information on material properties is also available via various websites, including eFunda and MatWeb, which are aimed at engineers. A range of information sources were searched during this study; the resulting data come from just the main bodies of information.

The main issue is the correct interpretation of published data for embodied CO_2 – whether or not it covers transportation and the energy used in production, and whether the correct energy source has been used in converting from kWh to CO_2.

PART B: CONCRETE INDUSTRY CO_2 DATA

In the second part of this research a number of specialist companies that make concrete products used in construction were asked to prepare a detailed summary of CO_2 emissions of their products to account for embodied CO_2, production CO_2 and transportation CO_2. These are the only accurate data in this book and as such will be used on the Construction CO_2 Audit statement when applicable.

The composite embodied CO_2 of materials

Part A reviewed all published sources of data on embodied CO_2, showing the variations in these values, and the best average values for making a comparative assessment of different construction approaches (see Table A.1).

The values shown are for individual materials and may take no account of composite materials' actual CO_2. For example, cement is only one-sixth of concrete; the other constituents are natural and have low embodied carbon. We can take these as zero for a quick assessment. So the reported figures could be artificially high, especially if low embodied cements were used. On the other hand, cement has to be transported to a ready-mixed concrete plant in a 40 tonne truck, and the resulting concrete is delivered to site by a truck mixer. The delivery mileage and CO_2 emissions of transportation have to be accounted for in computing the total CO_2, plus the energy of running the cement factory and batching plant, and also the home-to-work journeys of the workforce. This last figure may not be significant but it should be taken into account.

For a more accurate project-based assessment, all the CO_2 figures have to be factored this way to give the total composite CO_2 on which to base design decisions. To do this, the supply chain and product manufacturers have to audit the CO_2 emissions accordingly. It is not difficult to do, as all the data are already being collected or recorded for economic purposes by the manufacturers.

A number of companies were contacted to provide data for a project-based assessment. This information has been used for monitoring the CO_2 in the construction CO_2 audit. The essential information required is the CO_2 emissions for the production and delivery of cement, aggregates, plywood formwork, reinforcement, ready-mixed concrete, precast concrete, admixtures, release agents and waterproof coatings.

Dredged or excavated natural sands and gravels and hired proprietary formwork support system and scaffolding (which are reused many times and not written off against the projects) are taken as carbon neutral. Plant and machinery are also assumed to be carbon neutral; it is only the fuel they consume that should be measured. Timber formwork that will be disposed of is not carbon neutral.

The following companies have completed a total CO_2 product audit:

— Castle Cement – Ribblesdale Cement Works
— UPM Kymmene (WISA) – film-faced plywood from Finland
— Celsa – reinforcement manufacture
— BRC – reinforcement processing and supply
— Aggregate Industries – ready-mixed concrete, concrete blocks and precast cladding panels.

The following companies provided CO_2 data for their products (not validated for site delivery, transport home to work, plant and machinery):

— RockTron – PFA
— CSMA – GGBS
— UKQAA – PFA
— Lime Technology – Hemcrete blocks
— Lignacite.

The details of the CO_2 data for individual products are given in the relevant sections of this chapter and are summarised in Table A.2 (see Appendix to Part I).

THE CONSTRUCTION CO_2 AUDIT

In this section the data required to assess and review the total construction CO_2 of a building will be discussed and described. It is a bit like a design exercise – undertaking value engineering of the construction options to find the optimum building solution.

In a cost-benefit appraisal of a building, the frame, the cladding and the services options are assessed for: (a) the cost of construction; (b) the finance cost for the construction, based on the programme time; and (c) whether an option provides more lettable floor space, with the extra space earning additional rental income.

The driver for the choice of the building form – steel or concrete frame, natural or forced ventilation system, glass or masonry cladding – has generally been the lowest cost, and not the total CO_2 the building will generate. But if a material can offer long-term savings on energy use by having greater fabric energy storage (FES; see Chapter 2), as well as reducing the mechanical and electrical (M&E) services installation costs, then the CO_2 credit that this offers should form part of the total assessment, in the same way as the savings on the M&E costs. It is for this reason that a number of leading architects have opted for building forms that offer FES advantages and thermal mass.

THE EMBODIED CO_2 OF MATERIALS

Table A.1 (see Appendix to Part I) presents the embodied CO_2 values for a range of building materials. The values were obtained through an extensive review of published sources of data on embodied energy; Table A.1 provides the best average values for making a comparative assessment of the construction CO_2.

The values shown are for the raw material and may take no account of transportation, production and site construction CO_2 emissions, although some of them claim to (without providing more details). The CO_2 sources may not be significant, but they should be accounted for. For example, cement is only one-sixth of concrete; the other constituents are natural materials and have low embodied CO_2 levels. We can take these as zero for a quick assessment. Cement has to be transported in a 40-tonne lorry to a ready-mixed concrete plant, where it is mixed with aggregates to form concrete. The resulting concrete is then delivered to site by a truck mixer. The delivery mileage and CO_2 emission of transportation have to be accounted for, plus the energy required to run the cement factory and batching plant and the home-to-work journeys of the workforce, in computing the total CO_2. Similar assessments must be compiled for steel and timber-framed structures as well as for concrete structures.

CONCRETE INDUSTRY INPUT

A number of concrete industry companies provided embodied CO_2 data for the project-based assessment shown in the CO_2 audit study. The essential information required for the audit is the CO_2 emissions from the production and manufacture of cement, aggregates, plywood formwork, reinforcement, ready-mixed concrete, precast concrete and blockwork.

The CO_2 emissions for specific construction materials are listed in Table A.2 (see Appendix to Part I).

Dredged or excavated natural sands and gravels, and proprietary formwork support systems and scaffolding (which are hired and reused many times and not written off against the projects), are assumed to be carbon neutral. Timber formwork, however, which has to be disposed of, is not carbon neutral.

EXAMPLE CO₂ AUDIT

Quantities for the audit

The bill of quantities on a project provides the volume, area, length or weight of all materials required, so we can use this to build up the total CO_2 emissions for the construction. By changing the form of construction from in-situ concrete to steel, changing the service installation from mechanical to natural ventilation, or reviewing alternative cladding systems, we can model the effects of these changes on total CO_2 emissions and come up with the optimum design for a given project or a part of the building.

The overriding conditions are that the cost of construction must not increase by much and the durability and integrity of the construction must not be impaired or diminish the useful life of the building.

The data for the quantities have been taken from the Cost Model Study published by the BCA in 1993. This study provides the quantities for constructing a three-storey and a seven-storey building in the M4 corridor, adopting an in-situ concrete frame and a steel frame option for each. The following codes are used:

— M4C3: M4 corridor, three-storey concrete-framed building
— M4S3: M4 corridor, three-storey steel-framed building
— M4C7: M4 corridor, seven-storey concrete-framed building
— M4S7: M4 corridor, seven-storey steel-framed building

The building designs were based on typical commercial offices located along the M4 motorway corridor and have a 7.5 metre by 7.5 metre structural grid, pad foundations (no basement) and a specification suited to local market conditions.

The design team for the project were:

— Architect: YRM Architects and Planners
— Structure: YRM Anthony Hunts
— Services: YRM Engineers
— Quantity surveyor: Gardiner and Theobald.

Planning and programming

Prelims and substructure: 5-day week; 1 week for site set up, excavation and foundation follow setting out; concrete lead time 1–3 weeks; steel lead time 10–12 weeks.

Frame: Concrete – first floor supported on ground floor slab; 2-week floor cycle time, four pours per floor, soffit deck stripped after 3 days with props remaining. Steel – erected at the rate of 22 pieces per day, 50 tonnes per week.

Cladding: Stick system assumed; cladding starts after three floors of frame completed, one elevation at a time.

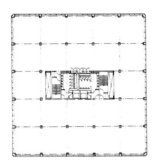

Typical floor plan

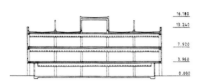

Typical section and detail

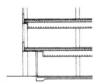

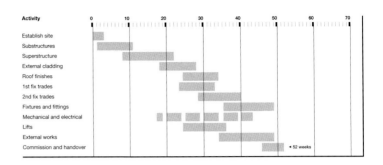

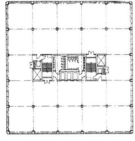

Typical floor plan

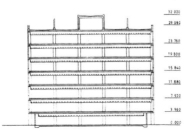

Typical section

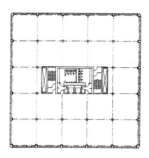

Typical floor plan

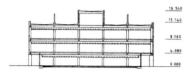

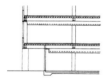

Typical section and detail

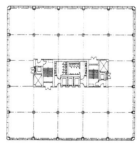

Typical floor plan

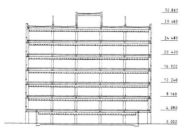

Typical section

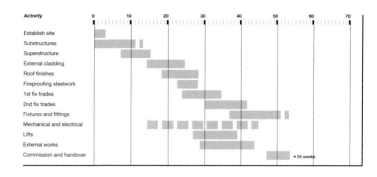

Left and above
M4S3: floor
plan, section
and programme

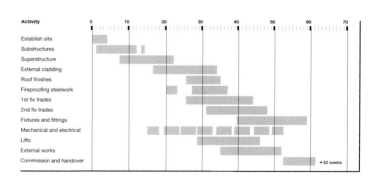

Left and above
M4S7: floor
plan, section
and programme

Fireproof steelwork: Fireboarding starts when floors are enclosed by the external cladding; progress from core to perimeter.

M&E: Services carcassing starts after first floor props removed or steel first floor deck cast.

CONSTRUCTION NOTES AND EMBODIED CO_2

Structure

— *All RC concrete:* 40 MPa, 50:50 OP/GGBS, cement 375 kg/m³, sand 700 kg, gravel 1,200 kg.

— *All RC concrete for metal deck:* 40 MPa, lightweight, 50:50 OP/GGBS, cement 400 kg/m³, Lytag 900 kg, sand 700 kg.

— *Galvanised steel decking:* 1.2 mm MD60, V2 trapezoidal, 60 mm depth, 300 mm centres.

— *Fire cladding:* 15 mm gypsum board, density 12.8 kN/m².

— *Holding-down bolts:* 20 mm dia., 600 mm long.

— Steel base plates: three-storey base plate 500 × 500 × 25 mm; seven-storey base plate 750 × 750 × 40 mm.

Zero CO_2 rated

— Excavation, fill, working space, support to excavations, granular bed, sand blinding.

— Temporary works, scaffolding, props, ladders and similar items that are on hire.

Internal planning

— 100 mm concrete blockwork.

— 200 mm concrete blockwork.

— Plasterboard 12 mm thick.

— Plasterboard, fire resistant, 15mm thick.

Finishes

— *Suspended ceiling:* mild steel Amstrong grillage support 1.5 kg/m², Orcal flat metal tile 5 kg/m².

— *Raised access floor:* Eurodek Fortress BSEN chipboard composite 29 mm, 2 mm galvanised steel, MD type metal pedestal legs, say 300 mm high.

— *Decorative plaster:* 10 mm thick.

— *Granite floor:* 15 mm thick tile on cement mortar bed (1:4 OP/sand) 10 mm thick.

— *Ceramic wall tiles:* 10 mm thick bedded on 2 mm polymer grout (cement polymer mix).

External cladding

— *Curtain wall:* 6 mm and 8 mm glass, aluminium transom 1.5 kg/m run, one per floor, aluminium mullions at 1.5 m centres, 1.5 kg/m run.

— *Cladding to external soffits:* columns, walls; 2 mm uPVC.

Mechanical and electrical (M&E) services

Mechanical plant, pipework, ducting for heating and cooling requirements for six service options, from passive systems to fully air conditioned. Assessed for 2,000 m² floor area by Cundall and arranged by Alan Forgarty.

Construction machinery and labour resources schedule

Assessed for all four buildings by Mansell Construction and arranged by Brian Flannery.

Items to be omitted from CO_2 audit

Precast concrete stairs, fixtures and fittings, electrical installations, lifts.

Audit results

The results of the building CO_2 audit are presented in Tables 1.8 and 1.9. The specifications and embodied CO_2 values for materials and components specified are presented in Table 1.10.

FES options

The CO_2 audit implications of alternative options for heating and ventilating the building have been assessed and are included in the main CO_2 audit (see Table 1.9, Options 1 to 6).

Note: all options are based on a treated floor area of 2,000 m².

Summary of the construction CO_2 audit

From this study, the estimated CO_2 embodied in the concrete frame and steel frame structures for the three-storey and seven-storey building options shows clearly that a concrete frame offers a significant saving in overall CO_2 emissions, by as much as 40 per cent.

CO_2 reductions are possible for the steel-frame building by specifying the use of only recycled steel, which has lower embodied CO_2 than virgin steel. However, if this approach were to be universally adopted it would, in the long term, mean closure of existing steelworks in the UK; therefore, a balance between the two production types would seem prudent.

Further reductions in CO_2 emissions are possible for concrete-framed buildings by the adoption of passive ventilation systems, which significantly reduce mechanical ductwork and pipework and eliminate the need for suspended ceilings. In addition, if all the ply formwork used for casting in-situ concrete were reused in the permanent construction, and not disposed of, quite a lot of CO_2 could be sequestered to offset the embodied CO_2 in plywood manufacture and concrete production. Alternatively, opting to build a precast composite frame would dramatically reduce the need for ply formwork, which would further reduce the construction CO_2 of the frame. Concrete offers designers a choice of frame options, enabling them to optimise on cost and minimise CO_2 emissions.

Concrete that combines low embodied CO_2 cements, such as PFA and GGBS, and natural aggregates is not a high-emission product, as has been shown by this audit and by the technical notes earlier in this chapter. Many designers who are not familiar with the constituents of concrete mistakenly believe that it is mainly composed of Portland cement, giving it a poor green rating. This perception should not be allowed to prevail.

Reducing waste, recycling formwork and not disposing of timber to a rubbish dump (thereby avoiding the creation of methane) should be part of good working practice. The use of public transport for home-to-work journeys reduces transport emissions for city-centre projects.

The key pointers from this study are that:

— the compilation of a detailed construction CO_2 audit of a building is very feasible
— the accuracy of CO_2 data, including the energy source and the collection of transport and production CO_2 data, is essential for making value judgements
— the supply chain must be encouraged to provide CO_2 data at tender stage, and such data must be validated, and
— knowledge of the constituents of concrete, the material choices and the construction options – in-situ, composite or precast – will lead to better management of construction CO_2.

Table 1.8.
Building CO_2 audit summary

Element	M4C3 Tonnes CO_2	%	M4S3 Tonnes CO_2	%	M4C7 Tonnes CO_2	%	M4S7 Tonnes CO_2	%
Substructure	136.19	10.3	94.7	4.1	253.91	8.7	159.77	3.0
Superstructure	349.61	26.5	1348.02	58.9	903.68	31.1	3410.50	63.7
External cladding	262.78	19.9	266.57	11.6	532.53	18.3	545.34	10.2
Finishes	431.73	32.7	433.52	18.9	892.60	30.7	910.85	17.0
M&E: fully air conditioned, Option 6	58.81	4.4	58.81	2.6	137.22	4.7	137.22	2.6
Plant and labour	82.50	6.2	88.98	3.9	189.69	6.5	188.97	3.5
Total (average)	1321.62	100	2290.60	100	2909.63	100	5352.65	100
Possible reductions in CO_2 for lean solution								
Superstructure: frame – all recycled steel	n.a.		−768		n.a.		−1972	
M&E: a) eliminate suspended ceilings	−59.63		n.a.		−148.50		n.a.	
b) reduce ductwork for Option 1, passive system	−53.16		n.a.		−124.03		n.a.	
Labour use public transport	−77.08		−83.45		−182.6		−181.69	
Total CO_2 reduction	−189.87	−14.4	−851.45	−37.2	−455.13	−15.6	−2153.69	−40.2
Low CO_2 total (tonnes)	1131.75		1439.15		2454.50		3198.96	

Table 1.9.
Building CO_2 audit

		Quantities				Embodied CO_2				
	Unit	No. units per building				kg CO_2 per unit	Total CO_2: tonnes			
		M4C3	M4S3	M4C7	M4S7		Total M4C3	Total M4S3	Total M4C7	Total M4S7
A. MATERIALS										
Substructures										
Site preparation	m²	1190	1190	1190	1190	[a]	–	–	–	–
Excavate oversite	m³	417	417	417	417	[a]	–	–	–	–
Excavate foundations	m³	599	293	1403	745	[a]	–	–	–	–
E/o hard excavation	m³	60	29	140	75	[a]	–	–	–	–
Backfill	m³	199	114	400	229	[a]	–	–	–	–
Disposal	m³	817	596	1434	934	[a]	–	–	–	–
Working space	m³	283	238	527	397	[b]	0	0	0	0
Support to excavations	m²	472	397	878	662	[b]	0	0	0	0
Level and compact	m³	1694	1474	2189	1764	[a]	–	–	–	–
Granular beds	m²	298	298	298	298	[b]	0	0	0	0
Sand blinding	m²	1190	1190	1190	1190	[b]	0	0	0	0
Vapour barrier	m²	1190	1190	1190	1190	11.06	13.16	13.16	13.16	13.16
Concrete blinding 50 mm	m²	1190	1190	1190	1190	4.1	4.88	4.88	4.88	4.88
Concrete blinding 75 mm	m²	504	284	999	574	6.2	3.12	1.76	6.19	3.56
Concrete foundations	m³	356	156	923	469	156.4	55.68	24.4	144.36	73.35
Columns	m³	5	6	9	8	156.4	0.78	0.94	1.41	1.25
Walls	m³	3	n.a.	5	n.a.	156.4	0.47	–	0.78	–
Concrete ground slab	m³	284	284	284	284	137.3	38.99	38.99	38.99	38.99
Reinforcement bar	t	30	14	77	40	485	14.55	6.79	37.35	19.4
Mesh (A142 @ 2.22 kg/m²)	t	2.64	2.64	2.64	2.64	510	1.35	1.35	1.35	1.35
Formwork to foundations	m²	305	221	580	410	7.25	2.21	1.60	4.21	2.97
Formwork to columns	m²	38	46	46	50	7.25	0.28	0.33	0.33	0.36
Formwork to walls	m²	31	n.a.	55	n.a.	7.25	0.22	–	0.40	–
Formwork to edges	m²	69	69	69	69	7.25	0.50	0.50	0.50	0.50
Superstructure										
Concrete walls	m³	50	n.a.	236	n.a.	156.4	7.82	–	36.91	–
Concrete cols <0.25 m²	m³	89	n.a.	0	n.a.	156.4	13.92	–	0	–
Concrete cols >0.25 m²	m³	0	n.a.	407	n.a.	156.4	0	–	63.65	–
Concrete beams	m³	2	n.a.	0	n.a.	156.4	0.31	–	0	–
Concrete suspended slab	m³	1335	n.a.	3025	n.a.	156.4	208.79	–	473.11	–
Plant room frame	m³	11	n.a.	11	n.a.	[c]	0	–	0	–
Lwt concrete slab	m³	n.a.	527	n.a.	1240	173.9	–	91.70	0	215.76
PC stair 1200 mm wide	no	8	0	0	0	[c]	0	–	–	–
PC stair 1500 mm wide	no	0	8	24	0	[c]	–	0	0	–
Steel stair 1200 mm wide	no	0	0	0	24	[c]	–	–	–	0
Steel stair 1500 mm wide	no	0	5	0	11	[c]	–	0	–	0
Reinforcement bar	t	158	5	452	11	485	76.63	2.43	219.22	5.34
Mesh (A142 @ 2.22 kg/m²)	t	n.a.	9.36	n.a.	22.02	510	–	4.77	–	11.23
Formwork to soffits	m²	4214	n.a.	9920	n.a.	7.25	30.55	–	71.92	–
Formwork to walls, 3 storeys	m²	567	n.a.	n.a.	n.a.	7.25	4.11	–	–	–
Formwork to walls, 7 storeys	m²	n.a.	n.a.	2573	n.a.	7.25	–	–	18.65	–
Formwork to columns <600 mm	m²	708	n.a.	0	n.a.	7.25	5.13	–	0	–
Formwork to columns >600 mm	m²	0	n.a.	2170	n.a.	7.25	0	–	15.73	–
Formwork to beams	m²	21	n.a.	0	n.a.	7.25	0.15	–	0	–
Formwork to edges	m²	204	n.a.	520	n.a.	7.25	1.48	–	3.77	–
Plant room frame	m²	99	n.a.	99	n.a.	7.25	0.72	–	0.72	–
Steel decking	m²	n.a.	4214	n.a.	9920	29.1	–	122.63	–	288.67
Steelwork, 3 storeys	t	n.a.	208	n.a.	n.a.	5216	–	1084.93	–	–
Steelwork, 7 storeys	t	n.a.	n.a.	n.a.	534	5216	–	–	–	2785.34
Studs	no	n.a.	2545	n.a.	5935	[c]	–	0	–	0
Holding down bolts	item	n.a.	36	n.a.	36	[d]	–	0.55	–	0.55

| | | Quantities | | | | Embodied CO_2 | | | | |
| | Unit | No. units per building | | | | kg CO_2 per unit | Total CO_2: tonnes | | | |
		M4C3	M4S3	M4C7	M4S7		Total M4C3	Total M4S3	Total M4C7	Total M4S7
Baseplates	item	n.a.	36	n.a.	36	[d]	–	4.68	–	16.39
Firecasing to beams	m²	n.a.	2553	n.a.	5964	10.44	–	26.65	–	62.26
Firecasing to columns	m²	n.a.	927	n.a.	2391	10.44	–	9.68	–	24.96
External cladding										
Glazed curtain wall	m²									
(a) 6 mm glass	m²	2013	2048	4497	4604	67.94	136.76	139.14	305.53	312.8
(b) Aluminium transoms	item	1	1	1	1	[d]	0.45	0.45	1.06	1.06
(c) Aluminium mullions	item	1	1	1	1	[d]	1.86	1.86	3.10	3.10
(d) Metal cladding	m²	2013	2048	4497	4604	40.4	81.33	82.74	181.68	186
Cladding to external soffit	m²	418	418	318	418	40.4	16.89	16.89	12.85	16.89
external columns	m²	140	140	210	210	40.4	5.66	5.66	8.48	5.66
plant room	m²	257	257	257	257	40.4	10.38	10.38	10.38	10.38
Screens to plant	m²	234	234	234	234	40.4	9.45	9.45	9.45	9.45
Window cleaning equipment	item	1	1	1	1	[c]	0	0	0	0
Revolving door	no	1	1	1	1	[c]	0	0	0	0
Entrance doors	no	4	4	6	6	[c]	0	0	0	0
Fire escape doors	no	2	2	2	2	[c]	0	0	0	0
Roof plant room door	no	1	1	1	1	[c]	0	0	0	0
Roof finishes										
Sand/cement screed	m²	1560	1560	1560	1560	20.1	31.36	31.36	31.36	31.36
Ashphalt to roof	m²	1560	1560	1560	1560	0.69	1.08	1.08	1.08	1.08
75 mm insulation	m²	1560	1560	1560	1560	33.4	52.1	52.1	52.1	52.1
Roof membrane	m²	1560	1560	1560	1560	11.06	17.25	17.25	17.25	17.25
Perimeter	m	280	280	280	280	[b]	0	0	0	0
Gravel	m²	1338	1338	1338	1338	[b]	0	0	0	0
Precast slabs 50 mm thick	m²	1560	1560	1560	1560	8.21	12.81	12.81	12.81	12.81
Internal planning										
100 mm Lignacite	m²	910	1880	1460	2957	0.6	0.55	1.13	0.88	1.77
200 mm Lignacite	m²	393	165	1021	1440	1.2	0.47	0.2	1.23	1.73
Plasterboard wall lining	m²	1102	821	2482	895	6.96	7.67	5.71	17.27	6.23
Fire-resistant plasterboard lining	m²	703	1322	1699	5464	10.4	7.31	13.75	17.67	56.83
Single doors	no	33	33	61	61	[c]	0	0	0	0
Double doors	no	13	12	30	30	[c]	0	0	0	0
Finishes										
Offices:										
raised floor	m²	3442	3405	8470	8345	69.2	238.19	235.63	586.12	577.47
suspended ceiling	m²	3442	3405	8470	8345	16.8	57.83	57.20	142.30	140.20
Reception:										
decorative plaster	m²	130	105	129	94	9.48	1.23	1	1.22	0.89
suspended ceiling	m²	107	129	107	116	16.8	1.80	2.17	1.80	1.95
granite floor	m²	107	129	107	116	3.6	0.39	0.46	0.39	0.42
Lobbies and corridors:										
terrazzo	m²	0	0	170	182	[b]	0	0	0	0
Toilets:										
wall tiles	m²	261	257	584	555	6.48	1.69	1.67	3.78	3.6
suspended ceiling	m²	0	0	262	253	16.8	0	0	4.40	4.25
floor tiles	m²	0	0	262	253	3.6	0	0	0.94	0.91
Lift installation										
3-storey passenger lift	no	2	2	n.a.	n.a.	[c]	0	0	–	–
7-storey passenger lift	no	n.a.	n.a.	3	3	[c]	–	–	0	0
7-storey fireman's lift	no	n.a.	n.a.	2	2	[c]	–	–	0	0

Table 1.9.
Building CO$_2$ audit (continued)

	Embodied CO$_2$ Total CO$_2$: tonnes			
	Total M4C3	Total M4S3	Total M4C7	Total M4S7
Mechanical services [e]				
Option 1 - passive ventilation, exposed concrete soffits, no raised access				
Polybutylene pipes	5.65	–	13.19	–
Option 2 - underfloor ventilation with exposed concrete soffits, raised access floor as plenum				
Steel ducts and pipes	10.91	–	25.60	–
Option 3 - exposed hollow core TermoDeck slabs, mechanical ventilation, raised access floors				
Steel ducts and pipes	32.80	–	76.53	–
Option 4 - water-cooled slab, precast Thermocast panels with embedded polybutylene pipes				
Steel ducts and pipes	21.04	–	49.09	–
Option 5 - chilled beams with exposed concrete soffit, raised access floor (ignore beam plates)				
Steel ducts and pipes	43.71	–	101.99	–
Option 6 - fully air conditioned, false ceiling, raised access floor (ignore fan-cooled units and plenum boxes and beam plates)				
Steel ducts and pipes	58.81	58.81	137.22	137.22

	Quantities					Embodied CO$_2$				
	Unit	No. units per building				kg CO$_2$ per unit	Total CO$_2$: tonnes			
		M4C3	M4S3	M4C7	M4S7		Total M4C3	Total M4S3	Total M4C7	Total M4S7
Electrical installation										
Transformer	item	1	1	1	1	[f]	0	0	0	0
LV electrical installation	m^2	4355	4355	10399	10399	[f]	0	0	0	0
Small power - offices	no	344	344	847	847	[f]	0	0	0	0
Small power - landlords	m^2	4355	4355	10399	10399	[f]	0	0	0	0
Communications 3-storey	item	1	1	n.a.	n.a.	[f]	0	0	–	–
Communications 7-storey	m^2	n.a.	n.a.	10399	10399	[f]	–	–	0	0
Preliminaries										
Establish site etc. 3-storey	item	1	1	n.a.	n.a.	[c]	0	0	–	–
Establish site etc. 7-storey	item	n.a.	n.a.	1	1	[c]	–	–	0	0
Supervision, hire etc. 3-storey	wks	52	54	n.a.	n.a.	[c]	0	0	–	–
Supervision, hire etc. 7-storey	wks	n.a.	n.a.	62	62	[c]	–	–	0	0
Total materials CO$_2$ (Option 1)							1185.96	2142.81	2595.91	5026.46
B. PLANT AND LABOUR										
See Tables 1.11 and 1.12										
Tower crane	wks	25	0	31	27	15.89	0.40	0	0.49	0.43
Mobile crane	wks	0	11	0	4	31.78	0	0.35	0	0.13
Excavator, Hymac	wks	10	12	10	12	10.9	0.11	0.13	0.11	0.13
Excavator, backacter	wks	4	4	4	4	10.9	0.04	0.04	0.04	0.04
Muck lorries	loads	91	66	160	104	4.15	0.34	0.23	0.66	0.43
Dumpers	wks	6	8	6	8	10.9	0.06	0.09	0.06	0.09
Generator, 400 kVA diesel	wks	28	0	35	34	10.9	0.31	0	0.39	0.37
Generator, 100 kVA, diesel	wks	24	54	27	28	2.73	0.06	0.15	0.07	0.08
Deliveries	no	454	500	580	615	9.08	4.12	4.54	5.27	5.58
Summary of labour (day shifts)	no	7460	8078	17677	17589	10.33	77.06	83.45	182.60	181.69
Total plant and labour							82.50	88.98	189.69	188.97

Notes:

n.a. Item not applicable to building.

[a] Included in CO$_2$ emissions from the plant and material deployed.

[b] Embodied CO$_2$ data not available for item or item not audited (assumed carbon neutral for the purposes of this example).

[c] Item shown as lump sum in the bill of quantities – could not be assessed for CO$_2$ as was not a measured item.

[d] Treated as single item for audit purposes.

[e] Detailed quantities were specially prepared by Cundalls to enable CO$_2$ emissions to be estimated for each building type and each services option, provided that thermal mass and low-energy systems could be incorporated.

[f] Electrical services shown as lump sums in the bill of quantities and too complex to evaluate without detailed drawings. Electrical provisions would be the same for steel frame and concrete frame buildings of the same height.

Table 1.10.
CO_2 calculation data for building audit

	Quantity	Unit		Quantity	Unit
SUBSTRUCTURES			Holding down bolts (S3 & S7)		
Vapour barrier 1000 gauge,1 mm thick, PVC	11.06	kg CO_2/m²	20 mm dia. 600 mm long; 144 no. volume = (314.16 × 0.6 × 144)/106 = 0.027 m³ = 20,209 kg CO_2/m³	546	kg CO_2
Concrete blinding 50 mm C20: 82 kg CO_2/m³ × 0.05	4.1	kg CO_2/m²	Baseplates (assume recycled steel) a) S3 - 500 × 500 × 25 each plate, 36 no. m³ = 6.25 × 0.01 × 36 = 0.23 CO_2 = 0.23 × 20,208 kg CO_2/m³ = 4648	4648	kg CO_2
Concrete blinding 75 mm C20: 82 kg CO_2/m³ × 0.075	6.2	kg CO_2/m²	b) S7 - 750 × 750 × 40 each plate, 36 no. m³ = 0.0225 × 36 = 0.81 CO_2 = 0.81 × 20,208 kg CO_2/m³	16,368	kg CO_2
Concrete foundations C40: 50/50 OP/GGBS (ignore ready-mix delivery)	156.4	kg CO_2/m³	Firecasing to beams	10.44	kg CO_2
Columns C40: 50/50 OP/GGBS	156.4	kg CO_2/m³	Firecasing to columns	10.44	kg CO_2
Walls (as columns) C40: 50/50 OP/GGBS	156.4	kg CO_2/m³	Firecasing calculations: 15 mm plasterbaord assume gypsum wallboard kg CO_2/m² = 696 kg CO_2/m³ × 0.015		
Concrete ground slab C30: 50/50 OP/GGBS	137.3	kg CO_2/m³	**EXTERNAL CLADDING**		
Reinforcement - bar (delivered to site) Celsa 422 + BRC 63	485	kg CO_2/t	Glazed curtain wall		
Reinforcement - mesh (delivered to site) Celsa 422 + BRC mesh 88.2 quantity: A142 2.22 kg/m² × 1190 = 2.64 tonnes	510	kg CO_2/t	a) Glass 14 mm thickness = 6 mm glass + 8 mm glass (assume laminated glass) kg CO_2/m² = 4853 kg CO_2/m³ × 0.014 m = 67.94	67.94	kg CO_2/m²
Formwork to foundations	7.25	kg CO_2/m²	b) Aluminium transoms 1.5 kg/m (assume recycled) 1 per floor, building width = 37.5, 4 no. elevations S3/C3: bulding perimeter = 150 m × 3 floors = 675 kg S7/C7: building perimeter = 150 m × 7 floors = 1575 kg S3/C3: kg CO_2/t = 674 kg CO_2/t × 0.675 t = 454.9 S7/C7: kg CO_2/t = 674 kg CO_2/t × 1.575 t = 1061.6	454.9 1061.6	kg CO_2 kg CO_2
Formwork to columns (disposable)	7.25	kg CO_2/m²			
Formwork to walls	7.25	kg CO_2/m²	c) Aluminium mullions 1.5 kg/m @ 1.5 m centres S3/C3: building height O/A = 13.14 m (length of mullions), 26 per elevation × 4 = 104 no. 104 × 13.14 m × 1.5 kg = 2759 kg	1860	kg CO_2
Formwork to edges	7.25	kg CO_2/m²	S7/C7: building height O/A = 29.47 m (length of mullions), 104 no. per elevation 104 × 29.46 m × 1.5 kg = 4596 kg S3/C3 kg CO_2/t = 674 × 2.759 = 1860 kg CO_2 S7/C7 kg CO_2/t = 674 × 4.596 = 3098 kg CO_2	3098	kg CO_2
Formwork calculations: 18 mm plywood WISA Birch, film-faced = 7.25 kg CO_2/m² Processed plywood = 676 kg CO_2/t WISA Birch 18 mm with 0.5 mm resin film face both sides: density 680 kg/m³ = 993 kg CO_2/m³ × 0.018 m = 17.9 kg CO_2/m² Phenolic resin (use PVC, Table A.1: 11,060 kg CO_2/m³) = 2 × 0.005 × 11,060 = 11.1 kg CO_2/m² 4 reuses = 29.00/4 = 7.25 kg CO_2/m²					
SUPERSTRUCTURE			d) Metal cladding (assume recycled), 2 mm thick, painted steel Cladding to:		
Concrete walls	156.4	kg CO_2/m³	external soffit	40.4	kg CO_2/m²
Concrete columns <0.25 m²	156.4	kg CO_2/m³	external columns	40.4	kg CO_2/m²
Concrete columns >0.25 m²	156.4	kg CO_2/m³	plant room	40.4	kg CO_2/m²
Concrete beams	156.4	kg CO_2/m³	Screens to plant kg CO_2/m² = 20,208 kg CO_2/m³ × 0.002 m = 40.4	40.4	kg CO_2/m²
Concrete suspended slab	156.4	kg CO_2/m³	**ROOF FINISHES**		
all C40: 50/50 OP/GGBS					
Lightweight aggregate concrete C40 mix, Lytag 810 kg/m³ (dry density 1800 kg/m³) kg CO_2/m³ OP = 152; GGBS = 10.4; sand = 1.5; Lytag = 10 Total = 173.9 kg CO_2/m³	173.9	kg CO_2/m³	Sand/cement screed 75 mm, 1 cement:4 sand, density 2200 kg/m³ cement 350:1400 kg CO_2/m³ OP 266 + 2.8 = 268 kg CO_2/m² = 268 kg CO_2/m³ × 0.075 m = 20.1	20.1	kg CO_2/m²
Reinforcement - bar Celsa 422 + BRC 63	485	kg CO_2/t	Asphalt to roof (source: Carbon Balance delivery and laying) 74 kg CO_2 + 91 kg CO_2/t = 165 kg CO_2/t installed assume: 5 mm thick, density ≈ linoleum = 1200 kg/m³ kg CO_2/m² = 165/1.2 × 0.005 = 0.69	0.69	kg CO_2/m²
Reinforcement - mesh A142 Celsa 422 + BRC mesh 88.2 = 510 A142 2.22 kg/m² × 1190 = 2.64 tonnes	510	kg CO_2/t			
Formwork to soffits	7.25	kg CO_2/m²	Insulation (75 mm) assume dense rigid polystyrene kg CO_2/m² = 445 kg CO_2/m³ × 0.075 m = 33.4	33.4	kg CO_2/m²
Formwork to walls - 3 storeys	7.25	kg CO_2/m²			
Formwork to walls - 7 storeys	7.25	kg CO_2/m²	Roof membrane assume 1 mm PVC sheet material (see vapour barrier)	11.06	kg CO_2/m²
Formwork to columns <600 mm	7.25	kg CO_2/m²			
Formwork to columns >600 mm	7.25	kg CO_2/m²	Precast slabs (50 mm) C30 mix as for ground slab kg CO_2/m² = 137.3 kg CO_2/m³ × 0.050 m = 6.87 add facory transport delivery CO_2 as Histon Plant kg CO_2/m² = 26.7 kg CO_2/m³ × 0.050 m = 1.34	8.21	kg CO_2/m²
Formwork to beams	7.25	kg CO_2/m²			
Formwork to edges	7.25	kg CO_2/m²			
all formwork disposable 18 mm film-faced plywood, WISA					
Steel metal decking 1.2 mm, 60 mm deep, 300 mm centres	29.1	kg CO_2/m²			
Steelwork (Corus UK)	5216	kg CO_2/t			

Table 1.10.
CO_2 calculation data for building audit (continued)

	Quantity	CO_2/unit		Quantity	CO_2/unit
INTERNAL PLANNING					
100 mm Lignacite blockwork kg CO_2/m^2 = 6 kg CO_2/m^3 (ex works) × 0.10 m = 0.6	0.6	kg CO_2/m^2	Option 3 - exposed hollow core TermoDeck slabs, mechanical ventilation, raised access floors		
200 mm Lignacite blockwork kg CO_2/m^2 = 6 kg CO_2/m^3 × 0.20 m =1.2	1.2	kg CO_2/m^2	C3 - steel ducts and pipes 0.541 × 20,209 × 3	32,799	kg CO_2
			C7 - steel ducts and pipes 0.541 × 20,209 × 7	76,531	kg CO_2
Plasterboard wall (10 mm gypsum) kg CO_2/m^2 = 696 kg CO_2/m^3 × 0.01 m = 6.96	6.96	kg CO_2/m^2	Option 4 - water-cooled slab, precast Thermocast panels with embedded polybutylene pipes		
Fire-resistant plasterboard (15 mm gypsum wallboard) kg CO_2/m^2 = 6.96 kg CO_2/m^3 × 0.015 m = 10.4	10.4	kg CO_2/m^2	C3 - steel ducts and pipes 0.347 × 20,209 × 3	21,037	kg CO_2
			C3 - polybutylene pipes 0.188 × 20,050 × 3	11,308	kg CO_2
FINISHES			C7 - steel ducts and pipes 0.347 × 20,209 × 7	49,088	kg CO_2
Raised floor			C7 - polybutylene pipes 0.347 × 20,209 × 7	26,386	kg CO_2
a) 29 mm chipboard (assume plywood), single use, no film coating kg CO_2/m^2 = 17.9 kg CO_2/m^2 × 0.029/0.018 m = 28.8	28.8	kg CO_2/m^2	Option 5 - chilled beams with exposed concrete soffits, raised access floor (ignore beam plates)		
b) 2 mm galvanised steel (assume recycled) kg CO_2/m^2 = 20,208 kg CO_2/m^3 × 0.002 m = 40.4	40.4	kg CO_2/m^2	C3 - steel ducts and pipes 0.721 × 20,209 × 3	43,712	kg CO_2
c) legs for pedesatal floor ignored	nil		C7 - steel ducts and pipes 0.721 × 20,209 × 7	101,995	kg CO_2
Suspended ceiling (steel grill, assume recycled) support: 1.5 kg/m^2 + flat tile: 5 kg/m^2 = 6.5 kg/m^2 recycled steel, assume average 2.590 kg CO_2/kg kg CO_2/m^2 =2.59 × 6.5 = 16.8	16.8	kg CO_2/m^2	Option 6 - fully air-conditioned, false ceiling, raised access floor (ignore fan, coiled units and plenum boxes, ignore beams plates)		
10 mm decorative plaster kg CO_2/m^2 = 948 kg CO_2/m^3 × 0.01 m = 9.48	9.48	kg CO_2/m^2	S3/C3 - steel ducts and pipes 0.97 × 20,209 × 3	58,808	kg CO_2
15 mm granite floor (assume local stone) kg CO_2/m^2 = 240 kg CO_2/m^3 × 0.015 m = 3.6	3.6	kg CO_2/m^2	S7/C7 - steel ducts and pipes 0.98 × 20,209 × 7	137,219	kg CO_2
10 mm wall tiles (assume clay tiles) kg CO_2/m^2 = 648 kg CO_2/m^3 × 0.010 m = 6.48	6.48	kg CO_2/m^2	**PLANT AND LABOUR[1]**		
15 mm floor tiles (assume local stone) kg CO_2/m^2 = 240 kg CO_2/m^3 × 0.025 m = 3.6	3.6	kg CO_2/m^2	Tower crane Assume 2-litre diesel engine, running 10 miles per day = 0.3027 kg CO_2/mile (Table A.9) × 10 miles × 5.25 days per week	15.89	kg CO_2/wk
MECHANICAL SERVICES			Mobile crane Assume 4-litre diesel engine, running 10 miles per day = 2 × 15.89	31.78	kg CO_2/wk
Assuming 2000 m^2 floor plate Ignore fan coils and chiller damper, plenum boxes etc. Assume steel ducting ≈ 20,209 kg CO_2/m^3; polybutylene pipe ≈ 20,056 kg CO_2/m^3			Excavators, dumpers, generators (400 kVA) Based on 3-litre diesel engine, running 5 miles per day = 0.4153 kg CO_2/mile (Table A.9) × 5 miles × 5.25 days	10.90	kg CO_2/wk
Volume of ducting: quantities = m^3 per storey			Muck-shifting lorries 3-litre diesel engine, each load travels 10 miles = 0.4154 kg CO_2/mile (Table A.9) × 10 miles	4.14	kg CO_2/load
Option 1 - passive ventilation, exposed concrete soffits, no raised access floor			Deliveries 2-litre engine, 30-mlle round trip = 0.3027 kg CO_2/ mile (Table A.9) × 30 miles. Concrete supply and reinforcement ignored as delivery mileage CO_2 inclded in London Concrete and BRC products	9.08	kg CO_2/ delivery
C3 - polybutylene pipe = 0.094 × 20,050 × 3	5,654	kg CO_2			
C7 - polybutylene pipe = 0.094 × 20,050 × 7	13,193	kg CO_2			
Option 2 - underfloor ventilation with exposed concrete soffits, raised access floor as plenum			Generator 100 kVA = 0.25 × 400 kVA	2.73	kg CO_2/wk
C3 - steel ducting and pipes 0.181 × 20,209 × 3	10,913	kg CO_2	Labour (transport) Assume travel by medium-sized car, 1.4–2-litre petrol engine, daily journey 30 miles = 0.3442 kg CO_2/mile (Table A.9) × 30	10.33	kg CO_2/shift
C7 - steel ducting and pipes 0.181 × 20,209 × 7	25,605	kg CO_2			

Notes:

1. Calculations for plant and labour CO_2: In the absence of accurate data on energy and fuel consumption of various heavy machines, lorries, cranes, commercial vehicles, electrical generators, heating and lighting for site accommodation etc., estimates have been made of the equivalent engine capacity and fuel consumption to provide an indication of CO_2 emissions. The CO_2 emissions from cars for home-to-work journeys by site staff and tradespeople have been approximated assuming a 30-mile round trip and a medium-sized car. For big city-centre projects, it is likely that people will travel by public transport and that the carbon footprint will be very small. On an actual project, all such data are readily available and should be collected to monitor CO_2 during construction and to build up a CO_2 construction database for future projects.

Table 1.11.
Plant breakdown

	Duration/unit	No.	M4C3	M4S3	M4C7	M4S7	Specifications/comments	kg CO$_2$ per unit	Total CO$_2$: tonnes			
									M4C3	M4S3	M4C7	M4S7
Tower crane	weeks	1	25	0	31	27	static saddle jib, 3 t at 25 m	15.89	0.397	0	0.493	0
Mobile crane	weeks	1	0	11	0	4	mobile, 100 t	31.78	0	0.350	0	0.127
Excavators	weeks	1	10	12	10	12	12 t Hymac type	10.9	0.109	0.131	0.109	0.131
	weeks	1	4	4	4	4	5 t JCB backacter	10.9	0.044	0.044	0.044	0.044
Muck-shifting lorries	loads	1	91	66	160	104	10 cu.yd lorries	4.15	0.378	0.274	0.664	0.432
Concrete pumps	visits	1	12	8	4	4	42 m reach, 25 m³/hr	n.a.	–	–	–	–
	weeks	1	0	0	20	9	static pump, similar spec to last	n.a.	–	–	–	–
Hoist	weeks	1	18	27	18	19	1 t passenger/goods electric hoist	n.a.	–	–	–	–
Site lighting	n.a.		0	0	0	0	via generator (below)	n.a.	–	–	–	–
Compressors	weeks	1	22	16	28	22	4 tool	n.a.	–	–	–	–
Dumpers	weeks	1	6	8	6	8	3 t	10.9	0.065	0.087	0.065	0.087
Heaters	n.a.		0	0	0	0	via generator (below)	n.a.	–	–	–	–
Mortar mixers	weeks	1	6	6	7	7		n.a.	–	–	–	–
Vibrators	weeks	1	21	15	27	20	poker via comp. air/side plate electric	n.a.	–	–	–	–
Power floats	n.a.		0	0	0	0	assume trowelled slabs	n.a.	–	–	–	–
Screed pump	days	1	12	12	24	24		n.a.	–	–	–	–
Generator	weeks	1	28	0	35	34	400 kVA diesel	10.9	0.305	0	0.381	0.371
	weeks	1	24	54	27	28	100 kVA diesel	2.73	0.065	0.147	0.074	0.076
Skips	no.		156	108	206	134	5.5 cu.yd	n.a.	–	–	–	–
Roller	weeks	1	19	19	21	21	sit-on Bomag 90	n.a.	–	–	–	–
Dewatering pump	weeks	1	14	15	14	15	3 in. diaphragm pump	n.a.	–	–	–	–
Site accommodation	weeks	5	52	54	62	62	2 × 32 ft office, 1 WC, 1 welfare, 1 canteen	n.a.	–	–	–	–
Deliveries	no.	1	12	12	28	28	scaffolding					
	no.	1	310	30	807	84	concrete*					
	no.	1	10	12	26	30	rebar/fabric*					
	no.	1	12	12	12	20	formwork/Holorib					
	no.	1	0	11	0	27	structural steel, 20 t articulated lorry					
	no.	1	430	465	540	540	other plant and materials					
	Net		454	500	580	615		9.08	4.122	4.540	5.266	5.584
Total plant and deliveries									5.486	5.573	5.266	5.584

* Delivery mileage included in material embodied CO$_2$

Table 1.12.
Labour breakdown

Trade	Discipline	Unit	M4C3	M4S3	M4C7	M4S7	kg CO$_2$ per unit	Total CO$_2$: tonnes			
								M4C3	M4S3	M4C7	M4S7
Substructure	labourers/machine drivers	day shift	147	103	277	177					
Superstructure	concrete gangs/steelworkers	day shift	602	617	1632	1507					
External cladding	skilled trades	day shift	1022	1034	1864	1899					
Roof finishes	skilled trades	day shift	256	256	256	256					
Internal planning	skilled trades	day shift	154	177	325	453					
Finishes	skilled trades	day shift	722	821	1984	1958					
Fixtures and fittings	skilled trades	day shift	52	52	100	100					
Lift installation	lift engineers	day shift	88	88	562	562					
Mechanical and PH	mechanical eng/support staff	day shift	1716	2072	4900	4900					
Electrical installation	electrical eng/support staff	day shift	972	1108	2586	2586					
BWIC with services	labourer/skilled trades	day shift	700	700	1703	1703					
External works	labourer/machine drivers	day shift	333	333	333	333					
Preliminaries	professional staff	day shift	696	717	1155	1155					
Total		day shift	7460	8078	17 677	17 589	10.33	77.06	83.45	182.60	181.69
Check on total resource											
Number of weeks (average 5.25 days/week)		weeks	1421	1539	3367	3350					
Contract period		weeks	52	54	62	62					
Average labour resource			27	28	54	54					

REDUCING
LONG-TERM
CO_2

C2

HEATING, COOLING AND THERMAL MASS

OVERVIEW

Building construction is inherently damaging
to the environment as it involves the extraction,
processing and transportation of large quantities
of high-energy materials. We rarely know the
source or the detailed composition of many
composite materials and, as designers, we
often have little control over the manufacturing
process. So we can either get very depressed
about this and worry our way through the
minutiae of decision-making, or we can wash
our hands of the materials and component
industries while assuming they are someone
else's problem.

The reality is that we operate in between
these extremes, trying to keep abreast of the
scarce and often contradictory information
that is available; making value judgements
about the key environmental issues and asking
manufacturers the questions that will encourage
them to take their own environmental agendas
seriously.

One of the best sources of environmental
information on materials is the BRE's *Green
Guide to Specification*, which includes the
rating of materials by Eco-points (and which
also forms the basis for ENVEST software).

The Green Guide to Specification attempts
to provide a full life-cycle cost analysis of
common methods of construction and is most
useful as an instant checklist. However, the
origin and weighting of the data used in the
software are not transparent, which makes it
rather difficult to interpret the information.
It is also rather limited in scope because the
software makes gross generalisations in terms
of building shapes and specifications. Hence, it
is really only useful for a quick comparison.

These two reference sources give slightly
different methods of analysis and focus on the
following issues:

— embodied energy and CO_2 emissions
— recycled materials
— ozone depletion potential

— toxicity to plant and animal life
— pollution of air during manufacture, use or
  disposal.

The Green Guide to Specification provides
some surprising data on the embodied
environmental impact of constituent elements
of a building over a lifetime. For example,
a pie chart shows the environmental impact
contribution of each element of a typical office
building.

The Construction CO_2 Audit section in
Chapter 1 of this book and the information on
how to use data on embodied CO_2 attempt to
help the designer by explaining how embodied
CO_2 can be evaluated realistically, transparently
and thoughtfully. This is the template on which
all building materials, construction options
and low-energy systems will be assessed in the
future.

PRINCIPLES OF HEATING AND COOLING

Thermal comfort depends on a variety of
factors – air temperature, radiant temperature,
humidity and air movement, as well as
clothing. But there are also psychological
aspects to thermal comfort, and one of the most
significant is the relationship between external
and internal conditions. We tend to be more
tolerant of lower temperatures in winter and
higher temperatures in summer.

As insulation standards improve, heating
loads go down, to the extent that buildings
become self-heating by their occupants and
through solar and equipment gains. But cooling
becomes more of a problem; the human body
has to get rid of 70–100 watts by convection,
radiation or transpiration for comfort. This
energy is useful in winter, but in summer it has
to be dissipated.

The following principles should be applied to
all new building design projects:

— A well-insulated building is more difficult
  to design for summer cooling.
— Place thermal mass inside the insulation. This
  damps down daily temperature fluctuations
  and provides radiant surfaces that are cooler
  in summer and warmer in winter.

— The new Environment Office sets a range of acceptable summertime temperature: above 25 °C for up to 5 per cent of the working year and above 28 °C for 1 per cent of the working year.

— As insulation standards go up, so does the impact of internal and solar gains; so ensure that the proportion, orientation and transparency of openings are examined thoroughly at the design stage.

— Design with the climate, rather than against it. Undertake a simple site microclimate investigation at an early stage and record wind direction, solar gain, shading, etc.

AIRTIGHTNESS

Adequate ventilation is essential for the health and comfort of a building's occupants. To avoid discomfort and energy waste it is important that this is controlled, rather than being the accidental result of uncontrolled air leakage through the building fabric. Mandatory standards for airtightness were not introduced into the Building Regulations until April 2002, and then they applied only to non-domestic buildings of over 1,000 m². In contrast, in Sweden, airtightness is a standard that is so ingrained in the construction industry that tests are no longer compulsory.

Specifying a building to achieve a high standard of airtightness requires the same level of rigour used to ensure that it is watertight and has no gaps in its insulation. The airtight layer is usually at or close to the inside surface of the external walls, restricting the passage of moist internal air into the fabric to prevent problems with condensation. There is an excellent checklist of typical air leakage paths in BSRIA Technical Note 19/2001, and there are some general principles that are worth considering:

— builders' work ducts formed in blockwork are notoriously leaky – for example, unfinished blockwork leaks between 0.1 and 60 m³/hr/m²

— in-situ concrete, concrete screens and plaster and render are good at forming an airtight seal

hollow-core concrete planks provide an air path from the middle of the building to the outside wall unless the ends and the joints between the planks are sealed.

Airtightness is an issue that cuts across many specifications and requires a dedicated specification to be written in the design preliminaries. Similarly, as airtightness depends on the quality of workmanship, it is recommended that an air permeability test is carried out.

Typically, a house can be tested in an hour or two using an electrically driven fan to pressurise the building. The AECB has a test kit that can be hired by builders. Buildings are best tested as a whole rather than in sections. Larger buildings require more powerful equipment such as the vehicle-powered fans used by BSRIA.

THERMAL MASS

The dynamic thermal response of high thermal mass buildings with exposed concrete is characterised by a slow response to changes in ambient conditions and the ability to reduce peak temperatures. This is particularly beneficial during the summer, when the concrete absorbs internal heat gains during the day, helping to prevent overheating. In addition to reducing peak internal temperatures,

Below
Stabilising effect
of thermal mass
on internal
temperature

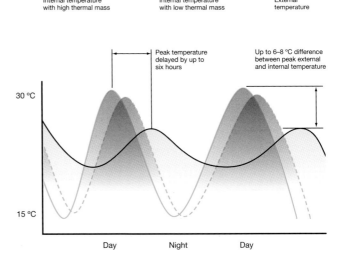

Internal temperature with high thermal mass	Internal temperature with low thermal mass	External temperature

Peak temperature delayed by up to six hours

Up to 6–8 °C difference between peak external and internal temperature

30 °C

15 °C

Day   Night   Day

a high thermal mass building can also delay the temperature peak by up to six hours. In an office environment this will typically occur in the late afternoon or in the evening, after the occupants have left, when solar gains are greatly diminished and little heat is generated by occupants, equipment and lighting.

During the evening, the external air temperature drops, making night ventilation an effective means of removing accumulated heat from the concrete and so lowering the temperature in preparation for the next day. The UK variation in diurnal temperature rarely drops below 5 °C, making night cooling relatively effective. Water can also be used to cool the slabs as an alternative, or addition, to night ventilation.

Concrete's ability to absorb heat and provide a cooling effect is determined by the difference between its surface temperature and the temperature of the internal air. Consequently, the greatest cooling capacity is provided when the internal temperature peaks. Therefore, to some extent a variable internal temperature is a prerequisite in fabric energy storage (FES) systems. However, to maintain comfortable conditions and limit overheating, peak temperatures should ideally not exceed 25 °C for more than 5 per cent of the occupied period and 28 °C for not more than 1 per cent.

Resultant temperature is an important measure of FES. It takes account of radiant and air temperatures, providing a more accurate indication of comfort than air temperature

alone. The relatively stable radiant temperature provided by the thermal mass in concrete is a significant factor in maintaining comfortable conditions. It enables higher air temperatures to be tolerated than in lighter-weight buildings, which are subject to higher radiant temperatures resulting from warmer internal surfaces.

Thermal mass, in the most general sense, describes the ability of any material to store heat. For a material to provide a useful level of thermal mass, a combination of three basic properties is required:

— high specific heat capacity – to maximise the heat that can be stored per kg of material

— high density – to maximise the overall mass of the material used

— moderate thermal conductivity – so that heat conduction is roughly in synchronisation with the diurnal heat flow in and out of the building.

Heavyweight construction materials such as concrete, brick and stone all have these properties (see Table 2.1). They combine a high storage capacity with moderate thermal conductivity. This means that heat transfers between the material's surface and the interior at a rate that matches the daily heating and cooling cycle of buildings. Some materials, such as wood, have a high heat capacity, but their thermal conductivity is low, which limits the rate at which heat is absorbed. Steel can also

Table 2.1.
Thermal properties of common building materials

Building material	Density kg/m^3	Thermal conductivity W/mK	Specific heat capacity J/kgK	Effective thermal mass
Timber	500	0.13	1600	Low
Steel	7800	50	450	Low
Lightweight aggregate blocks	1400	0.57	1000	Medium–high
Precast and in-situ concrete	2300	1.75	1000	High
Bricks and dense blocks	1750	0.77	1000	High
Sandstone	2300	1.80	1000	High

store a lot of heat but, in contrast to wood, steel has a very high rate of thermal conductivity, which means heat is absorbed and released too quickly to create the lag effect required for the diurnal temperature cycle in buildings.

Using thermal mass

False ceilings, raised floors and carpets in buildings, particularly offices, effectively isolate the thermal mass of the concrete structure underfoot and overhead. They can severely limit the concrete's ability to absorb and release heat within the occupied space. Buildings like this can be described as thermally lightweight, even though they may be structurally heavyweight. Consequently, it does not necessarily follow that a structurally heavyweight building will

automatically provide high thermal mass; this depends on the extent to which the structural elements can thermally interact with the occupied space, a relationship that is known as 'thermal linking'.

In existing buildings, thermal linking can often be improved during refurbishment by removing wall and floor coverings. Removing false ceilings or introducing a permeable ceiling will unlock the thermal mass in the slab. Hard floorings such as tiles and stone flags work well from a thermal perspective, but are rarely practical. Raised floors prevent radiant heat transfer to the concrete slab below, but they do allow good convective heat transfer when used as a plenum for underfloor ventilation.

Table 2.2.
Admittance values for different building constructions

	Admittance: W/m²K
Wall constructions:	
Dense cast concrete: 100 mm dense cast concrete, no plaster*	6.57
Precast concrete sandwich panel wall: 19 mm render, 80 mm dense concrete, 50 mm EPS insulation, 100 mm dense concrete, 13 mm dense plaster	5.48
Brick/dense concrete block cavity walls: 105 mm brick, EPS insulation, 100 mm dense concrete block, 13 mm dense plaster	5.75
Brick and block cavity wall: 105 mm brick, 25 mm airspace, 25 mm EPS insulation, 100 mm lightweight aggregate concrete block, 13 mm dense plaster	2.95
Timber frame wall: 105 mm brick, 50 mm air space, 19 mm plywood sheathing, 140 mm studding, 140 mm mineral fibre insulation between studs, 13 mm plasterboard	0.86
Internal partitions:	
Block partition: 13 mm lightweight plaster, 100 mm lightweight concrete block, 13 mm lightweight plaster	2.09
Timber studding: 12 mm plasterboard, timber studding, 12 mm plasterboard	0.69
Internal floor/ceiling constructions:	
Dense cast concrete: 100 mm dense cast concrete, no plaster*	6.57
Cast concrete: 50 mm screed, 150 mm cast concrete, 13 mm dense plaster	5.09
Timber flooring: 19 mm timber flooring or chipboard on 100 mm joists, 12 mm plasterboard ceiling	1.89

Higher values indicate a better ability to exchange heat with the environment and provide good FES performance.

Improvements to the level of insulation specified in these constructions to meet current Building Regulations will have little impact on the values of admittance shown.

*Barnard N., *Dynamic Energy Storage in the Building Fabric*, Technical Report TR9/94, BSRIA, 1995.

Source: adapted from TCC *Thermal Mass: A concrete solution for the changing climate* (2005); unless otherwise indicated, data is from CIBSE *Guide A – Environmental Design* (1999), Tables 3.54 & 3.56.

How do we know that a building specification has adequate thermal mass? During the early stages of design, the admittance value of a material can provide a useful means of assessing the FES, the operative term for thermal mass. Admittance describes the ability of a material or a construction to exchange heat with the environment when subjected to a cyclic variation in temperature (typically 24 hours for buildings). It is measured in W/m^2K, where the temperature is the difference between the mean value and actual value within the space at a specific point in time.

Table 2.2 provides some comparative values for the admittance values of different constructions. A more accurate indication of FES performance requires detailed thermal modelling, taking into account real weather patterns and the more varied nature of heat flow to and from the building fabric.

PASSIVE SOLAR DESIGN

Passive solar energy is nothing new – if you have ever sat in a car on a sunny day you will have noticed how hot it can get. About 50 per cent of space heating in an ordinary home comes from solar energy through walls and windows. Passive solar design tries to optimise the amount of energy that can be derived directly from the sun, by carefully planning the building to collect the sun's heat. Similar careful consideration of the building materials and the fabric of the building can further help to reduce the need for space heating and even artificial lighting.

How does passive solar design use the sun's power?

Passive solar houses are designed to let heat into the building during the winter months and block out the sun during hot summer days. This can be achieved by positioning deciduous trees or bushes to the south of the building so that during the summer their leaves will block out some of the sunlight. During the winter, the trees lose their leaves, allowing an increase in solar gain during the colder months. Buildings

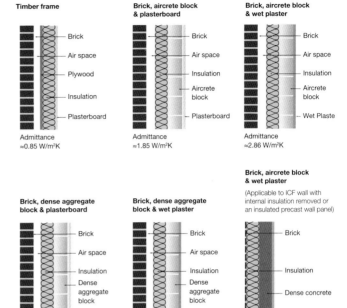

Timber frame

- Brick
- Air space
- Plywood
- Insulation
- Plasterboard

Admittance
≈0.85 W/m^2K

Brick, aircrete block & plasterboard

- Brick
- Air space
- Insulation
- Aircrete block
- Plasterboard

Admittance
≈1.85 W/m^2K

Brick, aircrete block & wet plaster

- Brick
- Air space
- Insulation
- Aircrete block
- Wet Plaster

Admittance
≈2.86 W/m^2K

Brick, dense aggregate block & plasterboard

- Brick
- Air space
- Insulation
- Dense aggregate block
- Plasterboard

Admittance
≈2.6 W/m^2K

Brick, dense aggregate block & wet plaster

- Brick
- Air space
- Insulation
- Dense aggregate block
- Wet plaster

Admittance
≈5.89 W/m^2K

Brick, aircrete block & wet plaster

(Applicable to ICF wall with internal insulation removed or an insulated precast wall panel)

- Brick
- Insulation
- Dense concrete
- Wet plaster

Admittance
≈5.5–6 W/m^2K

can also be designed to have louvres, awnings, shutter systems or green vegetation screens to block out the sun when it is high in the sky, while allowing sunlight in during the winter when the sun is lower.

Simple features can be incorporated into the design, such as large south-facing windows, and building materials with high thermal mass, such as concrete, can be used to absorb and slowly release the sun's heat. Passive solar designs can also include natural ventilation for cooling.

Direct gain systems are the simplest passive solar designs, whereby the sun's energy heats up the building's interior directly, and the heat is stored by the building's thermal mass. In this system, sunlight passes through the windows and its heat energy is trapped by the thermal mass in the room.

During winter, the thermal mass absorbs solar heat by being exposed to direct sunlight, and then radiates that heat back into the space during the cooler night. During the summer, thermal mass is prevented from receiving direct sunlight by screening; it then helps keep the room cool by absorbing the excess heat in the room.

In an indirect gain system, thermal mass is positioned between the sun and the space to be heated. The sun's heat is collected and trapped in a narrow space between a window and a thick dense concrete wall positioned behind it. This heats the air in the gap, which rises and permeates into the room through vents at the top of the dense wall. Cool air then moves in to take its place at the bottom of the wall; the heated air circulates through the room by convection. The thermal mass continues to absorb and store heat during the day, releasing it into the room after the sun has gone. During the summer months the process is reversed, with the thermal mass prevented from receiving direct sunlight. This allows it to absorb heat from the room, helping it to keep the temperature lower.

Economics of passive solar design

Passive solar design is best applied to new buildings, where the orientation of the building, the size and position of the glazed areas and the materials can be designed to maximise solar gain. Designing a building to maximise solar gain does not add to the cost of construction.

By incorporating passive solar design into new buildings, annual fuel bills can be cut by as much as 30 per cent, alongside the CO_2 savings. In addition, the increased daylight means that the need for electric lighting is reduced. Studies on houses in Milton Keynes have shown that low-cost passive solar design, airtight construction and insulation measures reduce heating bills by 40 per cent. The savings in energy costs offset the additional costs of construction within two years.

The best thing about passive solar design is that there are no moving parts. The systems perform effortlessly and quietly without mechanical or electrical assistance. Furthermore, most designs can be implemented using standard building materials and basic construction skills.

COOLING BY PASSIVE ENERGY DESIGN

Even an energy-efficient air conditioning system can add 40–50 kg $CO_2/m^2/yr$ to a building's CO_2 emissions, or as much as 175 kg $CO_2/m^2/yr$ in the case of a local 'split system' packaged air conditioner.

How can we keep cool indoors without the cost and complexity of installing air conditioning systems, particularly with the prospect of increasing summer temperatures? Potential sources of cooling are summer night-time air, which can be used to cool buildings overnight, and water or groundwater, which can be used to maintain temperatures below ambient. There are a variety of ways in which these two sources can be utilised, ranging from fully passive systems through to sophisticated mechanical ventilation and heat pumps.

Night-time passive cooling

The following points should be considered in order to maximise night-time passive cooling:

— Make sure that the system is independent of wind direction by careful design of vent openings.

— Make sure the openings seal properly and the controls work.

— Make sure the controls do not over-cool the space and produce uncomfortable conditions first thing in the morning.

— In the UK climate, cross-ventilation will generally override stack ventilation.

— Adding mechanical systems for night-time mechanical ventilation means adding fan power; so use large ducts and/or low flow rates. Fans give improved control and ability to increase cooling if necessary.

Groundwater cooling

Groundwater temperatures are generally a constant 10–12 °C at a depth of 2 m or more below ground level, but it is important to monitor groundwater temperatures locally as they can vary. Unusually high temperatures of around 15 °C can significantly reduce the performance of groundwater cooling. Systems either use water extraction or a heat exchange system within a borehole or attached to pipes buried 1 m in the ground. The water extraction system requires deep and expensive drilling work unless the building is near a lake or deep water. The heat exchange system requires a large surface area for heat transfer.

The quality of groundwater can vary significantly. Hard water can cause difficulties for water extraction systems due to the problem of scaling (unless water softening systems are included).

The effectiveness and control of a groundwater cooling system can be improved dramatically by connecting the source to a heat pump. Heat pumps can be used for heating as well as cooling.

GROUND SOURCE HEAT PUMPS

Ground source heat pumps (GSHP) make use of renewable energy stored in the ground, providing one of the most energy-efficient ways of heating and cooling a building. They are suitable for a wide variety of building types, and the only energy used by GSHP systems is electricity to power the pumps.

Typically, a GSHP will deliver three to four times as much thermal energy (heat) as is used in electrical energy to drive the system. They cost more to install than conventional heating systems but the payback period is relatively short, typically between three and five years. They have very low maintenance costs and can be expected to provide reliable and environmentally friendly heating or cooling for the duration of the building's life.

GSHPs are environmentally friendly because:

—   they do not use fossil fuels for heating or cooling a building

—   the fluids used in the system are designed to be biodegradable, non-toxic and non-corrosive

—   they minimise ozone layer depletion by using sealed refrigeration systems, which seldom or never have to be recharged

—   they use underground loops to transfer heat, with no external venting and no air pollution

—   they are energy efficient, with the earth providing over 70 per cent of the energy used to heat and cool a building.

GSHPs are installed in either open-loop systems or closed-loop systems. The system used will depend on the available land area and the soil and rock types at the site. These factors determine the most economical option.

The design of the installation is determined by the ground's thermal conductivity and temperature, the heating and cooling power needed and the balance between the amounts of heat rejected to and absorbed from the ground during the course of the year.

Closed-loop systems

For closed-loop systems, water or an antifreeze solution is circulated through plastic pipes buried beneath the ground surface. In a closed-loop system there is no direct interaction between the fluid and the earth; only heat transfer through the plastic pipe. The ground temperature, below a certain depth, is considerably higher than the ambient air temperature in winter. For example, it is estimated that a few metres below the surface, the ground temperature in London remains constant throughout the year at approx 12 °C.

During the winter, the circulating fluid collects heat from the ground and carries it through the system and into the building. During the summer, the system reverses itself, to cool the building by taking heat from the building, carrying it through the system and transferring it to the ground. This process creates almost free cooling in the summer and delivers substantial heat in the winter.

The vertical closed-loop system uses a single well (or bore hole), with the fluid in the pipe constantly circulated to and from the well. If a bore hole is used it is usually filled with a bentonite slurry to provide a good thermal connection between the pipe and the surrounding rock or soil. To install this system, a hole is bored in the ground, typically 45–75 m deep, and a U-shaped length of pipe is placed inside. A vertical closed-loop field will typically be used where there is only a limited area of land available.

A horizontal closed-loop field is composed of pipes that run horizontally below the frost line. A long horizontal trench is dug and U-shaped coils are placed horizontally inside the trench. Horizontal loop fields are common where sufficient land is available.

Open-loop systems

Open-loop systems operate on a similar principle to closed-loop systems and can be installed where there is an adequate supply of suitable groundwater and an appropriate place to discharge the water.

An open-loop system draws water from a well or lake, passes it through a heat exchanger in the building and then discharges it. Because the open-loop system removes water from the source and discharges it to a different location, an abstraction licence and a discharge consent are required. The appointed consultant should contact the Environment Agency or Defra as soon as possible to discuss plans and requirements for an open-loop GSHP and to obtain the required consents.

INSULATION

As long as energy production remains reliant on fossil fuel consumption, the energy used in manufacturing building components will be responsible for a large proportion of CO_2 production. However, over the life of a building, the energy used in manufacturing, transporting and disposing of the insulation materials can represent a negligible proportion of the total energy consumption of the building. It is therefore possible to say that the performance of the insulation material is of greater significance than its embodied energy, but if we have an opportunity to reduce CO_2 and the toxic pollutants in insulation, we should do so.

In the past, chlorofluorocarbons (CFCs) were used as blowing agents in the manufacture of the majority of closed-cell insulation. Because of the damaging effect of CFCs on the ozone layer, some years ago they were replaced by hydrochlorofluorocarbons (HCFCs), and these in turn are being replaced with new blowing agents called hydrofluorocarbons (HFCs). Although HFCs have no effect on the ozone layer, they are significant greenhouse gases and so contribute global warming. To overcome this, manufacturers are beginning to switch to using hydrocarbons such as pentanes or to CO_2.

TYPES OF INSULATION

Insulation materials can generally be categorised as three groups:

— *Cellular plastics* – these are generally foamed petrochemical products and include rigid polyurethane, phenolic foam and expanded or extruded polystyrene.
— *Mineral fibres* – typically made by spinning molten rock or glass and adding binders to create the required degree of rigidity for quilts or boards.
— *Plant or animal fibres* – these include cellulose, sheep wool, hemp and straw.

CHOICE OF INSULATION

The performance of insulation materials generally can vary by a factor of 2 across the product range. In other words, the best insulants are about twice as effective as the worst. The petrochemical foams perform best, but these products have the greatest environmental impact, in both their production and their disposal.

When specifying insulation materials, it is important to consider both the energy in use and the global warming potential:

— ensure the U-values are optimised
— specify high-performance materials or increase the thickness of less efficient ones
— ensure that the performance of the insulation will be maintained over the life of the building
— avoid specifying inappropriate materials in locations where they are liable to become waterlogged, compacted or otherwise degraded; this tends to mean specifying synthetic materials in such conditions
— ensure that the materials specified have zero ozone depletion potential (ODP); this simply means avoiding synthetic foams that are not specified as zero ODP
— ensure that the embodied energy in production and disposal are minimised.

DUNDEE UNIVERSITY RESEARCH ON U-VALUES

The following text is extracted from the report 'U Value Assessment of Various Construction Building Materials', by Dr Rod Jones and Dr Li Zheng of the Concrete Technology Unit, University of Dundee, commissioned by The Concrete Centre. This extract is reproduced with permission.

TEST RESULTS

Concrete and reinforced concrete

Indicative thermal conductivity, λ_{ind} and calculated U-value, U_{cal} of the concrete and reinforced concrete specimens are given in Table 2.3.

Effect of cement combinations

Three cement combinations, i.e. PC, PC/GGBS and PC/PFA, were tested. It can be seen that the λ_{ind} of the PC specimen is slighty higher than that of PC/GGBS and PC/PFA specimens. The calculated U-values for all three cement combinations are similar, ranging from 4.99 to 5.06 W/m²K.

Effect of lightweight aggregates

The λ_{ind} of the lightweight aggregate concrete tested is much lower than that of the normal weight concrete. Its λ_{ind} is about 64 per cent of the normal concrete while its density is about 80 per cent of the normal concrete. The U-values of the lightweight aggregate concrete are also lower than the normal weight concrete.

Effect of thickness of the specimen

The λ_{ind} of the 50 mm thickness specimen is slightly lower than that of 100 mm thickness specimens. For both normal and lightweight specimens, the λ_{ind} of 50 mm specimens is about 88 per cent of the 100 mm ones.

As mentioned above, λ [thermal conductivity] is an intrinsic property of the material and independent of testing conditions. However, λ_{ind} is a specific value, corresponding to a fixed set of testing conditions. The observed variation of λ_{ind} with thickness of the specimen in this work is only equipment associated.

The U-values of the 100 mm thickness specimens are about 0.5–0.6 W/m²K lower than that of 50 mm thickness specimens.

Effect of reinforcement

The λ_{ind} of the reinforced specimens are higher than that of the corresponding plain concrete specimens, about 14 per cent higher for normal concrete and 11 per cent for lightweight concrete. However, the U-values of the reinforced

Table 2.3.
λ_{ind} and U_{cal} of the concrete and reinforced concrete specimens

Specimen no.	Description	Moisture content % by mass	Density during test kg/m³	λ_{ind} W/mK	U_{cal} * W/m²K
1	PC, 50 mm	4.9	2295	1.81	5.06
		5.1	2330	1.77	5.05
2	PC/GGBS, 50 mm	4.5	2305	1.67	5.00
		4.8	2300	1.68	5.01
3	PC/PFA, 50 mm	3.9	2290	1.66	5.00
		3.7	2290	1.65	4.99
4	PC, lightweight, 50 mm	9.7	1900	1.15	4.68
		8.7	1880	1.14	4.67
9	PC, 100 mm	5.8	2335	2.00	4.55
10	PC, rebar, 100 mm	5.1	2420	2.28	4.68
11	PC lightweight, 100 mm	11.1	1920	1.31	4.06
12	PC lightweight, rebar, 100 mm	10.9	2000	1.45	4.19

* Calculation was according to BS EN ISO 6946.

specimens are only about 0.13 W/m²K (3 per cent) higher than that of the plain specimens.

Dense and lightweight blocks

Indicative thermal conductivity, λ_{ind} and calculated U-value, U_{cal} of the block specimens are given in Table 2.4.

Effect of densities

The λ_{ind} of the lightweight blocks is much lower than that of the dense blocks. Its λ_{ind} is about 61 per cent of the dense blocks and its density is about 75 per cent of the dense blocks. The

U-values of the lightweight blocks are about 0.5 W/m²K lower than the dense blocks.

Effect of joint materials

The λ_{ind} of the blocks with resin joints is slightly lower than that of blocks with mortar joints. The differences in λ_{ind} are between 0.06 and 0.07 W/mK. The differences in U-values are between 0.04 and 0.09 W/m²K.

Typical published U-values for masonry

The thermal conductivity of masonry materials from BRE Digest 108 are given in Table 2.5.

Table 2.4.
λ_{ind} and U_{cal} of the block specimens

Specimen no.	Description	Moisture content % by mass	Density during test kg/m³	λ_{ind} W/mK	U_{cal} * W/m²K
5	Dense mortar	2.2	2070	1.36	4.84
		2.1	2070	1.34	4.82
6	Dense resin	2.3	2066	1.29	4.79
		2.1	2062	1.28	4.78
7	Light mortar	6.6	1601	0.85	4.37
		6.1	1593	0.83	4.35
8	Light resin	8.9	1595	0.78	4.27
		5.6	1548	0.77	4.25

* Calculation was according to BS EN ISO 6946.

Table 2.5.
Thermal conductivity of masonry materials

Bulk dry density kg/m³	Thermal conductivity, W/mK		
	Brickwork protected from rain, Ψ = 1%	Concrete protected from rain, Ψ = 3%	Brickwork or concrete exposed to rain, Ψ = 5%
400	0.12	0.15	0.16
600	0.15	0.19	0.20
800	0.19	0.23	0.26
1000	0.24	0.30	0.33
1200	0.31	0.38	0.42
1400	0.42	0.51	0.57
1600	0.54	0.66	0.73
1800	0.71	0.87	0.96
2000	0.92	1.13	1.24
2200	1.18	1.45	1.60
2400	1.49	1.83	2.00

Ψ = moisture content volume by volume, m³/m³.

EXAMPLES OF CO_2 REDUCTION

This section describes methods used in practice to reduce the energy consumed in heating and cooling a building. The principal approach is to utilise concrete's thermal mass, combined with passive ventilation and other low-energy cooling systems, and examples are described for both office buildings and residential buildings.

It can be seen from the examples below, and *especially in the case studies in Part II*, that concrete buildings can offset the CO_2 embodied in their construction and can provide the greatest long-term reductions in energy consumption by deploying thermal mass and passive cooling.

OFFICE BUILDINGS

In-situ and precast composite slabs

The structural weight and the large surface area provided by concrete floor slabs are central to the design of most FES systems using thermal mass. The high thermal mass of cast in-situ and precast slabs is most effective if the slabs are 200 to 400 mm thick and if the surfaces are exposed. Additionally, a profiled finish, such as a ribbed or coffered slab, will increase the surface area for heat transfer.

Putting a greater reliance on the structural form to provide a comfortable environment avoids the need for suspended ceilings and a lot of overhead ventilation ductwork, enabling much simpler building installation. This can provide significant building cost savings and reductions in construction CO_2 and long-term energy use.

A further benefit of exposed concrete floor slabs is that they allow a range of FES design options to be considered. These systems can provide a bespoke solution to specific project requirements, making it a relatively flexible approach to both passive and mixed-mode cooling. Water can also be used to good effect in water-cooled slabs and chilled beams, which offer the highest cooling capacity of all the options featured.

Optimal slab thickness

All the structural elements of an office building – the walls, frame and floors – can contribute to thermal mass. However, it is the concrete slabs that provide the bulk of thermal mass. The factors for assessing the optimum slab thickness for good FES are indicated below:

— It is generally accepted that in naturally ventilated buildings with exposed concrete soffits and a floor surface that is covered, a concrete slab approximately 100 mm thick will provide sufficient thermal mass, assuming the current cycles of warm and cold weather prevail.

— For extended periods of warm weather, as forecast for the future, slabs of 100 mm thickness will not provide sufficient thermal mass to prevent overheating.

— Slabs with thermal linking on both sides, e.g. exposed soffit and exposed surface with underfloor ventilation or cooling, will therefore be required.

— Profiled slabs provide an increased surface contact area, enhancing convective heat transfer and improving FES performance.

— Taking account of these points, a building with exposed soffits and exposed floor surfaces should be capable of FES during extended periods of warm weather provided the concrete floor slab has a minimum thickness of 200 to 250 mm.

FES options

1. Natural ventilation: *with exposed soffits*

Description:
Flat or profiled floor slabs used in conjunction with natural ventilation. This may be wind driven, or a combination of wind and stack ventilation.

Typical applications:
Offices, schools, universities.

FES cooling capacity:
15–20 W/m² (flat slab); 20–25 W/m² (profiled slab).

Key benefits:
• Simple
• No fan energy
• Minimal maintenance
• Can be used in many existing buildings.

Key considerations:
• Application limited to environments with low to moderate heat gains
• Performance is particularly weather dependent and requires good occupant control
• External noise and security may preclude the use of opening windows
• Careful design and operation is required to ensure heating energy is minimised.

2. Underfloor ventilation: *with exposed soffits*

Description:
The void created by a raised floor is used as a plenum for mechanical ventilation. Air enters the occupied space through floor diffusers. This solution is often used in conjunction with an exposed, profiled slab and as part of a mixed-mode system.

Typical applications:
Offices, public and commercial buildings.

FES cooling capacity:
25–35 W/m² (exposed, profiled soffits);
20–30 W/m² (exposed, flat soffits).

Key benefits:
• Enables thermal linking of the upper slab surface in buildings with raised floors

• Turbulent air in the floor void can provide good convective heat transfer, enabling higher cooling capacities than in naturally ventilated systems
• Good flexibility and the ability to accommodate changes in building use
• Can provide the benefits of mixed-mode ventilation.

Key considerations:
• Space requirement for air-handling plant
• Higher capital and operating costs than passive solutions.

3. Permeable ceilings: *with exposed soffits*

Description:
Suspended ceiling with perforated tiles, allowing some thermal linking between the slab and occupied space.

Typical applications:
New build, and the retrofit of existing office buildings from the 1960s/70s.

FES cooling capacity:
Dependent on open area and ceiling type, but should provide approximately 10 W/m² in naturally ventilated buildings.

Key benefits:
• A low-cost solution that can prevent or reduce the frequency of overheating in new and existing offices, and avoid/reduce the use of mechanical air-conditioning
• Allows the use of a suspended ceiling, avoiding the need to route services elsewhere to exploit the thermal mass available in the slab.

Key considerations:
• Overall effectiveness is a compromise between maximising FES performance and concealing services.

4. Exposed hollowcore slabs: *with mechanical ventilation*

Description:
Precast, hollowcore concrete slabs with mechanical ventilation via the cores, which provides good convective heat transfer between the air and the slab. Further heat transfer is provided by the exposed underside of the slab. The system is typically referred to by the trade name TermoDeck.

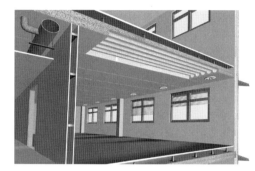

Typical applications:
Universities, schools, theatres, offices.

FES cooling capacity:
40 W/m^2 (basic system); 50 W/m^2 (with cooling); 60 W/m^2 (with cooling and switch-flow).

Key benefits:
- Well-established technology with good year-round performance
- Can be used as a full mechanical or mixed-mode system
- Air can be introduced at high level from diffusers linked to the slab cores, or at low level using an underfloor supply system, with the floor void acting as a plenum.

Key considerations:
- The slab cores may require periodic cleaning (access points are provided)
- Typical applications in the UK suggest it is a system suited to owner occupied buildings.

5. Water-cooled slabs: *with exposed surfaces*

Description:
Precast or in-situ slabs with water cooling via embedded polybutylene pipework, which can be used in conjunction with a night-time ventilation strategy. The precast option is trademarked Thermocast.

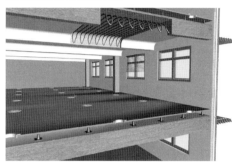

Typical applications:
Offices, museums, hotels, universities, showrooms.

FES cooling capacity:
64 W/m^2 (flat slab); 80 W/m^2 (profiled slab).

Key benefits:
- Minimal maintenance
- High cooling capacity
- Provides a combined solution for heating and cooling
- The ability to use high temperature cooling water may allow the option of free cooling from boreholes, lakes and evaporative coolers.

Key considerations:
- The control system must ensure that the slab temperature does not fall below the dew point of the internal air, or condensation may form
- For high-load applications, cooling water from free sources may need to be supplemented with mechanical chilling under peak load conditions.

6. Chilled beams: *with exposed soffits*

Description:
Concrete soffits (flat or coffered) with chilled beams suspended directly below. A permeable ceiling may be used, or the soffit left exposed.

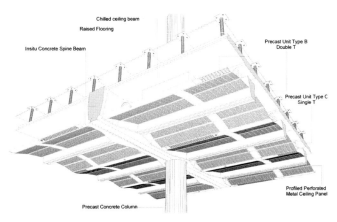

Chilled ceiling beam
Raised Flooring
Insitu Concrete Spine Beam
Precast Unit Type B Double T
Precast Unit Type C Single T
Profiled Perforated Metal Ceiling Panel
Precast Concrete Column

Typical applications:
Offices, universities, refurbished 1960s/70s office buildings.

FES cooling capacity:
15–30 W/m² (FES only). Cooling capacity is dependent on the type of ventilation and surface area of the soffit. Chilled beams can provide additional cooling as required, up to a maximum of 100–160 W/m².

Key benefits:
· Low maintenance (compared with other ceiling-based air-conditioning systems)
· Quiet, draught-free operation
· Relatively shallow unit depth makes chilled beams ideal for refurbishment projects with a low slab-to-slab height, especially where a raised floor is required
· Provides a high cooling capacity while still making effective use of FES
· The use of high cooling water temperatures may allow free cooling from boreholes, lakes and evaporative coolers, etc.

Key considerations:
· Water flow temperatures must be carefully controlled to avoid condensation problems
· Where possible, beam positions should not restrict air flow across the soffit
· If used in conjunction with a permeable ceiling, the open area must be maximised to promote air flow in the void.

RESIDENTIAL BUILDINGS

Unlike in office buildings, where the floors generally provide the greatest overall thermal mass, in houses and apartments where internal partitions are made from in-situ concrete or concrete blocks, the walls and partitions are the primary source of thermal mass. To ensure good thermal linking between the wall and the air in the room, a fair-faced surface with no plaster is the most effective option. However, a thin wet plaster finish on blockwork will not affect the admittance but will improve airtightness and sound insulation, but the use of plasterboard with dabs will reduce admittance, particularly when overlaying dense aggregate blocks, because of the air gaps at the interface.

Aircrete blocks

A complete insulation solution is achievable using Aircrete blocks. The inherent thermal qualities of these blocks provide a highly effective barrier against the penetration of moisture and frost. They can be used with full or partial fill insulation without necessarily increasing cavity widths, and if used below the ground can reduce heat loss by up to 25 per cent. Although Aircrete has a relatively low density (460–730 kg/m³), it still provides a useful amount of thermal mass. Plasterboard fixed using dabs produces an admittance value of 1.85 W/m²K, while blockwork with a 13 mm wet plaster finish provides a value of around 2.86 W/m²K. The use of plasterboard appears to have little impact on the thermal mass available in Aircrete.

Aggregate blocks

A wide range of concrete aggregate blocks is available, with densities varying from around 1,400 kg/m³ for a lightweight block to around 2,000 kg/m³ for a heavyweight block which, when used with a wet plaster finish, can provide a very high admittance of 5.88 W/m²K. A conventional plasterboard finish will halve the admittance value to around 2.6 W/m²K because heat flow is restricted by the air gap formed by the dabs.

Twin-Wall

(See Chapter 1, page 45.) A Twin-Wall with a simple painted system will provide a high level of thermal mass, with an admittance value in the order of 5–6 W/m²K. Twin-Wall also offers excellent acoustic performance, making it especially useful for separating wall situations. It can also be supplied with integral insulation for external walls.

Crosswall

(See Chapter 1, page 44.) Crosswall provides a high level of thermal mass, with an admittance value in the order of 5–6 W/m²K.

CASE STUDY/
TIMBER WHARF, MANCHESTER

Glenn Howells, Glenn Howells Architects

Brief/project function

Timber Wharf occupies a site bordering the Bridgewater Canal, and is part of the industrial Britannia Basin/St George's area. This area already houses Britannia Mills and The Box Works, both conversion projects by Urban Splash. It was envisaged that Timber Wharf would further enhance this new residential and working community in an area previously home to derelict factories and warehouses. The robust structure provides a very clear, strong identity,

creating a form which is not immediately recognisable as housing but instead continues the scale and simplicity of an industrial aesthetic, consistent with its surroundings.

Design

The design for Timber Wharf focuses on achieving optimum quality of space and materials within a modest budget, comparable in cost to the volume housebuilders' product. This was delivered by the use of high-quality components, including factory-produced precast concrete wall panels and bespoke glazing systems. These elements were subject to strict financial control and delivered by liaising with the manufacturers and subcontractors from the outset and throughout the design process. The factory production of the principal components of the building permitted a highly rationalised, fast-track construction, where the fit-out was commenced on lower levels as the superstructure was progressed on upper floors.

The building was designed as a precast concrete Crosswall solution on a continuous 6 m grid, supported on a two-storey in-situ concrete transfer structure.

Left
Timber Wharf

Concrete aspects

Crosswall construction offers the benefit of providing an efficient frame without structural downstands. This resulted in a vertical structural zone of 150–200 mm, permitting generous internal finished ceiling heights. One of the main objectives of this method of construction was to provide an early 'dry box', allowing subsequent trades prompt access into the building, creating programme efficiencies and reducing the number of wet trades on site. Load-bearing transverse walls provide the primary means of support, with longitudinal stability achieved by external wall panels or diaphragm action back to the lift cores or staircases. The system provided a structurally efficient building incorporating main division walls between apartments. It also offered a high level of sound reduction between dwellings. Internal division walls were manufactured to a high standard of finish using vertical casting, avoiding the need for plaster or other decorative finish.

In order to maximise economies of production, the quantity of casts per mould and their complexity were carefully analysed. The balcony division walls were connected to the grey concrete Crosswalls, and the balcony floor units to tie beams, for installation as single units, thus significantly reducing the number of individual lifts required, and so the construction period and costs. Stainless steel brackets were attached to the division walls, allowing the insulation and damp-proof membrane to be fixed between two precast units in the factory.

Balcony floor units and tie beams were cast in a two-stage process. The white concrete balcony section was cast first, with a stainless steel connector protruding from the back of the unit to connect to the tie beam behind. The next process was to place the insulation and damp-proof membrane in position, followed by pouring the grey concrete tie beam behind. Insulation and damp-proof membranes were left oversize so that they could be overlapped and jointed on site, providing a continuous barrier. Glazing installation followed behind the Crosswalls, commencing at the ground floor. This was fundamental in providing the early dry working box.

Site installation was undertaken using two tower cranes within a contract period of 24 weeks, equating to an erection period of three weeks per floor. The structure includes over 1,400 precast architectural and structural concrete components and 12,000 m^2 of hollow-core flooring units and structural steel members.

Top
Crosswall construction

Above
Interior

Insulating concrete formwork

Insulating concrete formwork (ICF), otherwise known as permanently insulated formwork (PIF), is an in-situ concrete building system that is quick to construct and provides a highly insulated structure. The system comprises large, hollow lightweight blocks or panels (typically made from expanded polystyrene) that lock together to provide a formwork system into which concrete is placed.

Once set, the concrete becomes a load-bearing structure and the formwork remains in place as thermal insulation, providing U-values ranging from 0.30 W/m²K down to 0.11 W/m²K.

As the permanent formwork is the insulation, the concrete's thermal mass is encapsulated by the insulation and so has little benefit. It may be necessary in this case to remove the internal insulation to expose the concrete, but this may compromise the U-value.

CASE STUDY/
CREO DEMONSTRATION PROJECT, BRE GARSTON

Duncan McKinnon, MJP Architects

The CREO project aims to demonstrate that high-quality affordable housing can meet the highest environmental standards in a cost-effective way. The project has been designed to meet Level 6 of the Code for Sustainable Homes, which means that it is a net zero carbon building.

The building's design represents a part of a larger apartment building, four and a half storeys high. There is a small commercial unit on the ground floor, and one 1-bed (2-person) flat and one 3-bed (5-person) duplex on the floors above. A core at the side contains the common staircase, a space for a lift and a vertical service riser.

Externally the building form progressively steps back from the corner, emphasising the corner entrance to the commercial unit and creating terraces for the apartments above. Adding emphasis to this modelling, bold use has been made of colour, with bright panels, particularly yellow, standing out against a neutral white background. External shading, or *brise soleil*,

Left
CREO demonstration house

Left
Insulating concrete formwork

Below
Construction detail

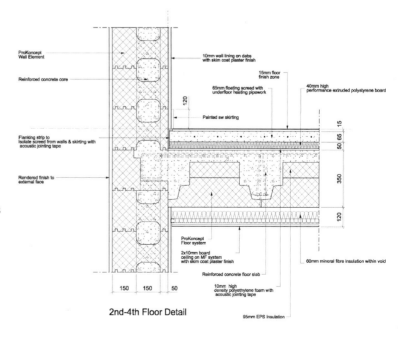

2nd-4th Floor Detail

to the south-facing windows tempers the solar gains on that part of the façade. The vertical core is clad in grey rainscreen panels. The pitched roof slope is angled to provide the best orientation for solar thermal heating panels and photovoltaic arrays.

The building is constructed using an ICF block for the external walls, and ICF trays forming floors and roofs. The lean-mix concrete core provides the structural frame. The system has inherently good thermal and sound insulation properties. Hot water is provided by air-source heat pump, and underfloor heating will be provided throughout. Grey water will be recycled and rainwater collected and reused.

Tunnel form

Tunnel formwork, also known as apartment formwork, is a factory-made steel formwork system that enables walls and slabs to be cast monolithically on the same day to achieve a one-day construction cycle. It has been developed for rapid construction of room

cells (i.e. walls and slabs) of varying sizes for housing projects, apartment blocks and hotels. The system has been used in the UK and is well-established in Europe and the USA. Provided that the room layouts or apartments of a building project can be rationalised into one-way spanning slabs of not more than 7.5 m spans, with a storey height not more than 3.5 m, then a tunnel form system can be made to work efficiently. Production rates of around two apartments a day are usual, equivalent to 450 m^2 of total wall and slab construction.

The key to developing this fast rhythm of production is to keep the immature concrete floor slab propped during the following morning, while removing a half-tunnel section of formwork. Minimum concrete striking strength is assured by tenting and heating the air space within the tunnel forms overnight.

The benefit of such a system is the reduction of site labour and the elimination of skilled finishing trades. Since the system is reliant on cranes to position and reset forms, labour is required only to wheel out and set down

forms, using simple hand-tools for jacking and clamping of the assembly. The accuracy of the wall forms and the exact positioning on successive lifts using specially cast kicker plates affords a high standard of surface finish and verticality, eliminating the need for plastering.

The architectural form and structural layout, within the concept of bearing walls and one-way spanning slabs, does not limit the scope for imaginative and dramatic building design using tunnel forms. Major improvements in speed of construction can be achieved over more traditional methods. The smooth face of the formwork used in tunnel form produces a high-quality finish that can be decorated directly, maximising the thermal mass admittance. This also reduces the need for finishing trades on site, thereby providing additional cost savings and speeding the building process.

Tunnel forms are especially well-suited to the construction of multiple residential dwellings (e.g. affordable attached apartment blocks, hotels and student flats). There are several versions of tunnel form systems, each version suitable for a multitude of customer preferences or project requirements.

Sandwich panel construction

(See Chapter 1, page 46.) One of the most structurally efficient building options for apartment buildings (and also for offices) is sandwich panel construction. The U-value and insulations thickness can be designed to meet or surpass all current codes and Building Regulations requirements.

Current standards (Finland) for sandwich panels are:

— with 160 mm rockwool:
U-value = 0.24 W/m²K

— with 240 mm rockwool:
U-value = 0.17 W/m²K

Low-density concrete (no insulation)

Low-density concrete can be used to form high thermal mass residential buildings, although there are limitations to the types of design where it can be used effectively.

CASE STUDY/
THE CHUR HOUSE, SWITZERLAND

Patrick Filipaj, Banz Choffat Filipaj Architekten, Zurich

Patrick Gartmann's two-storey house in Switzerland is an extraordinary achievement in monolithic, single-skin concrete construction. Its sculptural outer form is produced from one solid material without a separate insulation layer, render, plaster, rain screen or cladding – it's just concrete. The external load-bearing wall is 450 mm thick and provides all the necessary insulation and protection against cold bridging and moisture penetration. Low-density concrete for the wall was developed using expanded shale coarse aggregates and expanded glass fines and was placed by pump and truck mixer.

The construction for the house was entirely made of one material – in-situ concrete. The concrete mix was specially designed to be truck-mixed and poured in place, and to have a low U-value so that it would be self-insulating. It was waterproof because there was sufficient cement in the mix to give the surface a dense, hard finish, which also meant it could be self-finished on both sides, just like normal concrete. The whole point of the construction was to eliminate the need for built-up external wall systems whose performance depended on maintaining a cavity in the wall, the long-term durability of a decorative render as the waterproof membrane and keeping the insulation material dry within the cavity.

By using a lightweight aggregate such as Liapor, it is possible to design a concrete with a low density and a relatively high strength. High-strength concrete of 80 MPa with a density of 1,800 kg/m³ and concrete of 30 MPa strength with a 1,400 kg/m³ density are quite common using Liapor aggregates and fines. But to achieve a concrete with a U-value of 0.5 W/m²K and to keep the wall thickness to an economical section, the Chur House concrete density had to be as low as 1,000 kg/m³. The lowest density Liapor aggregate – at 400 kg/m³, with aggregate size of 4–8 mm – was combined with a fine aggregate made from expanded recycled glass, called Liaver, and mixed with the cement and water. A chemical agent was then added to help stabilise the mix and improve the cohesion of materials to make it workable.

The single-skin wall thickness of 450 mm achieved a U–value of 0. 55 W/m²K, while the 650-mm thick roof slab had a U-value of 0.45 W/m²K. These values were proven by rigorous tests carried out at the ETH in Zurich.

As building laws concerning thermal conductivity get stricter, Swiss architects become more and more uneasy with multilayer construction and the deeper cavity spaces that are necessary. How well is the insulation in the cavity performing? Is the original depth of the cavity being maintained? How well is the external skin tied to the internal wall?

A monolithic, self-insulating concrete seems to be a positive and innovative way to overcome these concerns, while at the same time creating a new style of architectural expression. Although the lightweight concrete was higher in cost – the expanded shale and glass fines are much more expensive to process than natural aggregates as they have to be heat-treated to above 1,000 °C – it offered savings by reducing on-site trades and shortening the building time.

As a material, the concrete is not especially carbon friendly, as the embodied CO_2 of the aggregates is higher than for standard concrete. However, its thermal mass and insulation properties mean that it will reduce energy required for heating or cooling, which may offset the material's embodied CO_2 after, say, seven to eight years.

A very important point to recognise is that self-insulating concrete can only be used for mass concrete structures and lightly reinforced slabs. It is not robust enough for framed structures.

Typical concrete characteristics:

— Density: 1,050 kg/m³
— Strength: 11.0 N/mm²
— E-modulus: 5,000 N/mm²
— U-value: 0.45 W/m²K at 650 mm thick.

Querschnitt C-C 1:50

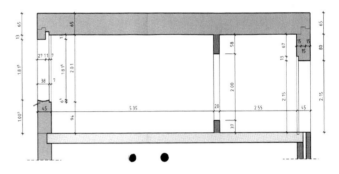

Querschnitt D-D 1:50

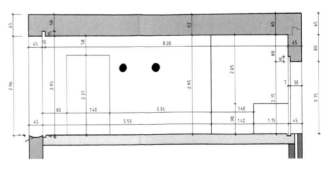

Top
Chur House, rear elevation
Above
Construction details

SUMMARY: LOWERING OPERATIONAL CO_2 AND ENERGY

The use of concrete in building construction often raises questions regarding its embodied CO_2. The Construction CO_2 Audit (see Chapter 1) has shown that concrete structures are significantly lower in embodied energy and CO_2 emissions than the equivalent steel-framed buildings, by as much as 40 per cent if low embodied CO_2 materials are specified, which are both cost-effective and readily available. Further reductions in construction CO_2 for concrete buildings can be realised if the advantages of concrete's thermal mass and passive cooling systems can be deployed, eliminating the need for suspended ceilings, air handling units and ventilation and heating ducts.

Significant reductions in the long-term operational CO_2 emissions over the lifetime of a building are also possible when FES systems are designed to take advantage of concrete's thermal mass, as shown by the examples in this chapter and in the case studies in Part II.

Designers often overlook this point, tending instead to focus on the impact of the embodied CO_2 of construction materials. In reality, the embodied CO_2 of concrete and masonry products can be lowered – even neutralised – by using the right combination of materials.

A concrete-framed building can support long spans and high imposed loads, and when the construction CO_2 and operational CO_2 are optimised the result is the most energy-efficient structure currently on the market.

FINDINGS OF WHOLE-LIFE CO_2 RESEARCH

Arup Research evaluated and compared the embodied and operational CO_2 emissions of a simple semi-detached house built using a lightweight timber frame with those for several masonry and concrete options with varying levels of thermal mass. The embodied CO_2 for each option was calculated and thermal modelling was undertaken to see how each performed, taking account of the likely impacts of climate change.

The results showed that there is a slightly higher construction CO_2 content in concrete and masonry buildings, and that this was around 4 per cent more than for a lightweight timber frame option. The research went on to show that this small additional amount of CO_2 in the construction would be offset within eleven years as a result of the energy savings provided by the concrete's thermal mass. The lowest whole-life CO_2 emissions were achieved by increasing the thermal mass in the house through including additional concrete elements.

Moreover, the reduction in CO_2 emissions over a 100-year period were even greater for the concrete and masonry options, with savings of 14–35 tonnes of CO_2 per house, depending on the level of thermal mass provided.

APPENDIX

EMBODIED CO$_2$ TABLES

Table A.1. Embodied CO$_2$ for construction materials

The data in this table are taken from published sources and are not validated by individual producers or manufacturers.

The ranges shown illustrate the variability of embodied CO$_2$ data for individual materials.

Material	kg CO$_2$/m³ (range)	Density kg/m³	kg CO$_2$/tonne (range)
Metals			
Lead	67,137	11,340	5920
Copper	56,725–74,566	8,930	6,352–8,350
Brass	61,381	8,600	7,137
Zinc	43,863	7,135	6,148
Aluminium, recycled	1,191–2,584	2,800	425–923
Aluminium, virgin	23,828–83,168	2,800	8,510–29,703
Steel, recycled	12,654–27,763	7,800	1,622–3,559
Steel, virgin	26,870–54,497	7,800	3,445–6,987
Oil-based materials			
Linoleum	17,831	1,180	15,111
Single ply roof membrane	20,046	–	–
Carpet, synthetic	10,030	190	52,789
Paint (liquid)	13,882	1,000	13,882
Polycarbonate	16,445	1,200	13,704
PVC	11,060	1,100	10,055
Plastics	20,046	1,100	18,224
Glass			
Tinted glass	44,356	2,400	18,482
Laminated glass	4,853	2,400	2,022
Toughened glass	7,800	2,400	3,250
Float glass	9,810	2,400	4,088
Clay materials			
Clay tiles	648	2,200	295
Bricks, engineering [1]	860	1,950	441
Bricks, Fletton [1]	128	1,950	66
Bricks, autoclaved [1]	341	1,950	175
Bricks, non Fletton [1]	624	1,950	320
Bricks [1]	1,895	1,950	972
Cement-based materials			
Particle board	520	–	–
Sand cement render	171	2,162	79
Concrete tiles	269	2,200	122
Concrete precast	328	2,400	137
Concrete, 1:3:6	256	2,400	107
Concrete	376	2,300	163
Autoclaved blocks	341	900	379
Lightweight blocks	256	600	427
Novacem	–	–	300

Material	kg CO$_2$/m^3 (range)	Density kg/m^3	kg CO$_2$/tonne (range)
Insulation products			
Woodwool, loose	384	–	–
Sheep wool	13	–	–
Foamed glass	320	–	–
Plastic	480	–	–
Polystyrene	445	–	–
Fibreglass	115	–	–
Mineral wool	98	–	–
Cellulose	57	–	–
Harvested materials			
Straw bale	4	–	–
Glulam	1,300	–	–
Local softwood	47	450	104
Local green oak	94	650	145
Plywood [2]	676	640	1,056
Prepared softwood	427	450	949
Local airdried timber	163	–	–
Chipboard	357	700	510
Quarried materials			
Gypsum wallboard	696	950	733
Plaster	948	950	998
Local stone	240	2,200	109
Local stone tiles	192	2,200	87
Local slate	230	2,200	105
Lightweight aggregate	128	1,200	107
Sand and gravel	19	2,000	10
Crushed granite/aggregate	64	2,400	27

Notes:
High and low figures show the range of values quoted for individual materials.
1. Density range of bricks is 1,700–2,200 kg/m^3; average 1,950 kg/m^3 used.
2. Density range for plywood is 500–780 kg/m^3; average of 640 kg/m^3 used.
– Where no value shown, no value found.

Sources:
The Environmental Handbook, Feilden Clegg Bradley; *The Green Building Bible,* vol 1; Simetric: www.simetric.co.uk; Engineering Toolbox: www.engineeringtoolbox.com/metal-alloys-densities-d_50.html; IEM: www.iem-inc.com/tooldens.html; Building Research Establishment Approved Environmental Profiles (1994); BIRSA: *Environmental Rules of Thumb* and *Environmental Code of Practice*; University of Wellington; *Canadian Architect*; Beyers Plastics; Association of Environmentally Conscious Building Architects.

Table A.2. Embodied CO₂ for construction products

The data in this table were provided by product manufacturers and have therefore been validated for use for the products listed.

(a) Charcon Precast Solutions: kg CO_2/tonne (delivered to site)

Location	Product	Material	Production	Transport	Employee	Total kg CO_2/tonne	Density kg/m³	kg CO_2/m³
Croft Plant	Dense aggregate blocks	75*	2.34	1.30	0.12	78.76	1800	141.8
Barnsley Plant	Precast stairs	312	7.05	3.12	2.08	324.25	2400	778.2
Stockton Plant	Precast stairs, carpark frames	312	5.16	3.12	1.94	322.21	2400	773.31
Histon Plant	Precast cladding panels, carpark frames, Crosswall	312	6.50	3.12	1.49	323.11	2400	775.46

* Estimated figure

(b) Lignacite blocks (ex works): kg CO_2/m³

Density kg/m³	Embodied material	Wood sequested	Reabsorbed CO_2 (20 yrs)	Total net
1500–1600 kg/m³, electricity	299	215	78	6

(c) London Concrete ready-mixed supply (delivered to site): kg CO_2/m³

Location	Product	Material	Production	Transport	Employee	Total kg CO_2/tonne	Density kg/m³	kg CO_2/m³
Bow	Ready mix	n.a.*	0.236	0.35	0.167	0.753	2400	1.81
Purley	Ready mix	n.a.*	0.166	0.463	0.043	0.672	2400	1.61

* Designer determines embodied CO_2 of the mix constituents

(d) Reinforcement: kg CO_2/tonne

Part A - raw material

Production	Meltshop	Rolling mill	Delivery to customer	Employee	Folklift (goods yard)	kg CO_2/tonne
Celsa Cardiff	284	138	n.a.	0.67	n.a.	422.4

Part B - process bar and mesh

	Fuel: gas	Fuel: electricity	Delivery to customer	Employee	Folklift (goods yard)	kg CO_2/tonne	Total delivered A + B
Bar: BRC Ltd Mansfield Depot (90,000 t/yr)	2.50	11.84	46.03	1.66	1.50	63.53	Bar = 486
Mesh: BRC Ltd Barnsley Depot (73,000 t/yr)	5.94	38.14	42.16	0.27	1.68	88.19	Mesh = 510

(e) Formwork panels (general): kg CO_2/m³

	Material	Production	Notes
WISA plywood	0	76	ex works (Finland)

(f) Cement and cement replacement: kg CO_2/tonne

(1) General (ex works)

	Fuel	Calcining	Total	Reabsorption	Net total	Notes
Portland cement (general)	360 approx.	570 approx.	930	−170	760	ex works 30% CO_2 reabsorption
GGBS (Civil & Marine)	n.a.	n.a.	52	n.a.	52	ex works
PFA	n.a.	n.a.	4	n.a.	4	ex works
RockTron	n.a.	n.a.	50	n.a.	50	ex works
Lime (general)	300	528	828	−445	383	ex works 90% CO_2 reabsorption

(2) Ribblesdale Cement

Calcining	All fuel (energy)	Deduct waste fuel	Net fuel	Total	Reabsorption	Net total	Notes
569.17 **(1)**	262.88	-44.88	218 **(2)**	787.17 **(1) + (2)**	−170.75	616.42	includes transport, employee, production, material, heating and lighting

(g) Lightweight aggregate: kg CO_2/tonne

Product	Material	Transport	Total	Notes
Lytag	15	65	80	made in Poland, includes transport by ship to UK
Liapor	5	n.a.	5	made in Germany (ex works)

CONSTRUCTION INDUSTRY CO$_2$ AUDITS

Table A.3. Aggregate Industries CO$_2$ audit

	Inner-city ready mix Bow	Outer city ready mix Purley	Block plant Croft	Precast factory Barnsley	Precast factory Stockton	Precast factory Histon
Materials						
Cement	105.29	105.29	53.93	119.84	119.84	119.84
Fine aggregate	1.08	1.08	1.03	0.94	0.99	1.04
Coarse aggregate	0.78	0.79	0.83	0.76	0.77	0.83
Water	0.00	0.00	0.00	0.00	0.00	0.00
Total: kg CO$_2$/tonne	107.15	107.16	55.79	121.54	121.60	121.71
Energy use						
kWh/tonne	0.44	0.31	4.36	13.12	9.60	12.10
kg CO$_2$/tonne	0.24	0.17	2.34	7.05	5.16	6.50
Delivery						
Distance to customer: miles	3.50	5.70	20.00	60.00	60.00	60.00
Payload: tonnes	20.00	20.00	20.00	25.00	25.00	25.00
Fuel efficiency: mpg	6.50	8.00	10.00	10.00	10.00	10.00
Fuel usage per delivery: gal	0.54	0.71	2.00	6.00	6.00	6.00
Mass fuel/delivery: kg	2.20	2.91	8.17	24.52	24.52	24.52
kg fuel/tonne delivered	0.11	0.15	0.41	0.98	0.98	0.98
Energy content fuel: MJ/kg	44.30	44.30	44.30	44.30	44.30	44.30
kg CO$_2$/GJ	71.80	71.80	71.80	71.80	71.80	71.80
kg CO$_2$/tonne	0.35	0.46	1.30	3.12	3.12	3.12
Employee travel						
Employees	3.00	2.00	18.00	22.00	17.00	15.00
Total shifts	822.00	548.00	4,932.00	6,028.00	4,658.00	4,110.00
Total mileage	19,728.00	13,152.00	118,368.00	144,672.00	111,792.00	98,640.00
Total CO$_2$: kg	2,984.85	1,989.90	17,909.08	21,888.87	16,914.13	14,924.23
Total plant output: tonnes	179,000.00	46,000.00	150,000.00	10,500.00	11,000.00	10,000.00
kg CO$_2$/tonne	0.02	0.04	0.12	2.08	1.54	1.49

Notes:
The data in this table cover several plants, producing ready-mixed concrete (Bow and Purley), concrete blocks (Croft) and precast concrete elements (Barnsley, Stockton and Histon). Products manufactured: Barnsley (Bespoke Precast): precast concrete stairs; Stockton (Rowecast): bespoke PCC stairs and landings, carpark units, Crosswalls; Histon: bespoke PCC stairs and landings, carpark units, Crosswalls.

Table A.4. Celsa Steel UK calculations for CO_2 emissions produced during the manufacturing of reinforced steel (annual)

(a) Production CO_2 emissions

	Units	Melt shop	Rolling mill	Total
Total energy consumption: coke, carbon, natural gas and electricity [1]	GJ	5,041,654	1,651,703	
Total CO_2 output [2]	tonnes	267,009	88,569	
Production volume	tonnes	941,690	640,712	
CO_2 per tonne of product	tonnes	0.284	0.138	0.422

(b) Transport CO_2 emissions: employee transport

	Units	Value
No. cars [3]	no.	600
Average journey	km	25
Annual journey distance [4]	km	3,405,000
Average CO_2 per km [5]	kg	0.17
Total CO_2 emissions, all employees	tonnes	578.85
Total CO_2 emissions, production employees [6]	tonnes	434.14
Total CO_2 emisions per tonne of rebar produced	kg	0.68

	Emissions (kg)
Production CO_2 at melt shop	283.54
Production CO_2 at rolling mill	138.23
Employee transport CO_2	0.68
Total per tonne of rebar produced	422.45

Notes:
1. Electricity use first calculated as primary, then factored by 2.6 (National Conversion Rate, Defra).
2. Conversion factors from Underlying Agreement (Defra):

	Unit	Electricity	Coke	Natural gas
Carbon	tonnes per GJ	12.6	32.8	16.0
CO_2	tonnes per GJ	46.2	120.3	58.7

3. 1,000 people, approx. 600 cars (some car sharing, some use public transport, some use motorcycles).
4. Assume each employee works a full year minus holidays: 227 days/year.
5. Assume 60% petrol, 40% diesel.
6. Assume 75% of employees work in the production facilities.

Table A.5. WISA production CO_2 audit

	kg CO_2/m^3
Carbon stored in the product	1070
GHG emissions from plywood production	15
GHG emissions associated with forest management and harvesting	10
GHG emissions associated with purchased electricity and steam	50
Raw material transport-related GHG emissions	1

Table A.6. Ribblesdale Works CO_2 audit

	kg CO_2/tonne cement
Direct CO_2 from calcination	569.17
Direct CO_2 from fossil fuel combustion	135.91
Direct CO_2 from waste combustion	44.88
Indirect CO_2 from electricity usage	79.55
Indirect CO_2 from employee travel	0.07
Indirect CO_2 from delivery of raw materials	0.51
Indirect CO_2 from delivery of fuels	1.97
Total direct kg CO_2/tonne cement: gross	749.97
Total direct kg CO_2/tonne cement: net	705.09
Total indirect kg CO_2/tonne cement	82.09
Total direct and indirect kg CO_2/tonne cement: gross	832.05
Total direct and indirect kg CO_2/tonne cement: net	787.17

Notes:
Data from 2007 using WBCSD cement sustainability initiative CO_2 protocol.

DEFRA CONVERSION TABLES

Table A.7. Defra energy conversion factors [1,2]

Fuel	Units	kg CO_2/unit
Grid electricity [3]	kWh	0.537
Renewable electricity	kWh	See footnotes [4] & [5]
Natural gas	kWh	0.185
	therms	5.421
LPG	kWh	0.214
	therms	6.277
	litres	1.495
Gas oil	tonnes	3,190
	kWh	0.252
	litres	2.674
Fuel oil	tonnes	3,223
	kWh	0.268
Burning oil [6]	tonnes	3,150
	kWh	0.245
Diesel	tonnes	3,164
	kWh	0.250
	litres	2.630
Petrol	tonnes	3,135
	kWh	0.240
	litres	2.315
Industrial coal	tonnes	2,457
	kWh	0.330
Wood pellets [7]	tonnes	132
	kWh	0.025

Notes:
1. http://www.defra.gov.uk/environment/business/reporting/conversion-factors.htm
2. The emissions factors shown are calculated on a gross calorific value (CV basis), as that is generally quoted by energy suppliers.
   For factors calculated on a net CV basis, visit the Defra website.[1]
3. This figure represents the average CO_2 emissions from the UK national grid per kWh of electricity delivered to site. The factor presented is the five year rolling average. It is suitable for calculating the emissions associated with a company's electricity use, and savings from a reduction in use.
4. For electricity purchased on a 'green tariff' the grid electricity factor above should generally be used. This factor incorporates UK renewable generation within it. For further information visit the Defra website.[1]
5. For electricity generated on-site using renewable energy, a factor of zero may be used, as long as Renewable Obligation Certificates (ROCs) and Levy Exemption Certificates (LECs) are not sold on to a third party.
6. Burning oil is otherwise known as kerosene or paraffin used for heating systems.
7. Wood pellets used in domestic biomass heating system. Biomass is a low carbon, sustainable renewable energy source, but cannot be classed as 'carbon free'. The carbon emissions associated with any agricultural and transport activities must be taken into account.

Table A.8. Conversion factors for energy units

From	to kWh
therms	29.31
Btu	2.931×10^{-4}
MJ	0.2778
toe	1.163×10^4
kcal	1.163×10^{-3}

Notes:
Btu = British thermal unit; MJ = megajoule; toe = tonnes of equivalent oil; kcal = kilocalorie

Example:
Conversion of 100,000 Btu to kWh:
100,000 Btu = 100,000 × 2.931×10^{-4} = 26.31 kWh

Converting CO_2 to carbon:
In certain circumstances you may wish to convert between kg C and kg CO_2.
- To convert from kg C to kg CO_2, multiply by 44/12
- To convert from kg CO_2 to kg C, multiply by 12/44

Example:
Conversion of 1,800 kg CO_2 into kg C:
1,800 kg CO_2 × (12/44) = 490.9 kg C

Common prefixes:
The following prefixes are used for multiples of joules, watts and watthours: kilo (k) = 10^3; mega (M) = 10^6; giga (G) = 10^9; tera (T) = 10^{12}; peta (P) = 10^{15}

Source:
Carbon Trust. (2008) *Energy and Carbon Conversions*, Fact sheet CTL018. 2008 Update, London, Carbon Trust.

Table A.9. Transport conversion factors

(a) Petrol and diesel cars

Size of car	Units	kg CO_2 per unit
Small, up to 1.4 litre petrol engine	km	0.1809
	miles	0.2912
Medium, 1.4–2.0 litre petrol engine	km	0.2139
	miles	0.3442
Large, over 2.0 litre petrol engine	km	0.2958
	miles	0.4760
Average petrol car	km	0.2070
	miles	0.3332
Small, up to 1.7 litre diesel engine	km	0.1513
	miles	0.2435
Medium, 1.7–2.0 litre diesel engine	km	0.1881
	miles	0.3027
Large, over 2.0 litre diesel engine	km	0.2580
	miles	0.4153
Average diesel car	km	0.1979
	miles	0.3185

Mode of transport	Units [1]	kg CO_2 per unit
Regular taxi	pkm	0.1593
Average bus and coach	pkm	0.0686
International rail (Eurostar)	pkm	0.0177
National rail	pkm	0.0602
Light rail and tram	pkm	0.0780
Underground	pkm	0.0650
Long haul international flight [2]	pkm	0.1206
Short haul international flight [2]	pkm	0.1071
Domestic flight [2]	pkm	0.1911

Notes:
1. pkm = passenger kilometers travelled
2. The air emission factors do not include non-CO_2 climate change impacts, such as Radiative Forcing. However, a 109% uplift factor has been built into the emission factors to take into account non-direct routes and delays/circling.

Source:
Carbon Trust. (2008) *Energy and Carbon Conversions*, Fact sheet CTL018. 2008 Update, London, Carbon Trust.

CASE STUDIES
IN SUSTAINABLE
CONCRETE
CONSTRUCTION

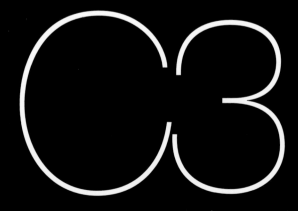

HOUSE IN HIGHGATE CEMETERY, LONDON

Piers Smerin, Eldridge Smerin

Architecture

Inspired by seeing Eldridge Smerin's Stirling Prize shortlisted house, The Lawns, on Highgate Hill in north London, the owner of a nearby house approached the practice about designing a new house to replace the one currently occupying the site. The existing house, dating from the 1970s, was designed by the noted architect John Winter and sat next to Highgate Cemetery, London's greatest Victorian cemetery. Although the site offered spectacular views over the cemetery, with Waterlow Park opposite and the city skyline beyond, replacing a John Winter house is a decision not to be taken lightly.

When we had investigated options for either retaining the corroding steel structure and/or reinstating it, it was clear that to restore the Winter house would have required complete reconstruction and would have compromised the greater potential benefit of a new house on such a unique site. The resulting new house is located on the footprint of the existing house. It is set out over four floors with a generous proportion of living to bedroom space, including balconies, terraces and a sizable sliding glass rooflight, enabling the top floor to become an open-air court. The new house is an additional storey higher than the previous one and is conceived with two strongly contrasting faces. To the street side, a sheer façade of honed black granite, translucent glass and black steel panels set flush against one another echoes the massiveness of the cemetery wall. This gives the house an air of mystery and intrigue, while at the same time making reference to the monumental masonry of the cemetery. In contrast, the elevations facing the cemetery are largely glazed, suffusing the interior with natural light and washing the fair-faced concrete structural frame and walls with sunlight. Unlike the lower part of the cemetery, where people often go to see Karl Marx's grave, the upper part where the house is located is overgrown and largely unvisited, allowing it to act as a stunning backdrop to the spaces within the house.

Building description

The full-height glazing to the elevation of the house
was enabled by the use of flat concrete slabs with long
cantilevers back to the four central columns supporting
each floor. The concrete supporting the internal and external
areas was kept separate to provide a thermal break between
inside and out. In contrast to the smooth fair-faced finish
of the concrete columns and soffits and the smooth stone
flooring, the concrete walls facing the street and adjoining
property to the north have a strong horizontal pattern derived
from the timber boards used for shuttering. The use of a
concrete frame with a high-quality exposed finish internally
also allowed a more sustainable environmental strategy
for the house to be developed than was permitted by the
lightweight construction of the original house.

The intention was to produce a house with significantly lower
energy usage than the original, despite an increased floor
area. The slow heat response characteristics of the concrete
allow the frame to act as an environmental modifier, slowing
down heat gain in summer and limiting heat loss in winter,
while the form of the house, with its large glazed openings
facing south, allows passive solar gain to be maximised
during winter months.

Below
The music room

Left
The kitchen, with
sliding rooflight
open

The use of stone cladding and a green sedum roof system similarly help to control temperature fluctuations. The use of concrete as a structure and finish, when sourced from a local plant that uses a proportion of recycled material, helps to minimise the embodied energy in the envelope of the house, as does the choice of generally natural materials for the internal finishes.

Internally, a low-temperature hot water underfloor heating system is used in conjunction with the thermal mass of the house to maintain comfortable conditions with minimised energy usage. The high natural light levels mean there is little need for artificial lighting during daylight hours, and all light fittings use low-energy lamps. The interior spaces are linked vertically by a series of large areas of clear glass floor panels, which filter daylight from the main sliding rooflight down to the entrance area that leads off the street. Full-height frameless pivoted doors, veneered in bog-aged oak, separate the living spaces and bedrooms from the main stair. The stair itself has precast concrete treads, cantilevered from the concrete walls on each side, with a clear glass fin to the centre supporting a stainless steel handrail, which is resin bonded to the glass. The fin is formed from two 4-m high sheets of toughened laminated glass, which were craned into position through a slot created in the roof slab.

Bathrooms on each floor are lined with white Corian and have white marble floors. Eldridge Smerin were also responsible for designing bespoke joinery and furniture throughout the house. Built-in storage is generally in timber behind white lacquered doors, but the music room on the first floor has a wall of storage units in high-gloss black lacquer and side tables in bog-aged oak.

The second floor study features a continuous work surface formed from and supported by clear frameless toughed glass sheets bonded together.

Prior to work starting on site, John Winter was philosophical about the demolition of the house he had designed, saying that there would be no hard feelings 'so long as the new house was better'. Reviewing the completed house for *Architecture Today* magazine, John Winter was generous enough to say he felt the new house was both better and 'as near to a faultless building as I have seen for a long time'.

Sustainability issues

While there is much interest in sustainability issues within the construction industry generally, there are as yet no clear accepted definitions of what makes a building sustainable. However, since 30 per cent of all UK-delivered energy is currently used to provide domestic heating, this far outweighs other energy uses and makes producing a house with low energy consumption the key environmental issue. The intention was to design a house with a significantly lower energy usage than the existing house, despite an increased floor area.

This was achieved in a number of ways. The form of the house, with a series of large glazed openings facing south, coupled with the use of a heavyweight concrete structure, allows passive solar gain to be maximised during winter months. The high thermal mass of the reinforced concrete structure acts as a temperature stabiliser, moderating temperature fluctuations; this is helped by the extent to which the house is set into the ground. The use of a heavy, stone-covered roof system similarly helps to control temperature fluctuations. The possibility of incorporating photovoltaic cells and of collecting and recycling wastewater was also considered. The use of concrete as a structure and finish, when sourced locally and with a proportion of recycled material, helps to minimise the embodied energy in the envelope of the building.

Internally, the low-temperature hot water underfloor heating system and the high thermal mass of the building's envelope maintain comfortable conditions with minimised energy usage.

Other finishes specified within the building were carefully audited to ensure that, as far as possible, they have zero ozone depleting potential (ODP) and are environmentally passive in manufacture and use.

Music room, with suspended
fireplace

Right
Cantilevered balconies looking
across Highgate Cemetery

Below
Section through stairwell and
west elevation

Energy data

Gross floor area	357 m²

Predicted annual energy consumption	kg CO₂/m²/yr
Gas space and water heating 25.5 MWh	13.88
Electrical usage 580 kWh	6.99
Total	20.87*

* Does not include non-regulated energy usage (see notes on page 256)

Description of heating and cooling provision

Condensing boiler – efficiency 90.4 per cent

Underfloor heating

Heat recovery ventilation unit

Compensated heating flow temperature within the house

Draught lobby to reduce heat loss

Cross-ventilation on floors to prevent summer overheating

Project team

Quantity surveyor	AB Associates
Structural engineer	Elliott Wood Partnership
Services engineer	Mendick Waring
Main contractor and concrete work	Harris Calnan
Concrete consultant	David Bennett

Building data

Number of floors	4

Building dimensions	
overall footprint	12 × 12 m
overall building height	8.75 m (from street level)
Year completed	2008

ABITO APARTMENTS, GREENGATE, MANCHESTER

Ian Palmer, Building Design Partnership

Introduction

Imagine that you could buy a city apartment that was cheaper than a one-bedroom apartment, but much, much better; that was specifically designed to reflect modern lifestyles; that could be customised to adapt to your own needs and personality; that was precision engineered to give you more, for less. Not bigger, just smarter. That's Abito.

BDP was approached by developers Ask to help them to design a new compact apartment scheme, aimed at both first-time buyers and people wanting a city 'crash pad'. The objective was to deliver high-quality design on a budget, with a brief to innovate and 'test assumptions'.

The design team initially had no specific brief to work with and developed the product from the inside out, creating a generic microflat which minimised dead space. Internally, the flats are a marvel of innovative spatial design, with clever features including a central 'fold-away' command module, creating bathroom space out of a corridor. The generous volume more than compensates for the compact floor and is flooded with daylight from the full-height windows which frame the view of the city.

Building description

The Greengate site forms part of a wider masterplan and presented a number of constraints resulting from its triangular shape. Corner options were appraised, but these paralysed much of the site and this led to the development of the courtyard option, which we called the 'Greengate Ark'.

The nine-storey 256-apartment building, with commercial units at its base, fills the plot. Pushing the apartments to the edge of the site creates a private, semi-external courtyard at its centre, protected from the weather by a fabric canopy that animates the skyline. Within the landscaped courtyard, occupants gain access to their flats via a single lift and stair core that rises up to just below the canopy. The grand central space is overlooked by open galleries and bridges, providing an open circuit and space for tenants to meet their neighbours.

The courtyard is also home to the residents' post boxes, bike racks, recycling bins and 24-hour concierge service – indeed, everything required to make urban living more practical, convenient and sustainable.

Apartment design

In order to test and validate the quality of the space, a full-sized mock-up was assembled off-site. Each apartment is 'split' into two areas – one for living and one for sleeping. Each apartment is fitted with a special full-sized fold-away bed, which faces the central 'pod'. This has a wardrobe with space for a television, utility space for washer/dryer/ironing board/vacuum cleaner on one side and a wheelchair-accessible bathroom containing a large shower, toilet and basin on the other. The kitchen comes with a combined microwave and oven, hob, sink, dishwasher and fridge freezer. All services and waste flow out through the riser, which runs vertically through all the Abito units above and below. Everything in the apartment is recessed and hidden – until opened, revealed or switched on.

Abito apartments are innovative, quirky and less expensive than many other city centre apartments and are designed with passion and a great deal of care.

Construction details

By definition, the building is extremely repetitive and modular and this certainly transposes itself onto the elevation. Although the designers were keen to embrace the nature of the building, it would have been all too easy for the building to become rather relentless. BDP's answer was to create a glazed elevation, maximising the daylight into the apartment, onto which a grid has been imposed to secure the 'clip on balconies'. Each balcony incorporates side cheeks, offering a private external space, with the splayed form creating interest and a social aspect.

The fact that each apartment is assembled from factory-built prefabricated elements, the designers were able to control the quality of the elements. Because of the unique nature of the design of the Abito apartments, 'tunnel form' construction was adopted, allowing ease of replication.

A canopy has been employed to protect the courtyard from inclement weather and also helps to articulate the skyline; an important consideration given that the building will be overlooked by the surrounding buildings proposed in the masterplan. The canopy is elevated from the roof deck, allowing the courtyard to breathe.

During daylight hours the tensile canopy acts as a giant light diffuser, protecting the courtyard from direct sun and levelling out the light and dark areas. It is an important device to aid the penetration of light through eight storeys to the ground floor.

On dark days (and during the night) advantage is taken of the inherent diffusing nature of the canopy by floodlighting it from below or, alternatively, from the outside. This removes the need for expensive 'heroic' architectural luminaries as light is directed in a 'natural' and more intuitive way, like a cloud in the sky.

Sustainability issues

Abito has been built on a brownfield site, just four minutes' walk from Manchester's retail core, making it an obvious choice for first-time buyers and city-centre lovers alike. Car parking provision was not required by the local authority, encouraging people to make use of public transport, which includes the nearby Manchester Victoria railway interchange, tram stops and local bus station.

Greengate is the first low-cost apartment block to be completed for Ask and we hope it will become an easily replicable and cost-effective way of providing affordable housing in cities throughout the UK. This ambition makes full use of the benefits of off-site modular construction and site-cast tunnel form construction, reducing the overall building time and site wastage.

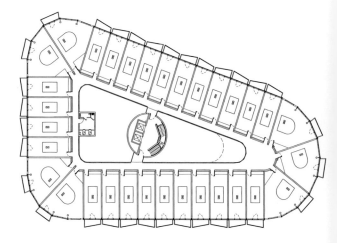

Tunnel formwork, or as it is sometimes called, 'apartment formwork', is a factory-made steel formwork system that enables walls and slabs to be cast monolithically on the same day, achieving a one-day construction cycle. It has been developed for rapid construction of room cells (i.e. walls and slabs) of varying sizes for housing projects, apartment blocks and hotels. Provided that the room layouts or apartments of a building project can be rationalised into one-way spanning slabs of not more than 7.5 m spans, with a storey height not greater than 3.5 m, then a tunnel form system can be made to work efficiently. Production rates of around two apartments a day are usual, equivalent to 450 m^2 of total wall and slab construction.

The key to developing this fast rhythm of production is to keep the immature concrete floor slab propped the following morning, while removing a half-tunnel section of formwork. Minimum concrete striking strength is assured by tenting and heating the air space within the tunnel forms overnight.

The benefits of such a system include the reduction of site labour and the elimination of skilled finishing trades. Since the system is reliant on cranage to position and reset forms, labour is required only to wheel out and set down forms,

using simple hand-tools for jacking and clamping of the assembly. The accuracy of the wall forms and the exact positioning on successive lifts, achieved by using specially cast kicker plates, affords a high standard of surface finish, eliminating the need for traditional plasterboard and plastering.

The smooth surface finish provided by the metal forms allows a thin white plaster coat to be spray-applied directly to the walls and ceilings, helping to reduce the need for artificial lighting. We liked not only the simplicity of this approach but also the fact that the use of concrete allowed us to accomplish complicated things in a very simple way. The concrete has a supporting role, it forms the walls, floor and ceiling, it removes the need for additional acoustic and fire protection and it helps to manage internal temperatures through its thermal mass.

One of the huge benefits of using a tunnel form system is the ability to reuse the shutters endlessly. This not only eliminates the problem of disposing of timber shuttering, but allows the forms to be used on the next Abito project. The concrete mix used recycled aggregates and 50 per cent GGBS cement replacement to halve the embodied CO_2 of the concrete.

Energy data

Commercial gross floor area	1,545 m^2
Residential treated floor area	9,263 m^2

Predicted annual residential energy consumption	*kg CO$_2$/m^2/yr*
Space heating 195 MWh	4.00
Water heating 431 MWh	9.00
Electrical usage 81 MWh	3.76*
Total	16.76

* Does not include non-regulated energy usage (see notes on page 256)

Description of energy-saving provisions

Each apartment is ventilated using the bathroom extractor, which is linked to a centralised fan at the top of each vertical stack of apartments. The extractor fan (like the bathroom lights) is activated when the doors are first opened and is linked to a moisture sensor. The WCs are fitted with a dual flush and taps with an aerated filter to help conserve water.

Along with the thermal store provided in the concrete, the thick wall insulation, high-performance glass and airtightness all help to minimise heat loss, enabling the apartment to be heated using only a small electric plinth heater. The clip-on balconies provide a degree of solar shading from the midday sun in summer

In these times, when consumption is carefully monitored, our resolve to design an apartment that was 'smarter not bigger' is sound and has helped to deliver a project that uses less, while creating more.

Project team

Structural engineer	Taylor Whalley Spa
Services engineer	Hulley & Kirkwood
Main contractor	Carillion
Concrete subcontractor	MPB

Building data

Number of floors	9
Building dimensions	length 60 m, width 38 m, height 36.5 m
Year completed	2007

Hannu Huttenen, Ark House

Architecture

The three residential apartment buildings of Arabianvillat are grouped on the plot so that the views from the apartments towards the surrounding environment and the town space are as wide and diverse as possible. With a cuboid shape, the buildings create a group of distinct bodies when viewed from the shore and the sea. The façades are characterised by continuous balconies, the free arrangement of window openings and the painted prefabricated concrete elements, enlivened by images of seagulls etched into on the concrete – the seagulls have already become the symbol of the group of buildings.

The core of each building is the sauna section – a lightweight pavilion-type structure that reaches above the roof level, providing a panoramic view of the landscape. On the courtyard side, the building cubes have been 'cut open' with a private entrance yard concealed behind the masonry wall and the gate. The hierarchical division of the outdoor space surrounding the buildings into sections with varying degrees of privacy gives the yard area a disciplined appearance. The masonry walls and the gates with their canopies form natural passages and create a human-sized scale for the courtyard milieu, lending the buildings a touch of detached-house atmosphere and a refined suburban feeling.

The starting point in the design of the apartments was to provide diversified views in several directions, both within the apartments and to the outdoor environment. In some of the apartments the number of rooms can be increased, and some apartments have a separate room with its own entrance. The apartments can also be combined through the front hall areas. The total number of apartments is 33 and the average apartment area is about 94 m^2.

The concrete frames of the buildings have been constructed using a mixture of techniques. The vertical load-bearing structures, the columns and the load-bearing walls, as well as the inner shells of the external walls, are prefabricated concrete elements, as are the side walls and the slabs of the balconies. The ground floor vault is a hollow-core slab structure and the landings in the stair halls are flat slabs.

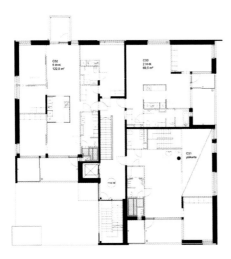

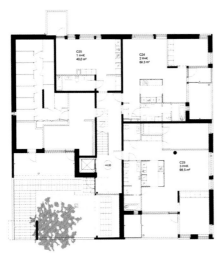

Construction details

Concrete façade

Arabianvillat is an example of high-quality concrete construction, with skilled architectural design and expert use of materials employed to produce a vivacious living environment. The internal precast panel has been combined with an external skin of precast concrete that utilises several other materials, such as brick, natural stone, glass and metal, in the surface matrix.

Continuous balconies, varying window openings, painted precast concrete units and the series of coloured graphic concrete bird figures fronting the shoreline give the façades a structured appearance. The birds are seagulls, which are used as the emblem of the building complex. Coloured concrete surfaces produced by different methods are placed in focal façade points to counteract the smooth light-coloured, thinly plastered surfaces.

The intensively coloured concrete surfaces of the façades, as well as the fences and the gates, are precast units. The coloured seagull units were created using a graphic concrete imprinting method. Concrete has also been used in the paving structures of the courtyard, as well as in various environmental products. The refined details and structures make the courtyard part of the building's complete façade system.

The 5 m wide by 15 m tall art walls were designed by artist Tiina Kuhanen and artist-architect Johanna Hyrkäs as 'courtyard tapestry walls', which join the interior and the outdoor spaces together. The figures on the art walls were painted on the precast concrete unit surface using varying degrees of gloss.

The complex is an example of a project where long-term, professional cooperation between different parties has produced a personalised end result of high quality.

The purpose of the newly established Betonikeskus ry [Finnish Concrete Centre] architectural award competition is to highlight successfully implemented precast concrete façade projects and their designers. The competition will be held biennially in the future.

Sandwich panel construction

The sandwich panels totalled around 1,800 pieces and each one was 10 m² in area. The surface was cast as normal grey concrete and painted on site by the main contractor. Casting beds were made of steel and each panel weighed, on average, 5 tonnes.

The exterior cladding panel was compacted on table moulds via an integrated shock-compacter. The interior load-bearing part of the sandwich structure was compacted with a poker vibrator. The product was kept inside the factory for up to two days after demoulding, to ensure sufficient strength levels. During that time, all fixing and minor repairs are carried out.

The size of the element panels varies, but is typically about 3.6 × 3 m. The thickness of the inner wall is 100 mm in those walls which are not load-bearing and 150 mm in the load-carrying walls. The insulation consists of 160 mm of mineral wool and the outer wall thickness varies between 70 and 100 mm. The surfaces of the external concrete elements have been etched and painted.

'Graphic concrete' is the term applied to a method of imprinting concrete patented in Finland, which uses a pattern-impregnated roll of fabric membrane carrying a dot matrix of surface retardants that etch the fresh concrete face, removing the surface skin of the cement paste to expose the aggregate. The depth of exposure will depend on the active ingredients in the retarder used. This is how the seagull motif was etched onto the surface of the precast panels.

Typical concrete mix details

Rapid hardening cement or white cement	350 kg/m³
Natural filler sand	150 kg/m³ (8%)
Aggregate sand 0–8 mm	950 kg (50%)
Aggregate gravel 8–16 mm	800 kg (42%)
w/c ratio	0.5
Superplasticiser	1.60% cement
Air-entraining agent	0.04% cement

Energy data

Heating energy consumption in apartment buildings	100 kWh/m²
Total energy consumption	135 kWh/m²

Description of heating and lighting provision
District heating via the national grid (coal, nuclear energy, hydroelectric energy – share of renewable energy unknown)

Mechanical heat recovery ventilation and cooling system in each dwelling

The windows are double and triple glazed, using low-energy (vacuum) glass in an aluminium–wood frame by Fenestra, U-value: 1.1 W/m²K

Project team

Client, project manager	VVO Rakennuttaja Oy/Housing Company Helsingin Arabianvillat
Structural engineer	Finnmap Engineering
Services engineer	Helsingin Kartech Oy
Main contractor	SVR Westerlund Oy
Precast concrete	Mikkelin Betoni Ltd, Parma Ltd

Building data

Group of three blocks of flats	33 apartments
Number of floors	4
Building plan dimensions	4,264 m²
Total dwellings area	3,460 m²
Year completed	2005

John Docherty, Elder and Cannon

Architecture

St Aloysius' Church and St Aloysius' College are part of the
Jesuit Order and have been established in the Garnethill area
of Glasgow for almost 150 years. The building is located
at the highest point of Garnethill, and sits on a corner site
commanding rollercoaster views across the Glasgow Grid.
This part of the city is a tableau of Glasgow in miniature
– the rigid Glasgow Grid, the long lines of sandstone
tenements, the impressive Victorian architecture of St
Aloysius, Edwardian townhouses, the brutalist extensions
to the School of Art, contemporary glass and concrete
extensions to the college campus and Glasgow's finest
building, Mackintosh's School of Art, all within a city block.
Unsurprisingly, this is a conservation area, but without a
dominant typology the test has been whether a building is of
sufficient quality to rub shoulders with its neighbours.

The Jesuit Residence is the third building completed
by Elder and Cannon within the campus of St Aloysius'
College, and brings together two independent facilities
with related roles to play in the St Aloysius and Garnethill
communities. On the ground floor, the Spirituality Centre
caters for the neighbouring college and local community,
providing religious education and counselling services. A
small conference facility, a prayer room and interview rooms
are also included. The residential part is a large house for up
to ten Jesuit priests and their guests. It occupies the upper
three floors and has a separate entrance from Hill Street.
This incorporates 12 bedrooms, a small chapel, visible to the
rear as a tall timber box, a reception and dining room around
an internal double volume, and an upper lounge leading to a
roof terrace.

The grid is the defining characteristic of the city, demanding
that certain conventions are followed: that blocks are empty
or complete, corners are clearly defined and important, and
massing is appropriate. Understanding this, the building
completes the block and, viewed in the round, resolves
its dual identity by presenting itself both as a residential
companion to the tenements in high-quality brick and as
a building of civic status, by book-ending the tenements
with an important gable in precast concrete. The building
also completes the intended gateway to Hill Street with the
college's Clavius Building opposite.

The concrete-framed building comprises four storeys, stepping back on the upper floor to reveal a generous sun terrace, the important issue of massing overcome by framing the Hill Street façade with a crisp concrete surround and colonnade to retain the street profile. The choice of precast concrete cladding as the predominant material freed us to consider the building as a sculptural object while achieving both urban and programmatic responses.

Our understanding of the client and their private but civic role in the context of other local institutions prompted a substantive materiality. While we considered a completely concrete building, such as we architects admire, we felt it would not be entirely appropriate for the priests' house. The building façade was softened and clad in a mix of glazing, brick and precast concrete components instead.

The carefully detailed gable reinterprets the high-quality stonework of its neighbours and reinforces the hard edge of the grid. On Hill Street, the rhythm and vertical emphasis of the tenements are respected but not aped by the bedroom windows, their proportions within the more domestic white masonry panels representative of their residential nature. Larger glazed screens are introduced to utility spaces, dining room and circulation areas and the major internal spaces are withdrawn from public view, creating a peaceful and private retreat for the priests. The colonnade above provides some privacy and represents a little classical composure, appropriate to the priests' house. Past the concrete gable, an entry court welcomes visitors, the timber-clad chapel tower marking the entrance to the Spirituality Centre.

Internally, the plan of the building intends to create an interesting sequence of spaces, which manage the priests' dual needs for privacy and welcome. By bringing light into the building in different ways, opening corridors to views and using fire engineering strategies, we have attempted to overcome the institutionalising strictures that are placed on residential buildings. The Spirituality Centre has a simpler organisation, gathering its main facilities around the entry lobby, but uses different scales of space and room height to create an appropriate atmosphere.

Given that the building sits 150 yards from the world-famous Glasgow School of Art, the character of the external envelope was critically important. Put simply, the School of Art is an exceptional example of exploiting the possibilities of a traditional material – stone – to create an appropriate representation of its function.

Glasgow is a city built in stone, a material that imbues the city with prestige, quality and identity. Here, in a succession of increasingly concrete-clad buildings, we have attempted to instil these same qualities within the parameters of the costs and labour skills available. Through an ongoing exploration of its potential with the same supplier, we have found that precast concrete panelling has properties that can match stone and be exploited in unique ways that display its virtues. Its ability to be cast in infinite variations, from small pieces to 5-m tall panels, enabled us to use the material to give scale and complexity to the elevation, creating both monolithic façades and slender framing surrounds, to bring a unifying control. Although it is only one of several materials used in a complementary palette, it is the concrete panelling which produces the hierarchy and identity of the building.

We focused on three attributes of concrete as cladding:

— as a containing material, where a modest amount can bring control to an elevation

— as a cladding material with the weight, quality and importance of stone in a modern aesthetic, and

— as a convincing means of achieving compatibility between different materials.

The uniformly smooth surface gives a pleasurable, high-quality finish to the touch and, through its consistency of colouring and fine tolerances, allowed us to feature the material on a larger scale. The size, precision, articulation and, in places, gravity-defying nature of the larger panels would have been difficult to achieve with more traditional materials, while the Skye sand–concrete mix has a surface complexity that gives the concrete its own special, sparkling quality.

In this particular context, the alternative choice of brick lacked identity, and natural stone was both too expensive and had its own limitations. While relatively economic, we felt there was an expressive modernity to the use of clean white concrete that gave the building an appropriate civic quality. Concrete also has an easy compatibility with other materials, giving the building a natural feel and allowing the harmonious use of different textures, such as brick and timber.

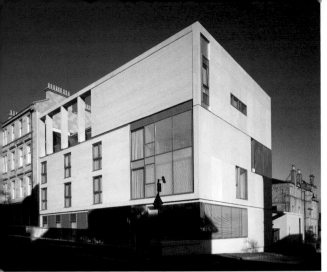

Left
The upper floors contain the
Residence

Bottom left
Fine joints and tolerances give the
concrete a monolithic appearance

The focus on precast concrete developed a unique but appropriate response to both functional and contextual aspirations. The building has solidity and presence and a kinship of material with the adjacent buildings which allow it to sit comfortably in the street and among its illustrious neighbours.

Material

The wet-cast concrete mix specified uses a limestone-based white Skye sand, which benefits from very consistent colouring but required scrupulous monitoring of the mix through precise measuring of materials in response to climatic conditions. The higher water to cement ratio required by the mix was susceptible to cold or damp weather, so care had to be taken to pour and cure the panels in the same conditions where possible, or to make very fine and controlled adjustments to maintain workability without compromising the end result. Although we were looking for uniformity in the panels, they have a life about them that benefits from natural variation.

Each intricate mould was custom-made by the fabricators' highly skilled joiners, reusing veneered and varnished plywood panels coated with releasing agents. While the units were sized to minimise the number of moulds required, on account of the many different fixings and profiles required to complete the envelope, 28 different moulds were used. Prior to delivery, the panelling was given an acid etch finish to remove laitance and was closely inspected for colour differentiation and flaws.

Working with the manufacturer, a great deal of thought was given to finding the right balance of size and weight to achieve the desired visual effect in the most cost-effective way. The final resolution reduced the panels to span single floor heights, below the maximum width of 2.5 m suitable for standard flat beds. Fixings were cast into the panels and companion fixings mounted on the building's concrete frame, which allowed three-dimensional adjustments to ensure a flush finish to very small tolerances. The precision of the completed panels and controlled installation quickly produced a defect-free façade, the gable panels taking just one week to install.

Right
The top floor terrace
colonnade

Below
Section through the
Residence building

Sustainability issues

As the building structure is a reinforced concrete frame, with large concrete cores to each stairwell and exposed structure and soffits in the larger spaces, the thermal mass this provides assists in the heating and cooling profile of the naturally ventilated building. In conjunction with the external envelope, which was insulated to exceed the Building Regulation requirements, the building was modelled to minimise the overall energy demand for the client.

Since it is an external application, the mass of the external concrete panelling does not contribute to thermal mass in the same manner, but it does make a particularly important contribution to the sustainability of the project by being an efficient and sustainable cladding material in its manufacture, construction requirements and lifespan.

The lead in of three or four months to design the panels and manufacture them off-site, coupled with the advantages of

quick construction and low impact on other activities on site, brought time and energy efficiencies to the contractor and reduced the environmental impact of the build.

The low environmental impact of the panel manufacture was also an important benefit. The timber moulds for the panels were reused time and again and, through sophisticated use of the formwork and inserts, there was minimal wastage between casts, despite the requirements for resizing. All timber used in the moulds was confirmed as FSC-sourced.

Over its lifespan, the use of concrete in the building should provide long-term benefits in terms of CO_2 reduction. The environmental impact of the precast panelling has also been considered and, by minimising waste, using a local supplier with good supply chain management, employing efficient methods to install and seal the panels, and given its durability, we believe there is a positive environmental rationale for its use.

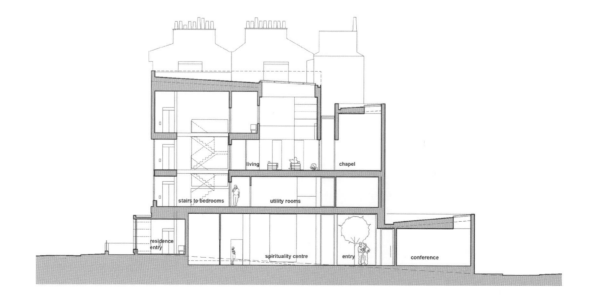

Energy data

Gross floor area	1,341 m²

Predicted annual energy consumption	kg CO₂/m²/yr
Space and water heating 440 MWh	62.3
Electrical usage 65 MWh	20.8
Total	83.1

Predicted annual energy consumption — *kg CO_2/m²/yr*

Description of heating and lighting provision

Shared plant room for both facilities despite independent management, for efficiency and to avoid duplication and individual metering

Hot-water-fed heating system, fed by highly efficient condensing gas boilers

Underfloor heating to main social spaces, radiators to bedrooms

Careful modelling of spaces to avoid oversizing of heating system

Passive ventilation to upper floors

Air conditioning to conference areas through highly efficient units

Solar shading to highly glazed top floor lounge through large canopy, elsewhere by solar control glazing to smaller bedroom and kitchen windows

Highly insulated fabric to achieve 20 per cent improvements on Building Regulations

Detailing to achieve airtight envelope

Project team

Structural engineers	Arup Scotland
Service engineers	Hawthorne Boyle
Quantity surveyors	Ross and Morton
Main contractor	Chard Construction
Precast contractor	Plean Precast

Building data

Number of floors	4
Building dimensions:	
ground floor	24 × 28 m
upper floors	24 × 14 m
Year completed	December 2006

Cathy Hawley, Riches Hawley Mikhail Architects

Overview

The project is based on a gentle 'minimalist' ecology, in keeping with its rural setting. The use of free energy was an important idea – all houses face south, maximising solar gain, and are highly insulated. A terrace consisting of three houses forms the basic building block of the scheme. The front façades are clad in continuous cedar weatherboards and shingles, gables in traditional lime render. Variety is brought to the elevations through the different positioning and sizes of windows, arranged to establish the optimal relationship between solar gain and daylight, as well as making the most of long views out. The low profile and varying scales of the buildings are designed to minimise overshadowing, enabling the low winter sun (typical of the area's flat landscape) to reach all properties.

The accommodation is arranged in groups of six houses, carefully positioned in distinctive groups around three low-maintenance communal gardens, including a wildflower meadow, allotments and a playground set in an orchard. A landscape of swales and dips drain the site, recalling ancient field patterns and promoting diversity of habitat. Residents have been consulted at every stage. The local primary school has been involved in the project from the beginning, with site visits and talks encouraging a real sense of ownership of both the homes and the spaces where the children will play.

The brief was to focus on two key aspects – modern architecture and sustainability. Moreover, the low-carbon homes were to be built without any 'greenwash' or highly visible environmental interventions. It had to be a design that would fit in with the local Suffolk barns as well as the surrounding bungalows. Further enhancing landscape features to soften the visual impact included sculptured gardens with a Japanese-inspired shingle coping that curves around the garden walls.

The Clay Fields housing mix includes 13 two-bedroom houses, 9 three-bedroom houses and 4 one-bedroom flats. These were based on the sizes of the families awaiting accommodation in the area, lending the project a genuine purpose, built for the local community.

The houses were laid out with one-half of the site resembling a regular chess board pattern. Homes were positioned in triple group clusters, as a compromise between a conventional terrace and a semi-detached pair. Each one overlooking an allotment plot or an area of field and, by offsetting each house, it was possible to avoid direct views between them.

However, it is not only the layout and design that makes Clay Fields stand out. The project can boast significant achievements in reducing the construction carbon footprint. Compared with the average 'house builder' development, it has managed a 60 per cent reduction in carbon emissions, both during the build process and over its lifetime use. The oversized glazing – covering approximately 40 per cent of the façade – achieves its full potential, with all houses facing due south, allowing each one to take in uninterrupted winter sun. For residents' comfort, the carefully positioned doors can be opened to adjust the temperature according to individual preference.

Also included in the community are four practical storage sheds. Rendered in clay brick, they also incorporate green roofs. With this subtle environmental technology on top, the storage areas blend in with the scheme.

Construction details

Instantly visible from the outside are the timber façades of each home. With their continuous cedar weatherboards, they are highly distinctive. For variety, differently sized windows are etched out of the cladding in a number of positions on each house, on both the façade and the roof.

The arrangement of the windows is by no means random. They are all positioned to make full use of daylight, with the exact locations specified by the services engineer. The focus was on the optimal relationship between daylight and solar gain, lessening the need for heating. Importantly, the windows do not face each other. Instead of looking out onto views of the other houses, each window is directed towards a picturesque landscape or open space.

Internally, the layout of space has been carefully planned. Living spaces have been organised over a staggered vertical section, meeting open-plan standards. The result of this was to enable whole-house ventilation through natural

Left
Folding sliding doors open from south-facing kitchen to the garden

Bottom left
Front doors are recessed from public paths

'Right
South-facing elevations, viewed over curved garden walls

Sustainability issues

While it was vital to keep environmental credentials high on the agenda, they had to be low key. The housing scheme combines a wide range of innovative methods aimed at keeping energy bills low and cutting out carbon.

Aiming for an EcoHomes Excellent rating and low in-use emissions, the project features a number of systems which yield low carbon emissions. A woodchip-fired biomass community heating network (fuelled by locally sourced woodchips) is installed to service the heating and instantaneous hot-water demands of each dwelling. Energy efficiency is primarily achieved through the use of whole-house ventilation with heat recovery, improved airtightness and highly insulated walls. These measures, together help the development to reduce carbon emissions by around 60 per cent compared with a standard Building Regulations compliant building.

The houses are constructed of timber frame, onto which Hemcrete (a mixture of lime and hemp) is sprayed. Hemcrete's high embodied CO_2 means that Clay Fields has managed to lock up a 65 tonnes of CO_2. Using traditional brick-and-block cavity wall methods, the site would have created approximately 100 kg of CO_2 for each square metre of wall. This construction ensures that the houses have very low embodied energy allied to high levels of insulation and airtightness. Garden walls are of unfired clay block.

Internally, the layout is carefully designed to maximise space, light and through-ventilation, making beautiful homes. Floors are staggered, with an open stairwell running from the kitchen to the rooflights allowing natural ventilation in summer. In winter, an additional mechanical system removes 80 per cent of heat from outgoing air and uses it to heat incoming air.

Other innovations include a system to recycle rainwater to flush toilets and water gardens. Clay Fields has been awarded an EcoHomes Excellent rating. The project is subject to post-occupancy evaluation by the Sustainability and Alternative Technologies Team at Buro Happold. Results to date indicate that the performance of the project is living up to expectations; for instance, CO_2 emissions to date equal 11.3 kg/m^2.

convection. This eliminated the need to hold open doors onto a closed stairwell.

In order to blend in with the neighbouring homes, the houses' large, deep shingle roofs were constructed at a level that matches the local bungalows' eaves. For a natural aesthetic, cedar cladding was also installed to some elevations, complementing the shingle roofing.

One of the major carbon-reducing aspects of the project was the use of Hemcrete insulating concrete, which was mixed on site and spray-applied to a timber frame. The walls were then finished with hydraulic lime renders to provide an aesthetically pleasing, low-maintenance and weathertight finish on top of the Hemcrete.

Energy data

Total floor area (all 26 properties)	1,830 m²

Predicted annual energy consumption	*kg CO$_2$/m²/yr*
Total space and water heating 170.45 MWh	17.70
Regulated electrical usage 25.95 MWh	6.10
Unregulated electrical usage 49.58 MWh	11.65
Renewables generation: biomass boiler output (district heating) 143.73 MWh	−14.92
Total	20.53

Description of heating and lighting provision
Biomass wood pellet boiler for all housed in the communal system

MVHR systems installed on each house

Passive techniques:
All houses face south and benefit from passive solar gain, even on the shortest day of the year. The position and size of glazing are carefully designed to maximise this effect. A rooflight allows for cooling using the stack effect

The massing of the houses on the site and their section have been designed to minimise overshadowing between properties

Whole-house ventilation system allied to airtight construction (3–4 m³/h/m² at 50 Pa)

Project team

Client	Orwell Housing Association
Structural engineer	BTA Structural Design Ltd
Services engineer	Buro Happold
Landscape architect	J & L Gibbons LLP
Civil engineer	Cameron Wilson Scott Taylor
Main contractor	O'Seaman and Son Ltd
Concrete insulation	Hemcrete – Quickseal

Building data

Total number of dwellings:	4 one-bedroom apartments
	13 two-bedroom houses
	9 three-bedroom houses
Year completed	2008

'NEW FOREST HOUSE', LYMINGTON

Wendy Perring, Perring Architecture & Design

Architecture

The site for our first major commission is located in the beautiful New Forest National Park and within a designated SSSI. The brief from our clients was to create with them a very contemporary sustainable home. This home should also sit comfortably within the landscape, which comprises 18 acres of stunning ancient woodland with far-reaching views towards the Isle of Wight.

From the outset of this project the clients were intimately involved. They wished to minimise the impact that the house would have on the site, both during construction and over its lifetime. Materials were selected that would be in harmony with the site and whose maintenance requirements would be minimal. While their accommodation brief was simple, they requested that a natural swimming pond be incorporated into the design. This would include a swimming area and separate regeneration area for aquatic plants that would filter the water, avoiding any need to introduce chemicals.

The initial concept for the building was formed quickly. Our aim was to recreate the sense of suspense experienced upon entering the site as the landscape gradually unfolded. Upon arrival one encounters magnificent ancient beech trees, with fallen trunks lying scattered among heather. The original wooden cottage dwelling on the site was hidden from view behind many trees and had to be sought out. Once the house had been discovered, the distant view was revealed as the landscape to the south of the house changed from woodland to open heath – dropping dramatically into a valley before rising up again to a distant pine forest. We decided to insert a long spine wall element on the plan, with a narrow entrance slot cut into it, both to focus views and to contain excavated earth. Instead of looking towards the distance, one's attention is immediately focused upon the beech trees.

The massing, form and orientation of the new buildings were carefully conceived in order that the proposals should have minimal impact on the site and its surroundings. The form of the main house and guest annexe were designed as very simple timber-clad boxes that echo each other and are linked by the spine wall. Both are low-rise volumes with green roofs planted with sedum native to the UK. This was supported by Natural England, who were consulted during the early stages of the design process because of the nature of the SSSI designation. They helped the client to develop a long-term maintenance strategy for the the site and woodland. Both bat and reptile surveys were required before the planning application was submitted. Before construction commenced, reptile fencing was erected around the working area and reptiles were relocated by a specialist. Slates were removed from the existing dwelling by hand and alternative roosting boxes provided for bats.

The buildings were orientated to maximise solar gain, open to the south and closed to the north. They utilise ground source heat pump technology, solar thermal panels and log burners for heating and hot water requirements. Provision for the future addition of photovoltaics was included at strategic points. The earth that was excavated to form the basement below the main dwelling and the natural swimming pond area was reused in an earth berm to the north of the spine wall, limiting the need to remove material from site. This helps to insulate the building, provides a visual screen to the north and acts as an acoustic baffle to nearby traffic noise.

The decision to use concrete was reached in response to a combination of environmental, structural and aesthetic requirements. We wished to create a building with a high thermal mass to give a stable thermal environment, not subject to excessive swings in temperature. The floor area of the building was restricted by planning legislation so, to maximise the sense of space, we created small rooms for sleeping with one generous open-plan living space with a glazed corner that completely opens up to dissolve the barriers between inside and out. The main element of the spine rises to 6 metres at one point, where the stair descends to the basement. Simultaneously, it acts as the retaining wall for the earth berm. Initially, we had hoped to use the excavated sand from the site to form the spine wall, aiming to create a structure that was derived from the

site itself, and the University of Bath made up a sample of stabilised rammed earth using the site material. However, the compressive strength of the material was not adequate to act as a retaining wall, necessitating a secondary concrete retaining wall behind the rammed earth, which would have been very expensive. At this point we made the collective decision to use concrete throughout. The use of concrete has allowed the different demands of the project to be addressed while also allowing us to explore its materiality.

New Forest Douglas fir was sourced from within 2 miles of the site and used to form the shuttering panels for the board-marked spine wall. We visited local sawmills to obtain samples (the colour, texture and quality varied between mills) and looked at the different textures that could be achieved using different cutting blades. This groundwork was essential in order to achieve the required relief on the finished concrete. To minimise wastage, the formwork was reused throughout. Larger areas were poured first and the formwork was gradually cut down in size to form smaller panels and return walls. After the spine wall was complete, the formwork was cleaned up and used to clad the interior of the workshop.

It was of great importance to us and to the clients that the colour of the concrete was correct and not contrasting starkly with the natural surroundings. With our clients we visited as many buildings as possible to examine the colour and texture possibilities of concrete. This was a vital learning process for us and for our clients as we gained knowledge of concrete along the way and became more convinced that it was the right material to use. David Bennett produced the finish specification for the exposed concrete. In order to avoid colour variations throughout, he asked the concrete supplier to develop a mix that would give consistency.

Construction

The main contract for the project was negotiated with one contractor, selected on the basis of his track record and his commitment to create something special on the site. The groundwork and concrete subcontractor engaged closely with the whole process, ensuring that the highest quality was achieved. Very early in the construction process a sample panel of the board-marked concrete was poured, which

enabled us to review tie bolt positions and concrete colour
and to decide on how to treat the Douglas fir boards to
achieve the best timber relief on the finished concrete. Half
of the Douglas fir boards in the sample panel were treated
with acrylic, and half with water (a process referred to as
'wetting up'). Although very similar in appearance, the acrylic
treatment picked up more of the colour from the shuttering
and had slightly more timber relief.

Although initially involving more work for the contractor, our
choice of acrylic treatment ultimately resulted in less work
between pours and fewer unknowns, as the shuttering
behaved more consistently and was subject to less swell and
shrinkage. We also decided to mastic the back face of the
Douglas fir between every joint to inhibit grout loss.

A small bone of contention arose with the selection of the
formwork. On David Bennett's recommendation, we had
specified Peri Vario formwork, which would better withstand
the increased pressures incurred in the fast pour needed
for a good finish while minimising grout loss. Critically, it
would also allow greater flexibility with regard to tie bolt
positions. To control the tie-bolt positions, we produced
drawings of all the board-marked walls detailing our intent

for both board thickness and tie bolt positions (especially
important on the double-height wall, which is visible against
the stair and would require two pours). We were unable to
persuade the contractor to use the specified formwork with
temporary works drawings that showed the corresponding
tie-bolt positions. The contractor insisted on using Peri Trio
formwork throughout, which was not an issue in areas where
the concrete was not exposed. However, the results across
the double-height stair wall were slightly disappointing as
some grout loss occurred between the pours. This was
attributed to the use of the Trio formwork, which did not lend
itself to such high pours and concrete pressure.

Overall, the contractor achieved good results and the quality
of the concrete improved with each successive pour. Light
falls down the concrete spine wall from the expansive
rooflight above the stairs, highlighting the timber markings,
and views of overhanging branches remind you that nature is
never far away.

Aside from its super insulation, renewable technologies and
responsibly sourced materials, we believe that this house has
the potential to be truly sustainable because it will be cared
for and enjoyed for many decades to come.

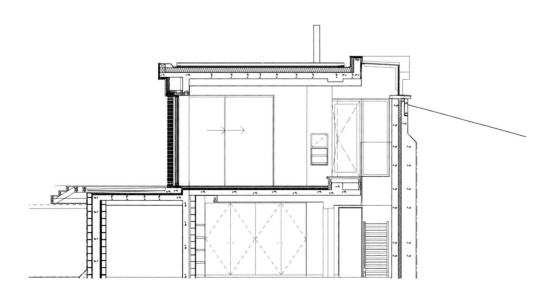

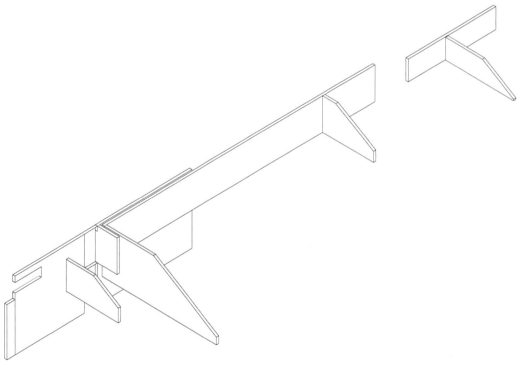

Sustainability issues

The design of the 'New Forest House' reduces energy demands by the incorporation of passive measures. The form and configuration of the main house have been considered to minimise active heating requirements.

The house is built into the ground and consists of a basement and ground floor level. The north side of the ground floor is set into an earth berm. This configuration increases the thermal mass around the envelope of the building and also provides wind protection and additional thermal insulation.

Increased thermal mass has an influence over temperature changes in the internal spaces, which will tend to cool down more slowly during cold periods and warm up at a slower rate during hot periods. The thermal mass acts to reduce peak heating and cooling loads, thereby reducing energy consumption.

The orientation of the building is another key factor. The main openings on the ground floor face south to maximise passive solar gains in colder periods. External shutters will provide a method of controlling excessive gains, predominantly in the summer months. A good standard of thermal insulation has also been provided in the fabric of the building to reduce heat losses.

Having minimised the energy demands by these passive measures, the remaining energy requirements are met by utilising renewable energy sources and low-carbon technologies where practical. The 'New Forest House' utilises renewable energy from the sun and biomass. The thermal mass of the ground is also used to improve the efficiency of active heating via a ground source heat pump system.

An array of ground loop pipes transfers energy collected in the ground (from the sun and rainwater) to a heat-pump unit. This increases the temperature of the water and supplies it to an underfloor heating system. During the summer the system can be used to provide free cooling by transferring the 'coolth' from the ground to the underfloor pipework system in the building.

The direct energy of the sun is collected in a solar thermal panel located on top of the main house. This combines with the ground source heat pump system to generate hot water for domestic use.

Energy demands are also met by using the wood fuel resource on the site. Some wood can be harvested as thinnings, as part of the sustainable management of the woodland. Once seasoned, this wood fuel can be used to provide heating and hot water. Firewood can also be bought from local suppliers. Wood fuel fires are located in both the main house and the annexe. The stove in the annexe has a back boiler, which transfers heat to a thermal store. The energy collected in the thermal store is used to heat domestic hot water instantaneously as required in the annexe.

There is an outdoor Japanese-style bath located next to the annexe. A woodburner is set adjacent to the bath, capable of heating the bath by thermosyphon via two water pipe connections. The woodburner can heat the bath from cold (if required) and then maintain the water temperature. In the summer, energy collected in the solar thermal panel can also be used to heat the Japanese bath. The bath is well-insulated and is supplied with a cover to reduce heat loss.

The site also reduces its reliance on the mains water system by utilising local groundwater collected via a well. This water is treated so that it is to a potable standard and is supplied to outlets around the site.

We have made an estimate of the CO_2 emissions due to energy consumption in the main house and annexe (based on the SAP calculations). The estimated figure is 5.7 tonnes of CO_2 per annum, derived from the amount of non-renewable energy consumed within the house in one year and would correspond to approximately 13 MWh per annum.

We stress this is just an estimate based on the SAP calculation (which is meant as a comparative tool and not an absolute calculation of energy consumption). Also, the amount of non-renewable energy used will be affected by occupation, use of wood fuel and availability of solar radiation.

Using benchmark figures for average British housing stock, a typical UK house of the same size would be expected to have CO_2 emissions due to energy consumption of 15.6 tonnes of CO_2 per annum (or almost three times as much).

Far left
Front entrance
by night

Left
Rooflight over
the staircase

Below
Architect's
planning image

Right
Fin wall to the
pond

Energy data

Gross floor area	273 m²

Predicted annual energy consumption	kg CO_2/m²/yr
(all mains electricity)	
Space heating 7 MWh	11.08
Water heating 2.6 MWh	4.07
Fan and pumps 1.3 MWh	2.08
Lighting 1.5 MWh	2.38
Renewables generation:	
photovoltaics 8.07 MWh	−12.72
Total	6.89*

* Does not include non-regulated energy usage (see notes on page 256)

Description of heating and lighting provision

Passive: solar thermal panels by Viessman

Active: biomass stove by Barbas and UFH by Warmafloor with comfort cooling

Ventilation: MVHR by Nuaire

Solar shading: timber sliding shutters to main south elevation designed by architects

Airtight construction: robust detailing and best practice used throughout

Project team

Client	private
Main contractor	HA and DB Kitchen
Structural engineer	Andrew Waring Associates
Services engineer	EDP Ltd
Landscape architect	PAD Architects
Concrete consultant	David Bennett

Building data

Number of floors	2 – ground and basement
Building dimensions:	
main house	length 16 m, width 10 m, height 4.5 m
annexe	length 6 m, width 8.7 m, height 4.5 m
Year completed	2009

Andrew Clancy, *Clancy Moore Architects*

Overview

The project comprises the reordering and extension of a
19th-century country house in the extreme south-west of
Ireland, a place characterised by intense contrasts, where
the full force of the Atlantic gales hit the island of Ireland,
carrying with them the tempering qualities of the north
Atlantic drift. It is a landscape of bare islands, mountaintops,
verdant forested valleys and rich agricultural lands.

Sitting on the edge of a lake addressing the surrounding hills,
the site enjoys a local microclimate, the potential of which
the original landowner, a prosperous German businessman
with an avid interest in botany, exploited. The house stands
on a manmade hill at the centre of an elaborately planted,
deceptively ordered, romantic landscape incorporating both
native species and many rare plants.

During the mid-20th century, the house was converted
to a hotel, entailing the demolition of a large ironwork
greenhouse, replaced by unconsidered guest
accommodation and service buildings which formed a
ragged entry courtyard to the existing house. The robust
dignity of the house was compromised further through
a number of crude extensions and internal interventions
during its lifetime as a hotel. The gardens, however, matured
under the careful attention of three generations of the same
family of gardeners in residence on site. The current owner
purchased the property on the close of the hotel in 2005; the
gardener remains.

The original house is what can be termed an Irish house of
the middle size. A common typology in 19th-century Ireland,
the classical house of the middle size is characterised by
a highly ordered plan containing a variety of rooms within
a square or rectangular form. On commencement of the
design we immediately reinstated this order, returning the
dwelling to its pure original form, somewhat abstract within
the broader landscape. The challenge then became to
accommodate the client's requirements by extending such a
singular, complete and direct structure.

Right
The dining area

Far right
Stairs to the
roof

Bottom right
Sections
through the
extension and
existing building

A strategy of elaborating the threshold between the reception rooms of the house and the garden was adopted by wrapping the house in a notional forest of columns, creating deep verandas to the south and west of the main living spaces. The grid of structural columns derived its proportions directly from the house. Clearings were made in this concrete forest where rooms were required, with a meandering weathering line creating a series of indoor and outdoor garden rooms for eating and entertaining. The columns became analogous with the mature oak and pine trees in the garden beyond, while the floor and ceiling were considered as landscapes in their own right, with the black floor forming hearth stone, kitchen island and basement cellar and the concrete roof inflected to hold rooflights, a chimney and a landscape on the roof above.

This language would be refined by the architects in the design and construction of an enclosed lap pool adjacent to the extension. Built hard against the edge of the hill on which the house stands, the vertical space of the pool acts as an inhabited retaining wall, enclosing a new private courtyard to the west and additional verandah spaces to the east and south.

Construction details

The expression of the concrete-framed extension, with its perceived honesty and simplicity, relied on preserving the legibility and integrity of the structure. This proved a challenge for the architects with regard to thermal transmittance through the concrete. Ultimately, a solution was developed that positioned the cast in-situ concrete structural frame as an outer leaf, achieving the desired visual depth, and on-site precast concrete panels providing the inner structure, with the joint between insulated and masked visually by the triple-glazed window system. The idea of an inter-reliant double structure was further elaborated during the design of the swimming pool, with each structural column being split into two more slender and elegantly proportioned concrete columns – a strategy similar to Aalto's bound columns at the Villa Mareia. The 5-m tall columns of the swimming pool were be precast on site to facilitate a single pour and ease of vibration. All concrete roof and floor slabs were similarly thermally broken from the outer beam

along all thresholds and supported on the inner columns. The build-up to the terrazzo-covered floor and roof provided a further weather check and thermal mass for underfloor heating.

The formwork to the extension was fabricated using plywood coated with phenolic-impregnated resin on both faces. This provided a pristine fair-faced finish on striking, the concrete carbonating quickly from a dark to a lighter shade of grey. Internally all infill panels to the frame were completed in timber, with all carcassing to concealed storage constructed in solid timber for reasons of durability. The marbling on the surface of the concrete, a chance 'mistake' considered beautiful by both client and architect, inspired the choice of a silver bird's-eye maple veneer finish to all infill panels, the pattern and colour of which complemented the marbled concrete, avoiding undue visual contrast between frame and infill. A further internal lining of deep green velvet curtains enclosing a series of more intimate spaces in the extension permits another layer of inhabitation and flexibility.

The existing house was insulated to modern standards, with a drained ventilated cavity allowing the deep stone walls to breathe. In a similar spirit to the extension, the main function rooms of the house were lined with veneered timber panels framed by solid sections to protect all edges and provide a sense of solidity in keeping with the age of the house.

Sustainability issues

The planting of the original gardens was carried out with the care and inherent local knowledge of a gardener of some skill. The house was raised artificially, on naturally draining soil sourced from the lake shore, to permit extensive panoramic views across the landscape to expose it to maximum sunlight. Belts of deciduous native Irish trees shelter it from the prevailing south-westerly winds, while their thin trunks welcome the lower winter sun. Planted shrubberies closer to the house provide further buffering. This deceptively simple strategy, which fostered a comfortable microclimate on the site, was adopted by Clancy Moore in their design of verandas, whose construction detail and orientation acted to shelter the house and create garden rooms capable of year-long inhabitation.

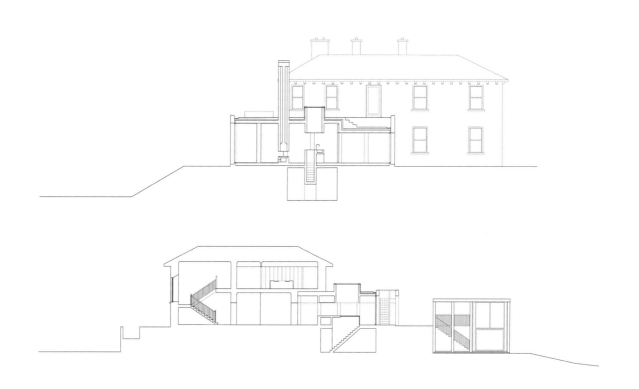

Right
The verandah
from the living
room

Below left
Fireplace and
kitchen

Below right
Kitchen detail

The massive stone walls of the existing dwelling act as a thermal sink deep in the heart of the house, allowing slow warming and cooling effects over the course of the year. All existing external walls were re-rendered to prevent them drinking in the driving rain, as well as being lined internally with a new drained and ventilated cavity and insulation system to achieve contemporary levels of insulation. This wall lining also enabled the delivery of a high level of airtightness, permitting the use of a heat recovery ventilation system to increase efficiencies in the heating system.

The lessons of this local 'massive' means of construction were elaborated by the architects in the construction of the extension to the house. The concrete exposed for its aesthetic quality removes the need for any further linings or finishes. The black terrazzo floor, grounding the extension in the dark soil, acts to hold the heat in both external and internal rooms, while the columns and exposed concrete ceiling soffit act as a thermal sink, creating a stable environment in both the extension and the existing house.

The repetitive nature of the grid, coupled with careful handling and storage of the European-sourced phenolic plywood formwork, enabled the reuse of all formwork three times before it was used elsewhere on site and in landscaping works by the contractor. All site spoil arising from the works was retained on site and used to provide additional grading to the western side of the house.

In addition to minimising the house's energy consumption, it was important that the house be self-sufficient. The energy requirements for the house and its future needs (including the modestly sized lap pool) are met by means of a large biomass boiler which uses a wood-pellet source. A well sunk on site provides potable water with no requirement for treatment, permitting the house to be disconnected from the local authority water scheme. Rainwater is harvested from the courtyards and roof and used to irrigate a new glasshouse to the west of the house, and as a grey water source for the service buildings.

In all cases materials and skills were sourced locally to exploit indigenous knowledge and support a sustainable local craft-based community. All joinery work, with timber sourced from storm-felled or sustainable sources, and fittings (including lights and ironmongery) were fabricated in local workshops.

Energy data

Annual consumption of wood pellets	42 tonnes using biomass CHP boiler
Total electricity usage for entire property	on average 6,400 units per month
Total built area of site	1,485 m^2 in six structures: office, gym, staff quarters, boathouse and sauna
Total	carbon-neutral energy system

Project team

Engineer	Malachy Walsh and Partners
Concrete consultant	David Bennett Associates
Project manager	Triona Costello
Contractor	S&T O'Shea Limited
Concrete subcontractor	Fix-Set Limited

Building data

Number of floors	2
Year completed	2008

Robert Romanis, Allford Hall Monaghan Morris

Architecture

The Tooley Street project is an 18,500 m^2 mixed-use development for Great Portland Estates and represents a significant step forward in the evolution of office design, embodying current thinking about how commercial buildings need to respond to the issue of sustainability. Part refurbishment and part new build, the scheme offers five floors of flexible, speculative office space and five residential units. The lower floors of the refurbished buildings accommodate a restaurant, bar and retail units and provide an active, urban edge to Tooley Street.

From inception, the ambition of the client and project team was to create a building that would serve as a new model for large-scale commercial office developments. An innovative approach has been adopted for all aspects of the building's design, procurement and construction. All of these can be loosely defined under the term 'lean office design'. While few of the technologies applied are in themselves ground-breaking, it is the way in which these technologies have been successfully brought together, coupled with the scale of application, that is visionary.

The building occupies a dense urban site on the south side of Tooley Street in Southwark. The form and mass of the building have been derived from analysis of daylight and rights of light, as well as a consideration of the characteristics and scale of surrounding buildings. The barrel-vaulted roofs are a direct response to the rights-of-light envelope. The idea was to maximise the internal volume and minimise the area of the cladding, while creating an interesting spatial experience and an identifiable external form.

The principal organising device in the scheme is an internal street, which accommodates the public areas of the building as well as the main vertical circulation and services zones. The floor plates are arranged as two wings, each having a depth of 19.5 m. Natural daylight penetrates these spaces from the fully glazed internal elevation to the atrium and rear courtyard and the large picture windows in the external façades. Broad connections are made between these spaces to provide a continuous series of lettable spaces.

A light-touch approach has been adopted for the refurbishment of the existing buildings, while providing a level of quality that is comparable with the new-build office space. Externally, little has been done to these buildings, other than a programme of repairs. Crucially, the fenestration has been replaced in all the buildings, giving a lift to their appearance and a hint of the new development behind.

An early inspiration for the scheme was taken from the Victorian warehouse buildings on the site. Termed 'New Warehouse Aesthetic' the inherent qualities of these buildings give them an ongoing life as flexible, robust, loose-fit space for a variety of uses. The internal spaces provide generous floor to soffit heights, robust use of materials with minimal linings, good levels of lighting and oversized windows.

Construction details

The façade is composed of a frame of precast concrete that mirrors the superstructure. As with most other construction elements, the elevations are composed of prefabricated, self-finished components, which are then assembled on site. Large glazed units were inserted into the frame with the symmetry of the window pattern offset on successive floors to create a staggered rhythm on the elevation. The use of coloured spandrel panels and opaque vertical units, particularly in the upper floors of the building, reduce solar gain by employing a high level of insulation to the solid parts and reducing the area of clear vision glazing to around 47 per cent, thus managing the energy load on the building.

Achieving the project ambitions – for a high-quality, flexible product and a low-energy building – demanded a close integration of architecture, structure and building services. Employing an exposed soffit as an important part of a displacement air-conditioning system meant that the engineering solutions became the architecture and therefore control of the finish became crucial.

The precast concrete soffit panels, or 'biscuits', were formed in steel moulds using self-compacting concrete, with an as-struck finish. These were used as permanent formwork for the post-tensioned in-situ slab. The steel reinforcement lattices cast into the top surface of the precast soffit slabs tie the composite floor together. The logic applied to the soffit was extended to other aspects of the superstructure.

Structural elements in the two main cores are fair-faced concrete, using steel formwork and strongbacks to largely eliminate the need for tie bars. The central columns act as structural ducts delivering cooled air from the rooftop plant directly to the perimeter zone of each floor plate, where the solar gain load is highest. The development of techniques for precasting these components involved a high degree of coordination between Malling, the precast supplier, and the design team.

The construction of the barrel-vaulted roof adheres to the aims of off-site prefabrication and repetition of components in controlled conditions, which are then brought to site for assembly. Extruded aluminium ribs infilled with identically sized solid and glazed overlapping units were prefinished internally and externally. A timber lining system softens the appearance of the anodised aluminium panels and provides a visual link with the finishes to the cores. Other prefabricated finishes to the interiors include the timber-veneered and white-finished joinery panels as well as high-level GRC units within cores and to the double-height barrel-vaulted space on Barnham Street.

The absence of lightweight finishes to ceilings and walls meant that there was no opportunity to conceal building services. This led to the development, in conjunction with Zumtobel, of a bespoke lighting system with fire detection installation. The floor void acts as a plenum for the displacement system and also contains the distribution network for small power and data.

At Tooley Street, the widespread application of prefabrication techniques, including the lighting systems and building services, was particularly innovative. This resulted in high-quality finished components, delivered to site on a just-in-time basis for rapid assembly.

Below
Barnham Street
barrel vault

Below right
Atrium looking
towards the
courtyard

Sustainability issues

A driving ambition of the project was to achieve a BREEAM Very Good rating. Throughout the design development, alternative strategies for a sustainable design were considered and solar gain was addressed through the form and façade design.

After planning permission was granted in 2005, the Greater London Authority's requirement for 10 per cent of the building's energy consumption to be provided from on-site renewable sources became mandatory. The inclusion of a biomass boiler, as well as solar thermal preheating of hot water using evacuated tubes on the west-facing roof were able to provide a total of 10 per cent of the building's energy use.

The most significant innovation was the integration of structure and services to create an aesthetically pleasing exposed concrete soffit to provide thermal mass. Post-tensioned slabs were poured onto a deck of permanent precast concrete panels, eliminating the need for ply formwork, with its related disposal requirements.

The precast central columns also act as structural ducts delivering cool air directly to the perimeter zone of each floor plate, where the solar load is highest. The 1.05 m diameter of the columns is constant at all levels of the building. The internal diameter reduces at lower levels, with a consequent increase in wall thickness. This reflects the increased structural load on the columns lower down the building and the reduction in the amount of cooled air to be supplied at

Left
Barnham Street
elevation

Below
Sections through
the external
courtyard (top) and
atrium (bottom),
looking south

these levels. The supporting walls are slender and densely reinforced, making the placement of concrete technically challenging. The walls were therefore filled from the bottom up, using a pump and manifold to force the concrete upwards under pressure.

Insulated permanent formwork is utilised inside the service ducts to keep the supply air cool as it passes through the floors. The use of prefabricated components offered a number of advantages, including greater integrity of quality and finish, reduced reliance on wet and finishing trades and reduced wastage. In addition to this, a rainwater harvesting system was incorporated into the scheme.

As a result of these measures the building was awarded an Energy Performance Certificate Rating B, placing it above the anticipated upper benchmark for similar new office buildings.

In designing a building to minimise environmental impact and reduce energy consumption in use, an immediate cost benefit accrues. The use of recycled water, solar heating and intelligent lighting systems as well as the cooling benefits of the exposed structure, coupled with durable low-maintenance finishes, has led to a building that will not only be a pleasure to work in but also be efficient in its operation and maintenance.

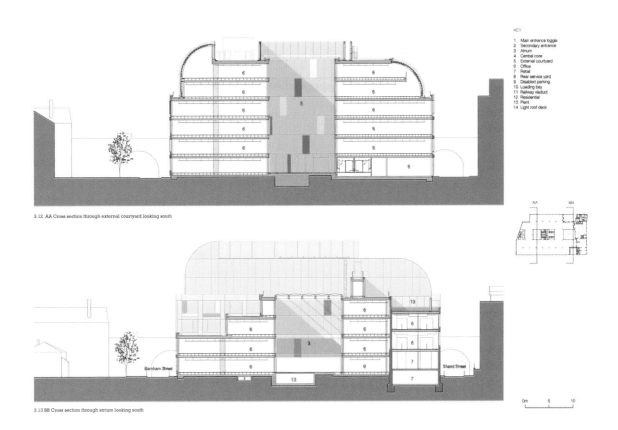

KEY

1 Main entrance loggia
2 Secondary entrance
3 Atrium
4 Central core
5 External courtyard
6 Office
7 Retail
8 Rear service yard
9 Disabled parking
10 Loading bay
11 Railway viaduct
12 Residential
13 Plant
14 Light roof deck

3.12 AA Cross section through external courtyard looking south

3.13 BB Cross section through atrium looking south

0m   5   10

Floor area:

gross	24,007 m²
treated	18,612 m²

Predicted annual energy consumption	*kg CO$_2$/m²/yr*
Net space and water heating (gas) 96 MWh	0.98

Net regulated electrical usage:	
lighting 958 MWh	22.13
fans, pumps, cooling 373 MWh	8.63
special electrical load 906 MWh	20.93

Renewables generation:	
solar panels (heating) 31 MWh	0
biomass boiler (heating) 180 MWh	negligible

Total	52.66

Description of heating and lighting provision

General: displacement ventilation exposed thermal mass for night-time cooling

Temperature criteria: the air-conditioning and heating systems are designed to deliver an occupied zone temperature of 21 °C in the winter and a maximum of 24 °C in the summer

Fresh air standard: the air-conditioning systems are designed to deliver 12 l/s per person, based on an occupancy density of 1 person per 10 m². There is flexibility in the system to deliver fresh air to an increased density of up to 1 person per 7 m²

Cool air is delivered directly to the perimeter zone of each floor plate via structural ducts

Façade: 47 per cent vision glazing; high performance glass (G-value 0.27); super-insulated solid parts; internal blind deals with glare as well as a minor portion of solar load

Structural engineer	Arup
Services engineer	Arup
Main contractor	Laing O'Rourke
Precast supplier	Malling

Floors	6

Typical floor area:	
second	4,155 m²
total	23,558 m²

Year completed	June 2008

Left
Entrance loggia

THE KATSAN BUILDING, STOCKHOLM

Bengt Svennson, White Architects

In Sweden, a project takes the name of the city block on which it is built. 'Katsan' is an old Swedish word for fishing equipment.

Architecture overview

In the city block, Katsan is at the western end of the North Hammarby docks in Stockholm, where White Architects have designed themselves an office building. The city block is part of the plan for Hammarby Sjöstad, the city's new residential precinct in what was previously industrial docklands. The new office lies in a spectacular urban landscape, where the horizontality of the Skanstull bridges extend over the back of the site and, to the front, the Hammarby locks, the gateway to Lake Mälaren, form the backdrop.

The Sjöstad or 'sea-city' has gradually evolved from an industrial dockland precinct into a modern city with a distinct urban pattern of city blocks and squares. The railway track along the quay is a reminder of the past, while the locks and the bridges indicate its continuing importance as an infrastructure node.

The building has an uncomplicated external form: a long and narrow rectangular glass box. The façade consists of a light metal cladding with glazing. On the roof, set back from the façade, is a timber volume with adjacent terrace landscaping. On the quay level, an opening through the middle punctures the building and becomes the building's main entrance, which can also be reached from the opposite side by a pedestrian bridge three storeys up. On the waterfront elevations, half the building juts out over the adjacent canal and, at dusk, the façade is mirrored on the water's surface.

The formal language of the architecture is characterised by hard-bitten structuralist thinking, clearly presented in the technical and mechanical systems, natural exposed materials and precise detailing. The building can be linked historically to the daylight-dependent industrial buildings, and the simple plan form is reminiscent of dockland sheds. The artist's studio, with its light, spacious and flexible space, has served as an important model for the workspace.

The project has embraced stringent environmental demands. Despite the glazed façades, low energy consumption is maintained. Climate is controlled by use of the building's thermal mass. Water is run through plastic piping cast in situ on the floor slab, thus increasing the cooling capacity of the building mass. This energy contribution is, by and large, free as it comes from the adjacent canal.

Construction details

The construction of the building consisted of the assembly of precast columns, beams and double T-beams. Columns are spaced 7.2 m from each other along the length of the building. The double T-beams (2.4 × 0.5 m) stretch 12.65 m from the edge beam to the central spine beam and 4.15 m for the corridor span.

The corridor span is the partitioned zone for archive storage, meeting rooms, the lifts and the services core. The columns were cast in double storey high lengths and were rather flimsy during erection and had to be temporarily braced until the beams were connected and toppings to the double T-beams were poured. The floor is stabilised on the top surface by a thin concrete topping into which is laid the underfloor heating pipes. The design load is 4 kN/m².

The large area of the floor slab constitutes a significant thermal mass that is used to regulate the indoor climate. To enable this process, the concrete soffit has to be exposed. The double T-beams house and contain the ventilation ducts,

the sprinkler system and electrical light fittings. The double T-soffits also act as acoustic diffusers in the open-plan office space.

In the smaller cellular room spaces, acoustic damping is resolved in another way. Here, sound-absorbent panels are mounted between the flanges of the T-cassettes.

The façade consists of a light metal framing with glazing panels on all four sides. The glass cladding extends vertically from floor to floor and follows the horizontal module of 24 m. In every module there is an openable window. The glazed eaves, in conjunction with the stepped corners, make a seamless mantel of glass around the building. The demand on the glass isolation is a U-value of 1.0 W/m²K. There is a 600 mm air space or cavity between the concrete construction and the glass façade, and a convector heater counteracts the cold airstream from the window.

The sun screen consists of an outdoor blinding of vertical transparent texture, combined with a certain reflection in the glass. The foot board on the outside of the façade makes it possible to shade the façade and provides access for cleaning the windows.

The interior materials of concrete and glass contrast with the floor and inner walls, which are made of wood in a warm yellow colour. The top of the floor slab is covered with parquet of oiled ash in squares of 600 × 600 mm. The inner walls consist of a flexible system of block walls covered by veneer of abachi timber.

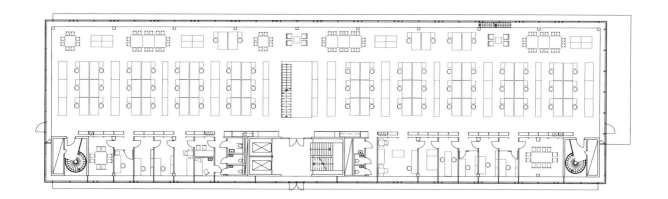

Right
Entrance space,
connecting three
levels

Below
Construction
systems: (left
to right) frame,
façade, heating
and cooling, and
interior

Sustainability issues

The brief for energy consumption set a goal of 85 kWh/m^2 per year for the building and 35 kWh/m^2 per year for usage, giving a total of 120 kWh/m^2 per year. The primary concern in an office building is to remove the excess heat that builds up during working hours.

The solution for an energy balance builds on the principle of a so-called 'heavy building', i.e. a building with a large thermal mass. The mass comprises 5,000 m^2 of concrete slab, which acts as a temperature regulator. Normally, the façade takes on this role, but in this case the slabs are three times as large. The flanges of each slab's double T-cassettes increase the exposed area of the concrete slab by 50 per cent. The slab's mass eliminates rapid temperature fluctuations by absorbing or emitting heat.

When staff come to work in the mornings, the air temperature rises. The difference in temperature between the air and the concrete activates the slab's cooling effect and the excess heat in the air is absorbed and transferred away through the slab. At night-time, when the internal temperature drops, the reverse activity takes place and the double T-beams are cooled down.

This technique has been tried and tested in old stone buildings. In our building, the effect is enhanced by having water pipes cast into the topping of the slab. The water passing through the pipes is about 18 °C in summertime and about 20 °C in wintertime, supplied from the Hammarby Canal at no cost. The cooling effect is 11 W/m^2 for each degree of temperature difference between the air and the slab. For the temperature regulation to work, the surface of the concrete slab must be exposed, thereby demanding an exposed ceiling without any acoustic ceiling panels between the slab and the rooms.

The heating and cooling system is deceptively simple. Its complexity lies in the extensive energy calculations required. The calculation has been validated by a research project, which the IMechE performed a few years after the building was put into operation.

As the concrete slab regulates the temperature, the ventilation in the building has a purely hygienic function in managing supply and return air. The ductwork is 'circuit fed', i.e. any given point in the ductwork is fed from two directions. The supply airshafts are placed furthest out in the short façades and are connected by a large collecting duct on each floor. The 'circuit feeding' therefore works vertically as well as horizontally. The ventilation system is built as an 'end pressure' system, where the pressure drop is taken at the ends of the ducts, i.e. at the air diffusers, thereby avoiding adjustment dampers, resulting in lower pressure losses in the ductwork and lower energy costs. To maintain temperature control, external sun shading is required.

The entire electrical system is computer-controlled by a BMS. The general lighting levels in the office space are thereby regulated according to the levels of daylight. For environmental reasons, all electrical cables are halogen-free. Exposed cabling is fed through metal OMG pipes.

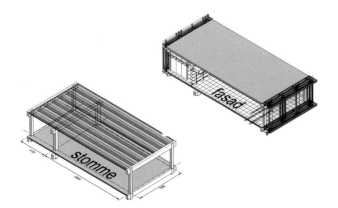

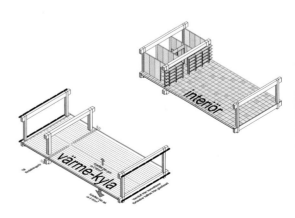

Energy data

Floor area:

gross	6,700 m²
treated	5,680 m²

Predicted annual energy consumption

Building (total)	70 kWh/m²
Usage (total)	70 kWh/m²

Annual CO_2 emissions

Electrical usage	7.3 kg CO_2/m²
Space and water heating	4.8 kg CO_2/m²

Description of heating and lighting provision

Heating from district heating supplied via convectors, slabs and supply air

Free cooling from nearby canal distributed passively via water-cooled slabs

Designed to have a large thermal mass to lower heating and cooling demand

Exhaust air heat recovery

Solar and wind-controlled automatic external solar shading

Daylight-controlled artificial lighting

Annual energy consumption:	120 kWh/m²

Project team

Client and architect	White Architects
Structural engineer	Scandiakonsult
Mechanical engineer	Angpanneforeningen
Electrical engineer	Elkonsult Lennart Goldring
Contractor/developer	PEAB
Precast manufacturer	Strangebeton

Building data

Number of floors	5 + roof
Total gross floor area	6,752 m²
Year completed	2003

Michael Cambden, Building Design Partnership

Architecture

BDP's new Manchester studio, at the junction of the Rochdale and Ashton canals in Manchester's Piccadilly Basin, creates a working environment that is open and transparent, comfortable, technologically advanced and conducive to integrated team working. It is also recognised as the first naturally ventilated office building in Manchester to achieve a BREEAM Excellent rating and has recently been certified as a Carbon Neutral Development.

The functional brief for the new studio at Ducie Street was to accommodate BDP's 250-strong Manchester-based staff in approximately 2,500 m^2 of large, open-plan studio space and provide a further 400 m^2 of ancillary accommodation, including an interactive 'linear hub' at ground floor level housing the BDP café, exhibition area, flexible meeting rooms and extended reception space. Perhaps more important to the brief, however, were the company's aims of providing the practice with a distinct and visible profile within Manchester, creating a sustainable building and providing an uplifting, high-quality workplace for its staff.

With the architecture, structure, services, sustainability, lighting and management strategy all being designed by BDP, the combined requirement was to create a building that would showcase the credentials of this multidisciplinary design practice and encapsulate BDP's workplace philosophy.

The Ducie Street site was selected because of the opportunities it created. Located within the city's most current regeneration zone, the Northern Quarter, the site sits in an area of global historic significance, often described as the cradle of the Industrial Revolution.

The form, massing, detail and materials of the building evolved and developed as an expressive response to the physical context of the area and the microclimate. It is surrounded by refurbished Victorian mills and contemporary residential blocks, generally six to eight storeys high and predominantly in brick.

Above
Stainless steel
south façade

Above
Open-plan studio
space

Viewed from the west end of Ducie Street, the shining steel form of the south façade can be seen leaning gently out across the pavement, to be glimpsed beyond its residential neighbour. Alongside its functional role of reducing solar gain, the machine aesthetic of this element has been designed as a contemporary reference to the industrial heritage of the surrounding area. A counterpoint is created by the more tactile timber soffits and reveals, the brick base and exposed concrete columns that surround and abut the steel.

Moving around the building, its form evolves to address the changing context. The main body of accommodation floats over the water, while the dramatically angled cantilevered stair responds to the geometry of the canal, to accentuate this prominent position and provide views beyond the city towards the Peak District. The highly glazed façade and external terrace at the uppermost level take full advantage of the historic waterside setting, while a new publicly accessible pontoon hovers above the water to extend the Victorian tow-path around the face of the studios.

Construction details

From the project outset, a close working relationship was formed between BDP's design team and the contractor to ensure quality of finish and also to explore opportunities for sourcing and utilising the most sustainable materials and products possible. Design workshops were held with subcontractors and suppliers during construction, and this team approach facilitated a full understanding of the design aspirations. It also enabled the quality of workmanship to be closely monitored and reviewed as work progressed.

A good example of this collaboration was the construction of the exposed concrete frame. BDP carried out a careful selection process with the contractor to determine the most appropriate formwork to use for the slabs. Off-site tests were undertaken to gain a full understanding of the visual qualities achievable by using different types of soffit formwork boards. A number of trial pours were undertaken, together with inspection of other sites, before the team elected to use a phenolic film faced ply. Careful consideration was also given to the way the formwork was to be jointed, the nailing patterns to be used and how the formwork would be dismantled and reassembled as the work progressed.

Formwork layouts were prepared for the contractor which optimised the use of 'standard' plywood sheet sizes as far as possible, and presented the board arrangement in a coordinated and symmetrical fashion. All boards were nailed in a neat and symmetrical manner. The slab and formwork design was also coordinated with the lighting design, with cast recesses being provided to accommodate lighting tracks. This facilitated a flexible and future-proof lighting solution which balances brightness ratios by reflecting light from the slab soffits.

The concrete mix uses 50 per cent GGBS, a by-product of iron-making blastfurnaces in Teeside, as a replacement for ordinary Portland cement. This not only reduced the embodied CO_2 of the concrete by 50 per cent, but also produced a lighter colour that was considered appropriate for the exposed concrete within the studios. Recycled aggregates were also considered; however, a guaranteed source of suitable material could not be found without adding substantial costs to the project.

Materials specified for both the interior and exterior construction – stainless steel cladding, concrete frame, timber rainscreen and brickwork – were selected for their durability and longevity in service, keeping to the first tenet of sustainable architecture that they must last for the building's design life.

Sustainability issues

In response to the brief's requirement for a highly sustainable building, research into a range of different environmental and energy-control strategies concluded that employing a low-tech, passive solution would be more effective in terms of usability and longevity, and also more economical than providing on-site renewable energy production. Given that a large proportion of a typical office building's energy consumption is dedicated to heating, cooling and ventilating the space, it was soon agreed that significant reductions should be targeted in these areas.

A highly integrated approach to the design of the architecture, structures and services engineering was undertaken to produce a naturally ventilated building with a substantial thermal mass provided by a concrete structural frame with exposed concrete soffits. A more latent but still

recognisable benefit of the exposed concrete frame was the strong visual aesthetic and sense of 'quality' that well-finished concrete imparts.

Perhaps the most striking architectural feature of the building is the punctuated stainless-steel southern façade, which rises above the Ducie Street colonnade to contain the studios before sweeping over to form the roof of the building. The reflective external finish, the heavily insulated build-up and narrow vertical apertures all serve to minimise solar heat gain while maximising privacy for the residential buildings opposite.

By contrast, the northern façade of the building is transparent. The floor-to-soffit glazing takes maximum advantage of north light to illuminate the full extent of studio spaces and reveal wonderful views of the city centre. The studio floors themselves have been designed with a maximum width of 16 m to enable natural ventilation and reduce the use of artificial lighting. Cantilevered slabs to the north elevation feature a tapered soffit to the canal-side elevation, which helps to maximise daylight penetration.

With the exception of the steel roof structure, the building has an in-situ concrete frame that provides substantial

thermal mass. Within the studio spaces, the suspended ceilings and mechanical plant generally associated with open-plan offices have been omitted and exposed slab soffits maximised to enhance the thermal performance of the building throughout the year. The desire to create open-plan, column-free flexible studio space was also a key driver in establishing the long-span, open-plan structural form, for which a post-tensioned slab solution was appropriate.

Natural ventilation, controlled by the BMS, is provided across the studios between acoustically attenuated louvres within the vertical slots to the south elevation and hardwood louvre panels and windows facing the canal. Air temperature is monitored via sensors on each floor, located at either end of the studio. These feed information back to the BMS, which opens or closes the louvres as required.

At night, the vents are automatically opened to cool the concrete which, in turn, absorbs the heat of the office during the day. In summer, the 'coolth' from the concrete negates the requirement for mechanical cooling, and during the winter the warmth from the concrete significantly reduces the requirements for heating. Further sensors within the concrete slabs enable the BMS to determine the optimum period for the louvres to be open.

The essentially low-tech solution ensured that it was cost effective to build, that the suitability and functionality of each part was proven and that the chance of unforeseen technical problems was minimised.

The SBEM calculations and TAS thermal model forecast annual CO_2 emissions of 40.8 kg/m². As a relevant benchmark, figures from ECG19 2003 illustrate that the annual carbon emissions expected from an air-conditioned prestige headquarters office of the same size would be 130.3 kg/m². (No actual figures were available at the time of publication due to the short period of occupation.)

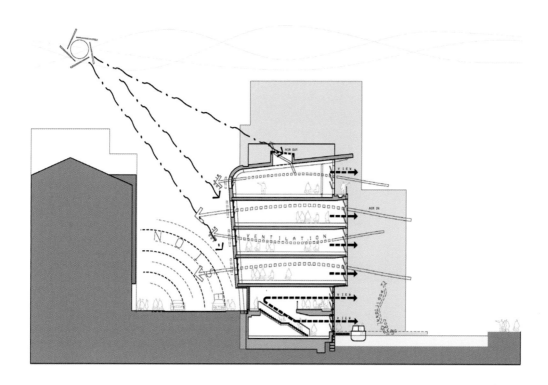

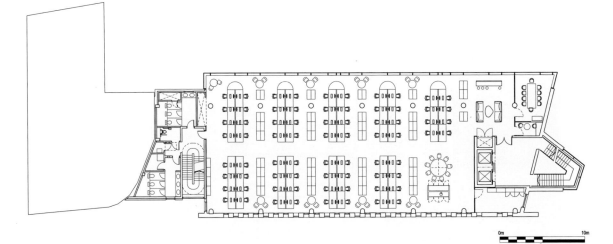

0m   5m   10m

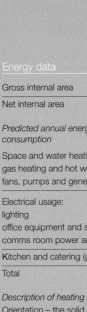

Energy data

Gross internal area	3,840 m²
Net internal area	3,073 m²

Predicted annual energy consumption	kWh/m²/yr (gross)	kg CO_2/m²/yr (gross)
Space and water heating:		
gas heating and hot water	39.6	7.7
fans, pumps and general cooling	13.5	5.7
Electrical usage:		
lighting	11.2	4.7
office equipment and small power	16.1	6.8
comms room power and cooling	24.2	10.2
Kitchen and catering (gas and electricity)	15.8	5.7
Total	120.4	40.8

Description of heating and lighting provision

Orientation – the solid, reflective south elevation minimises solar gain while the transparent north elevation maximises use of north light

Thermal mass – the exposed concrete soffits of the structural frame enhance thermal performance throughout the year

Natural ventilation – the BMS controls the flow of air across studios between acoustically attenuated louvres on either side of the plan

Night-time cooling – the BMS also controls actuated hoppers on either side of the building that are opened at night to cool the exposed concrete slabs

Lighting – natural daylight is supplemented by energy-efficient luminaires positioned directly above the working planes and linked to both presence and daylight sensors

Project team

Client	Town Centre Securities PLC and BDP
Main contractor	Kier North West and Styles & Wood
Structural engineer	BDP
Services engineer	BDP
Cost consultant	AYH Arcadis
Concrete contractor	Adana Construction Ltd

Building data

Number of floors	6
Plan depth	15.5–16.0 m (varies due to raking elevation)
Plan length	45.5 m + 5.5 m cantilevered stair
Column grid	6.0 m along length, 11.5–12.5 m across depth
Floor-to-floor height	4.05 m
Finished floor-to-ceiling height	3.17 m
Year completed	2008

Jo Wright, Feilden Clegg Bradley Studios

Architecture

For their new central office, the National Trust chose an intriguing site that once formed part of Brunel's Great Western Railway Works close to the centre of Swindon. It was the adjacent 19th-century engineering sheds that provided us with a concept for the new offices. These buildings are lofty, two-storey buildings with high-quality daylighting and ventilation achieved through a regular rhythm of pitched roofs, designed before the days of artificial lighting. The design that emerged uses a very similar form, with the orientation of the ridge turned so as to provide south-facing roof slopes for solar collection and north-facing rooflights for daylighting. The orientation of the building provides a powerful diagonal line, which picks up the natural desire line across the site leading to a tunnel under the railway and thence to the town centre. The building is truncated on the remaining three sides, with the pattern of the gable walls revealed, clad in blue engineering bricks, picking up on the decorative detail of many of the remaining buildings.

One of the key requirements of the National Trust was that the disparate parts of the organisation that were coming together into the new building all needed to feel part of one organisation. The regular rhythm of an all-embracing roof supported on slender columns, visible from all workstations on ground or mezzanine floors, seemed to fulfil this objective. The deep plan that this building form suggested initially seemed to be counter-intuitive, though redefining the building with the roof as the major connection to the environment means that, in effect, each workstation is no more than 7 m from daylight and ventilation. The internal courtyard was added to provide indoor garden spaces and a greater connection to the outside.

The design concept also derived from Max Fordham's philosophy that in office environments it is important to maximise natural lighting and the most efficient way of doing this is to use roof apertures.

The design team agreed that each workspace should have a view of the sky; the most difficult zones in which to achieve this were, obviously, under the mezzanine floor areas, which were designed to be 9 m wide to provide reasonable flexibility and workstation layout. Various geometrical analyses were carried out to generate voids between mezzanine floor plates of 6 m and floor-to-ceiling heights on the ground floor of 4.5 m so as to provide an even distribution of daylight to the ground floor. Detailed studies were carried out, first using ECOTECT and then using an artificial sky. Anticipated daylight factors range from 3 per cent at the centre of the underside of the mezzanine floors to an average of 9 per cent on the mezzanines themselves.

The rooflights are shaded by extending the leading edge of the south-facing slope over the ridge to shade from high-level summer sun, and by incorporating ventilators at, at least, 9 m centres, which consist of a raised enclosure around the section of the rooflight that is providing shading

from both east and west low-level elevations. Because of the extent of the roof aperture, however, internal roller blinds will also be installed to provide a finer degree of control should clear sky radiation result in glare.

The ventilators at roof level are designed to operate independently of the wind direction and also to provide rain protection to the opening sections of rooflight. They are controlled automatically, as are a series of vertical openings around the perimeter of the building. This system will be automated to provide night cooling in summer and daytime ventilation from spring to autumn, with vents being controlled by a BMS with local manual override. One of the problems with naturally ventilated buildings is the provision of the very low rates of ventilation that are required to maintain oxygen levels during the winter. Casement windows or even trickle vents tend to admit too much air and cause draughts. A very low level mechanical ventilation system has therefore been installed with an integral heat recovery system, which

Top
General layout
view of Heelis

Above
Schematic
section

Right
Site plan

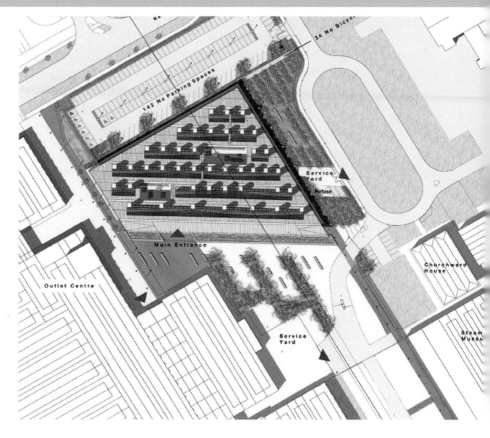

introduces air to raised floor plenums and provides a single point of extraction adjacent to the fan unit itself to provide heat recovery. Calculations show that this should have a dramatic effect on the building's overall heat requirement.

We estimated during the design stage that heating and hot water combined would come to 36 kWh/m² per year – this is 45 per cent below the benchmark for good practice for offices. However, we actually recorded 86 kWh/m² per year, which is 9 per cent above best practice. This was due to various control issues, such as a window which had been wired back to front and which therefore remained open during the winter, and excessive hot water use by the kitchen. We have not been able to obtain any further data from the client to review current use.

Naturally ventilated buildings often incorporate 'safety net' measures to deal with excessive summertime conditions. Rather than making provision for extensive cooling, the solution at the National Trust has been to incorporate an extract ventilation system in five of the roof ventilation 'snouts' to enhance cooling potential and air movement through the building if absolutely necessary. It is not anticipated that these units would be used in other than exceptional summertime circumstances. Both the daylighting and ventilation strategy will therefore result in the electrical consumption of the building being kept to a minimum.

Power consumption by office equipment, however, is more difficult for the design team to control, and will remain the largest source of CO_2 emissions in a low-energy office building. The only way to meet this electrical load without importing electricity is to incorporate on-site photovoltaic generation. The roof form of the National Trust building maximises this potential with a total potential area of 1,400 m² of ideally oriented collection area, facing due south at 30° to the horizontal. Around one-third of the collection area consists of the extensions to the south-facing roof slope that form shades for the north lights. The remainder is located on the south-facing roof itself in a position where it is exposed to direct sunlight above an altitude of 20° due south. Various photovoltaic options were considered, resulting in different capital costs and outputs, and the most cost-effective solution for the client was to use a low-cost thin-film amorphous silicon panel.

Significantly, however, desktop studies which looked at the use of high-efficiency polycrystalline silicon cells showed that the maximum installation over the roof area would result in an annual contribution of 70 per cent of the total electrical load of the building, thus reducing CO_2 emissions virtually to zero. What this study shows is that the concept of maximising daylighting and natural ventilation combined with photovoltaic collection is much more likely to reduce CO_2 emissions than the alternative of taller buildings where walls become the solar apertures rather than the roof. This is not necessarily to say that one- and two-storey buildings are optimal, because of the impact this would have on land take and urban design, but it does show that buildings where roof

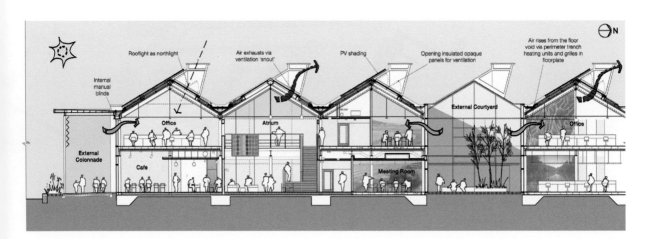

area dominates wall area are more likely to meet the elusive target of zero CO_2 emissions.

The National Trust's sustainability agenda extends far beyond energy use. Studies of water usage showed that, by installing 4-litre flush WCs and waterless urinals, spray taps and class A kitchen appliances, it will be possible to reduce water consumption by 60 per cent. Because of this, the studies that were carried out on a rainwater recycling system proved not to yield a cost-effective result. However, the site is subject to flooding and attenuation of surface water was required by the Environment Agency. This was achieved by creating a bunded tank under the car park area using the natural clay of

the ground to retain the water prior to discharge into mains drainage. An alternative system – which took rainwater from the roof and from the car park, passed it through a series of wetland swales that ran down one side of the building, providing natural filtration, and thence into a tank, from which it was pumped back into the building to flush WCs – proved to be too expensive.

The materials selected for use in the buildings are also subject to scrutiny by, among other things, checking them against the rating in *The Green Guide to Specification*. Blue engineering bricks chosen for the outer walls of the building will be laid in lime mortar to ensure that they can be recycled.

Sustainable Concrete Architecture

168

Right
Interior use of
timber

It is interesting that Brunel originally incorporated these into his early buildings, and they formed the canal that once ran adjacent to the site.

Both the roof and the windows are made out of aluminium, which now consists of a very high percentage of recycled stock. Various options were examined in relation to the superstructure frame, with timber solutions evaluated against steel. Surprisingly, studies showed that the embodied energy of highly processed timber, as opposed to steel sections with a high percentage of recycled steel, made very little difference to the overall embodied energy. The refinement of the steel frame and the reduction in thickness of the concrete slab were of greater consequence.

The National Trust is very keen on utilising materials from its own estates, and one of the more significant undervalued products is the wool from its flock of Herdwick sheep on the Lake District fells. At considerable extra cost, this will be used to provide insulation in walls and roof. Elsewhere, it is hoped that the internal fittings of the building will utilise timber from nearby estates.

Sustainability issues

The National Trust's sustainability policy also extends to the transportation strategy for the building as well as its management. The site was selected because of its proximity to the mainline station, and the number of car spaces provided has been reduced to below the number that commercial developers might expect and the planning authority might accept. One car space for every three workers will mean that a green transport plan will be required, which will enforce reduced car dependence.

Social facilities for both staff and public form the heart of the building. There will be no cellular office spaces, giving greater credence to the organisation's democratic working principles. Thorough post-occupancy evaluation is proposed, and a display of the building's energy consumption, which will be constantly monitored, will be available in the reception area. This approach should ensure that maximum benefit is derived from feedback in what ought to be the lowest energy consumption office building in the country.

The sustainability features extend well beyond Part L requirements:

— water use: by installing 4-litre flush WCs and waterless urinals, spray taps and class A kitchen appliances, water consumption will be reduced by 60 per cent

— materials: the rating of all materials selected for use in the buildings is checked against *The Green Guide to Specification*. Blue engineering bricks chosen for the outer walls of the building will be laid in lime mortar to ensure recyclability. Both the roof and the windows are made out of aluminium, which now has a very high percentage of recycled stock. For the superstructure frame, various options were examined; however, studies showed, surprisingly, that an engineered timber or steel frame made a similar contribution to the overall embodied energy. Is the *Green Guide* flawed, we wonder, in this instance?

— transport: the site was selected because of its proximity to the mainline station, and the number of car spaces has been reduced to below a number that commercial developers might expect and the planning authority might accept. Less than one car space for every three workers will mean that a green transport plan will be needed.

Energy data

Gross floor area		7,300 m²
Predicted annual energy consumption	*kWh/m²/yr*	*kg CO₂/m²/yr*
Electrical usage		
cooling and plant	29.15	12.53
lighting	22.00	9.46
unregulated electrical, Part L	81.50	35.05
Renewables generation:		
electric + heat	11.63	–5.00
Gas usage, all sources (total)	195.10	37.07
Total	316.12	89.1

Project team

Structural engineer	Adams Kara Taylor
Services engineer	Max Fordham
Main contractor	Moss Construction

Building data

Number of floors	2
Total floor area	7,300 m²
Year completed	2005

Sarah Hunneyball, Allford Hall Monaghan Morris

Architecture

The Yellow Building is a seven-storey headquarters building to house all head office staff and design departments of Monsoon Accessorize and showcase the unique Monsoon Art Collection. Commissioned by Peter Simon, founder of Monsoon, the new building is the first of four phases of a development set to transform the edge of Notting Hill into a vibrant new urban quarter.

The building rises over the low-level studios and warehouses of White City with a bold, striped façade of highly transparent low-e glass and sunflower yellow spandrels. The colour yellow, selected for its charismatic and unique associations, also augments the Monsoon brand itself in terms of its vibrancy and energy.

In addition to meeting the specific needs of the Monsoon organisation, the building must also work as a speculative office building, with floors designed to be sublet, and it must also serve as a public building at ground floor level, with a staff restaurant and areas for events and fashion shows. The building has a gallery for showcasing pieces from the Monsoon Art Collection and provides a connection to the cultures and places that give Monsoon its brand identity.

The brief from Monsoon Accessorize was for a building that would facilitate connectivity and visibility between the various departments and fashion brands to encourage collaboration. The seven-storey building is organised as open, unobstructed floor plates on either side of a linear atrium. Rising through this dramatic space is a great open staircase, whose landings provide links between the floors and informal meeting spaces.

As early proposals for the scheme were developed, an idea for a triangulated structure reminded Peter Simon of an early version of the Monsoon logo and the concept was progressed. Working closely with structural engineer Adams Kara Taylor, a dramatic, diagonal concrete grid evolved that wrapped around the building, providing structural rigidity without the need for supporting cores. The unique structure also defined the form and look of the building, while the diagonal geometry of the exposed concrete structure provides a cathedral-like drama to the atrium space, which is the focus of the building's architecture.

Right
The reception area

Far right
East elevation,
looking south

Bottom right
Section showing
diagrid frame and
roof beams

The services concept aimed to provide the client with a high-quality, flexible headquarters building which is also robust and energy-efficient. Much thought was given to designing the building to reduce energy consumption, mirroring the company's sustainability and corporate social responsibility ethos. This has been achieved by employing displacement ventilation and passive energy-saving methods and through reducing solar gain by the use of high-performance glass combined with external shading and building orientation.

The service tower, which houses lifts, lavatories and escape stairs to each floor, is located at the south end of the building. The tower is clad in aluminium to reflect its functionality and the east and west elevations have white vertical louvres. At the north end a second service tower is located within the atrium, which contains all the air-handling ducts and an escape staircase.

Construction

The exposed diagonal concrete structure, or diagrid, was developed to provide both gravity and lateral support to the structure, removing the need for shear walls or stability cores within the frame. The floor is an in-situ flat slab, with an exposed soffit, supported on a column grid typically 9.0 m by 7.5 m, although this varies at the perimeters with the inclined columns of the diagrid. The exposed concrete soffits and walls provide thermal mass, in addition to their aesthetic qualities, which works well with the displacement ventilation system used to heat and cool the building.

Buildability and critical path studies in terms of reinforcement layouts, floor repetition and formwork cycle time were undertaken at an early stage. The main contractor, Laing O'Rourke, and their concrete frame subcontractor, Expanded Structures, proposed to replace the 325 mm flat slab with a 275 mm post-tensioned flat slab, delivering programme and cost benefits.

In discussion with Expanded Structures, the formwork proposal for the in-situ inclined columns was a significant innovation, because it demonstrated that the columns could be cast in a controlled and relatively straightforward fashion. Rather than taking a traditional column form and inclining it, Expanded Structures proposed to utilise reusable wall forms, with inclined partitions built within to form the V shape of each column pour. This enabled the position and verticality of the forms to be controlled, and minimised the complexity of the plywood formwork and falsework propping.

In addition to the inclined columns, at lower levels there are inclined walls at the entrance area to the building. The inclination of these walls matches both the columns and further inclined walls to the external restaurant building, which also has an exposed concrete structure. The concrete canopy linking the atrium to the restaurant, which hangs from beneath the first floor slab, presented challenges in terms of thermal breaks at the envelope line and the need for rotation to allow differential settlements between the main piled building and the raft foundation to the restaurant. Both issues were solved by placing a number of breaks in the canopy, at locations specifically chosen to minimise their visibility and to maximise the continuity of the structure.

Overall, the building has a 'studio' type feel and an aesthetic which is reflected in the sawtooth or north-light roof. This roof profile, which has rooflights on the north-facing pitch over the atrium space, provides a large amount of daylight at the upper levels. The roof trusses are formed from steelwork, allowing the roof to be lightweight and enabling the internal concrete columns to stop beneath the uppermost occupied level. This arrangement also creates a natural and defined 'top' to the structure. The roof trusses are supported by V-shaped steel beams, which spring from the tips of the concrete lattice. This interface between the steel and concrete structure required a bespoke detail to accommodate the required tolerances and movements.

Sustainability issues

Within the design and construction of the Yellow Building a number of features were developed specifically to address carbon emissions. While the embodied energy within the concrete structure can be relatively high during the construction phase, over the lifetime of the building these figures become insignificant and hardly measurable as they are offset by the benefits of concrete's thermal mass.

The use of exposed concrete soffits has yielded an approximate 2 per cent saving in CO_2 emissions, which

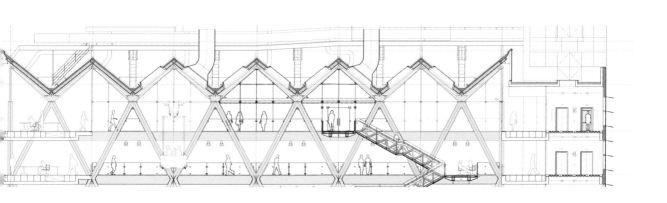

equates to over 6 tonnes of CO_2 per year. The overall effect of these energy-saving measures has been to achieve an approximate 35 per cent reduction in CO_2 emissions relative to the Building Regulations' notional building.

The large linear atrium provides excellent natural light. It is also used to extract air, both for ventilation and in a smoke extraction capacity, and acts as a smoke reservoir. Tall floor-to-ceiling heights on all the floors have also improved daylight penetration to the floor plates. The lighting system has movement-sensitive 'Dali' controls to minimise electricity usage when rooms are not occupied.

The use of post-tensioned slabs allowed the floor to be slimmed down, and the wall to the basement was removed and replaced with sheet piles. Expanded Structures worked very hard to recycle and reuse the formwork wherever possible. They used and reused standard wall forms with infills for casting the inclined columns to simplify the process as much as possible and to minimise waste.

Careful consideration was given to minimising the effect of solar overheating of the office areas by providing a façade with a very high level of solar control. This has been achieved using a combination of external shading, high-performance glazing and internal blinds. The use of vertical 'fin' shading on the east and west façades helps to reduce the solar gain through these façades. A great deal of work was done to optimise the fins, with material, size and angle all being considered carefully.

The Yellow Building has been designed as a building with a very long life span, and with built-in sustainability for the long term. The open-plan areas make the space highly adaptable, meaning that, in future, the building could accommodate a change of use without requiring any physical work to be carried out on any of the primary elements.

Energy data

Floor area:	
gross	15,951 m²
treated	15,323 m²

Predicted annual energy consumption	*kg CO$_2$/m²/yr*
Space and water heating 550 MWh	6.83
Electrical usage 640 MWh	17.90
Total	24.73*

* Does not include non-regulated energy usage (see notes on page 256)

Description of heating and cooling provision
Displacement ventilation

Project team

Structural engineer	Adams Kara Taylor
Services engineer	Norman Disney and Young
Main contractor	Laing O'Rourke
Concrete frame contractor	Expanded Structures

Building data

Floors	7
Total floor area	15,000 m²
Year completed	2008

David Henderson, Bennetts Associates

New Street Square is a speculative office and retail development which creates a new destination between High Holborn and Fleet Street serving the 'mid-town' area of the City of London.

The project comprises a group of five new buildings set around a new public square. A tightly planned series of pedestrian routes integrates the new development with the lanes and courts that characterise the adjacent Fleet Street conservation area. These pedestrian routes converge on the new square, with cafés and shops animating the street scene alongside office entrances. A programme of public art and planned performance encompasses all the main spaces.

When Bennetts Associates became involved with the project in 2002, the site was occupied by a series of office buildings from the 1950s and 1960s. These buildings were inefficient, energy-intensive and lacking in flexibility for modern office occupiers and their space requirements. From an urban design perspective, they were unresponsive to the historic street pattern and this manifested itself in public spaces which were difficult to access, did not encourage casual use and which felt generally uninviting. A previous proposal for redevelopment had carpeted the site with a single, very large and deep-plan office floor plate, but this had attracted criticism on account of its overall bulk and was, ultimately, regarded as too inflexible in a changeable office market.

The post-war development of the site cut off many of the natural 'desire lines' for pedestrians, crossing between one business district and another or to the four nearby Underground stations. The development reinstates these desire lines to help to make the site busy once again, bringing back life to the area at street level and re-establishing the address.

Historic city centres are often characterised by a consistent pattern of construction and building sizes. The remnants of such a pattern can be seen in older buildings on Fleet Street and this is a philosophy which was embraced when formulating the redevelopment proposal. The New Street Square site was certainly large enough to establish a pattern of its own that confers scale and civic identity to the development.

The overlaying of a regular pattern of spaces or routes with the irregular site boundary generates plots around a new public square for major buildings of differing sizes and plan form. The result is to ensure a degree of economic flexibility, combined with the essential ingredients for a townscape of identity, variety and drama.

In addition to one high-rise tower, two medium-rise atrium buildings and one low-rise block, there is a small pavilion that serves as a management suite and access point to car and cycle parking at basement level. Quite apart from urban design considerations, the varying heights of the buildings ensures the maximum level of sunlight penetration into the square, with the tallest building to the north and the lowest to the south. Scale and materiality are also used to establish appropriate relationships between the scheme and its surroundings, with the tallest building being the most assertive; its sharply pointed corner signalling the development from Holborn Circus.

The square at the heart of the development has a point of access at each corner. The layout of this space means that each of the four main buildings has a prominent position for its entrance, with axial views from the main approaches. The composition of the square is rectilinear but informal and its approaches ensure that there are no enclosed corners or symmetrical views. Its dimensions, and those of the surrounding buildings, are chosen to ensure that a sense of enclosure can be achieved without overshadowing.

A development based around arcades and squares needs people as its lifeblood and should feel like an extension of the existing city fabric. The intensified population created through the development also requires access to a range of facilities outside the workplace. Much of the ground level is devoted to non-office uses, enlivening the street scene and drawing people to the development throughout the day. External spaces are orientated so that café seating inhabits sunny outdoor areas in the square. The intention is to create a sense of street life long after normal working hours.

By City of London office standards, the New Street Square development is unusually versatile and site-specific. Although all four of the main office buildings differ in scale and detail in response to their own particular local context within the overall masterplan, they also share a number of key characteristics:

— all buildings feature simple, adaptable floor plates, which can be subdivided to provide a number of separate office tenancies on any floor and which can accommodate a range of cellular or open-plan office arrangements

— all floor levels adhere to a consistent datum throughout the development so that individual buildings can be linked by bridges for use by large occupiers

— the buildings are all constructed in concrete with flat, post-tensioned floor slabs of 12 m span. An intermediate column is located asymmetrically within the floor plate to facilitate fit-out space planning

— structural cores are of slip-formed reinforced concrete; the cores were constructed well in advance of the floorplates to facilitate a very rapid construction programme

— a family of external cladding elements, including extensive use of precast concrete to frame sun shading and to define cores and corners.

Construction

The selection of in-situ concrete as the structural framing material was relatively uncommon in the context of other contemporary city office buildings, where steel frames with cellular beams are the predominant type. While steel framing usually claims to offer programme benefits, on this project thorough preplanning and expertise by the main contractor and their concrete specialists negated any advantage of a steel frame in the overall build time.

Another characteristic of the steel frame with cellular beams is that it tends towards a bespoke servicing regime, requiring special air supply ducts and fan coil air-conditioning units. A key motivation for opting for a post-tensioned flat slab structure was its inherent flexibility in terms of the coordination of building services. Even more importantly, the flat slab conferred the ability for tenants to choose to fit out their spaces with lower energy solutions, such as chilled beams, rather than the standard approach using energy-intensive fan coil air-conditioning units.

The free cooling benefits gained by exposing the concrete soffit within the space, coupled with the provision of high-level opening vents, was also important in realising the potential for even greater energy saving.

Left
View from Holborn
Circus

Bottom left
Scale and materiality
are used to establish
appropriate
relationships between
the scheme and its
surroundings

Sustainability issues

From the outset, the New Street Square development was intended to represent a new benchmark for sustainable development, embracing a holistic approach towards social and economic issues, as well as incorporating the most advanced thinking on minimising energy in use and in the carbon footprint of the construction and materials selected.

Low CO_2 emissions were targeted for the buildings in operation. The design allows for the inclusion of alternative means of comfort control, such as chilled ceilings, active or passive chilled rafts, mixed-mode ventilation and so on, in a way that can be discussed and agreed with tenants in advance of fit-out. These options can drastically reduce CO_2 emissions while the building is in operation and offer maximum choice to the occupier.

A range of cladding options was designed to minimise the amount of solar gain, and therefore reduce the cooling requirement for the building. External timber solar shading, suited to the differing orientations and local conditions of each building, was installed and the ratio of glass to solid cladding was balanced against external heat gains and losses to achieve optimum performance.

The solar shading was designed so that the shading effect was not achieved at the cost of reduced daylight levels within the spaces. End-users need not depend on electric lighting during the day, offering a direct saving in electricity consumption and reducing internal heat gains from artificial lighting.

Assessment and reduction of embodied energy in the construction process played a key part in specification. By using several tools, such as ENVEST and Environmental Profiles, developed by BRE, the design team minimised the impact of the materials used to create the development, i.e. the embodied energy of the materials, by adhering to the following principles:

— substituting materials of known high embodied energy

— recycling materials and using recycled materials where possible

— designing to minimise the quantity of materials used and to minimise waste

Left
The new public
square provides a
place for relaxation

Right
East elevation of
scheme

Below
Ground floor plan

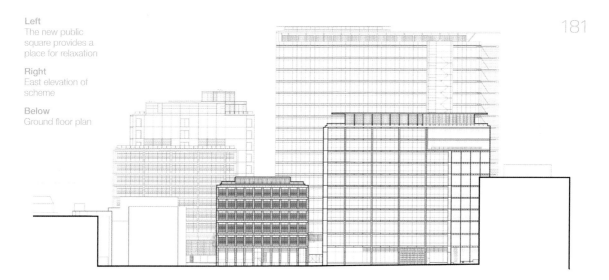

designing for long life and to reduce the need to refurbish
— specifying materials after due consideration of transport distance and energy used to produce them (concrete, aluminium, timber and carpets, in particular).

The main contractor and their specialist subcontractor teams were fully engaged in the construction process. Reuse of the materials, furniture and carpets from the demolition of the existing buildings was undertaken to minimise the volume of waste created. This also reduced the amount of embodied energy in the scheme. Maximum use was made of off-site prefabrication and preassembly, with key components trialled using mock-ups, and as much standardisation as practicable was undertaken to minimise waste of materials. On-site segregation of waste, reuse and recycling also minimised the material sent to landfill.

Freshwater use was considered from the outset and the design minimises the use of this increasingly important resource in the development through the installation of dual-flush toilets, flow restrictors to taps and grey-water recycling to soft landscaping. Sedum-covered green roofs also minimise the rate of rainwater run-off and reduce the pollutants going into the drainage system.

The redevelopment provided an opportunity to improve local biodiversity. The previous buildings had limited brownfield biodiversity, primarily limited to plant and small tree species in brick planters. The new development includes semi-mature trees in planters, along with a range of other flora, and a number of 'green walls' on the management pavilion. The scheme also has green roofs on several of the main buildings – both extensive and intensive – to adhere to the City of London green roof initiative.

Both demolition and main contractors embraced the principles of the Respect for People initiative and the Considerate Contractor scheme, with particular reference to good neighbour relations. The tender required employment policies, evidence of high levels of site welfare and proof of site cleanliness and safety. Care was taken to ensure that construction components and assemblies were obtained in a way that is consistent with the terms of ethical investment.

The development's links to transport hubs are emphasised through its layout, access and approaches to encourage pedestrian connectivity. Cycle parking has been provided, with shower and locker facilities and a cycle ramp, to be managed by the building owner, next to the cycle parking area.

The outdated 1960s buildings previously on the site had little appeal to tenants. Their inefficient building systems, lack of accommodation for technology and obtrusive layout with no

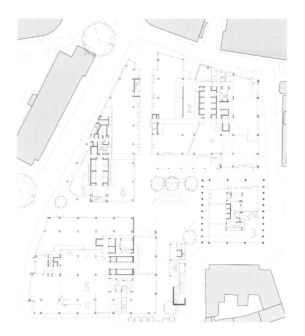

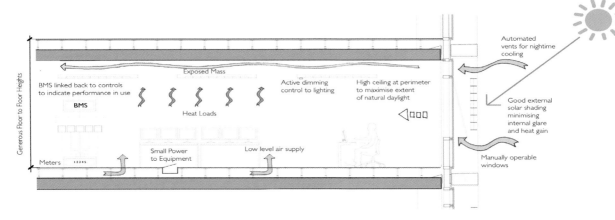

retail provision were quickly causing the site to become an economic wasteland in the heart of the city.

New Street Square, on the other hand, offers flexible, energy-efficient office space with the latest technology. The addition of retail provides further economic viability and transforms the area from a Monday-to-Friday commuter destination into a seven-days-a-week local destination, creating valuable economic activity at the weekends.

Summary

The New Street Square design earned a BREEAM Excellent rating. The predicted CO_2 emissions across all the buildings in the New Street Square development are 49 kg/m^2 per year (with fan coil air-conditioning) for regulated asset energy.

Also noteworthy is that 93 per cent of demolition materials were recycled and every trade contractor was obliged to measure transport impacts.

Moreover, the developer, Land Securities, has achieved the highest ever rents in the City of London for the space inside the tallest building, No. 6 New Street Square, proving that an environmentally friendly building can also be a highly profitable one.

Energy data

Floor area:	
gross	85,119 m²
treated	64,225 m²

Predicted annual CO_2 emissions	kg CO_2/m²/yr
Space and water heating	12.8
Regulated electrical usage	52.7
Unregulated electrical usage	74.5
Total	140.0

Description of heating and lighting provision
Passive measures:
optimised glass/insulation ratios capability of night purging and exposed thermal mass
external sun shading

Active measures:
low-energy lighting and pumps
daylight dimming
capability to accept alternative environmental control systems

Project team

Client	Land Securities
Structural engineer	Pell Frischman
Services engineer	Cundall
Project manager	Davis Langdon
Quantity surveyor	Davis Langdon
Main contractor	Sir Robert McAlpine
Concrete subcontractor	Byrne Brothers

Building data

Number of floors	9–18 floors, building to building
Building dimensions:	
plan depth	18 m
column grid	9 × 12 m and 9 × 6 m
floor-to-floor height	3.81 m
Year completed	2008

Tim Pettigrew, Swanke Hayden Connell

Architecture

The new office building at One Coleman Street is the new headquarters for Legal & General and replaces its 1960s predecessor. It provides 22,000 m^2 of highly flexible and efficient column-free office space, with enhanced sustainability credentials. This was achieved through significant reductions in energy usage and the use of secondary concrete materials.

The design set out to unite the disparate urban context of the eastern end of London Wall in the City of London. To the south and east of the site, the context is mainly pre-20th century buildings located within the historic street pattern of the City's core. To the north and west of the site the context is defined by post-war development of parallel high-rise tower blocks set at an angle to the straightened London Wall and connected by the podium high-walk. The proposals set out to re-establish the street wall along London Wall and Coleman Street, and create gardens on the southern side of the new building. The mass of the building was further defined by the existing rights of light of the Girdlers Hall and the Armourers Hall and the height was defined by the St Paul's viewing corridors. The main entrance on the east end of the building opens directly onto the new pedestrian section of Coleman Street, which will become a major pedestrian route once the Crossrail station at Moorgate is complete.

The nine-storey office building contains typical floor plates of 1,906 m^2 and the rigorous plan and tight core provide a net-to-gross ratio of 88 per cent, making it one of the most space-efficient buildings in London. The structural design and compact central T-core maximise the floor area and provide floor plates with clear spans of up to 14 m. There are areas of deep floor space that have additional load capacity, allowing the tenant to install centralised facilities including archiving, servers and tea-points, freeing up the façade to provide maximum natural lighting to the premium office areas.

The façade is clad in precast concrete panels and stainless steel elements, configured in a geometric arrangement. This form is generated by the curvature of the building floors and expressed through a series of interlocking and alternating triangulated surfaces.

The window fenestration is set at an angle to the edge of the floor plate, enhancing tangential views from the building while creating a robustly modelled surface to the external building face. This arrangement follows the curvature of the floor, creating directional movement to the precast façade by alternating the panel angles on successive floors. This changing geometry is also resolved by the triangulation of the spandrel and results in a richly modelled curvilinear façade.

Construction

The basic structural scheme used contiguous bored piles, and where a tunnel passed underneath it was bridged by a concrete diaphragm wall integrated into the pile wall. The superstructure was a steel frame with a composite concrete floor plate, which was stabilised by the main concrete core and a small satellite core to the west of the building.

The two cores were carefully coordinated during the design process and were built using the Twin-Wall system. Here, the core walls were designed as two skins of thin precast concrete with the rebar already attached and then filled with in-situ concrete. This method of construction was more expensive, but ultimately saved money by reducing the preliminary cost and shortening the programme. The risk of delay was reduced as the cores were taken off the critical path of the construction programme.

One Coleman Street was designed prior to the implementation of the Building Regulations Part L 2006; however, the design was developed to follow the draft regulations where possible. The completed project in any case exceeds the Part L 2002 requirements by more than 30 per cent. The large quantities of concrete cladding meant that the proportion of glazing on the façade was only 60 per cent, which made a significant contribution towards achieving the ambitious Part L targets. When seen from the inside of the building, the reduction in glazing is marginal as the average windows make up approximately 80 per cent of the internal façade and there are no louvres to obstruct the views.

The precast concrete cladding, which was manufactured by Decomo in Belgium, was complicated by the curvature of the façade intersecting a 6 m grid. This meant that the sections between every column varied in size. To reduce cost it was essential to standardise moulds and increase repetition of the precast elements where possible. A construction analysis showed that varying the lengths of the spandrels and standardising the column spacing minimised the number of moulds required. The final spandrel mould design allowed the variation to be taken up within only two moulds. The precast moulds were designed using complex 3D geometric modelling and rigorous quality control. The moulds were designed to allow micro-adjustment in terms of length and the angle of the ends and this allowed the spandrels and mullions to be delivered on-site within the tight tolerance limits of ±6 mm.

The installation of the panels caused a number of other complex issues as there were no plumb lines and the large radii of the curves meant that the installation had to be undertaken using GPS coordinates. GPS points were added to all the columns and the spandrels were offered up and manoeuvred into the residual gap between. As a result of the close coordination and quality control, all of the precast panels fitted well and follow-on trades found that the space for window openings was well within the tolerance levels.

Sustainability issues

During the design development phase a number of different building scenarios were evolved for raising the profile of the building's sustainability credentials. These specifically addressed the impact of concrete on the construction in terms of the cladding and especially the structure.

Both embodied carbon and resource/waste issues were targeted by the use of cement replacements and secondary aggregates. The design team recommended the use of china clay stent as a substitute for quarried primary aggregate, which equated to a saving of 6,000 tonnes of spoil from the china clay quarries and a saving of 6,000 tonnes of primary

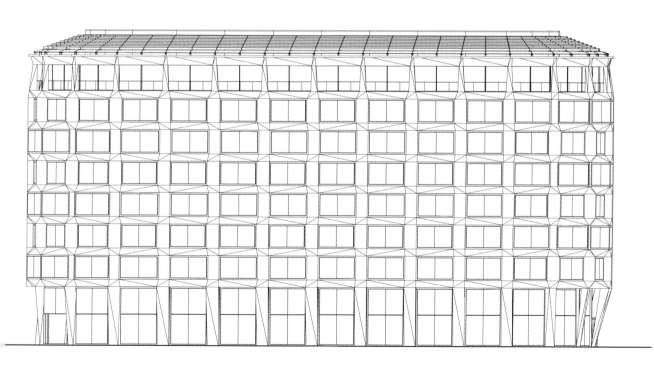

aggregate quarried. The use of pulverised fuel ash (fly ash) as a cement replacement material, at the exceptionally high volume of up to 40 per cent, reduced the embodied CO_2 of the concrete significantly. This approach was incorporated in the watertight basement slab and the pile caps. By reducing the Portland cement content of the mix, approximately 500 tonnes of embodied CO_2 has been omitted from the construction. As a result of this, the project won the 2007 Concrete Centre Award for Sustainability.

The rationalisation of the façade construction through the clever use of adjustable moulding by the precast manufacturer created an efficient cladding scheme. The 400+ cladding panels required just two moulds for casting all of the panel variations, which made a significant contribution to the reduction of building waste during the precast concrete manufacture.

The façade was designed to anticipate the higher performance requirements of Part L of the 2006 Building Regulations and was optimised for solar heat gains and natural daylight. The building envelope was specified to achieve a leakage rate of less than 5 m^3/h per m^2, half that required by the Building Regulations.

The building services were designed prior to the introduction of Part L 2006 but pre-empted its requirements by aiming to achieve 30–40 per cent below the CO_2 emissions targets in Part L 2002. The shell and core plant includes low specific fan-power air-handling units, fitted with heat recovery coils. High-efficiency air-cooled chillers were selected, along with condensing gas boilers to recover flue waste heat. Pressure drop, and therefore fan energy, was kept to a minimum by designing a simple distribution network based around generous risers.

Energy data

Gross floor area		21,203 m²
Predicted annual energy consumption	*kWh/m²/yr*	*kg CO₂/m²/yr*

	kWh/m²/yr	kg CO₂/m²/yr
Gas usage:		
heating and hot water	55.0	10.45
Electical usage:		
heating and hot water	38.6	16.60
fans, pumps, cooling (electric)	52.4	22.53
office equipment	23.0	9.89
Total	169.0	59.5*

* Does not include non-regulated energy usage (see notes on page 256)

Project team

Client	Union Investments
Development manager	Stanhope plc
Structural engineer	ARUP
Service engineer	ARUP
Quantity surveyor	Davis Langdon
Façade engineer	ARUP Facades
Landscape architect	Robert Townshend Landscape Architects
Main contractor	Bovis Lendlease Ltd
Precast concrete	Decomo Ltd, Belgium

Building data

Number of floors	ground plus 8 floors
Building dimensions	72 m (longest) × 40 m (widest)
Year completed	2007

Bennetts Associates Architects in association with
Lomax Cassidy & Edwards

Introduction

Judging from the extraordinary public and press reaction
to the opening of Brighton and Hove's new central library,
this is the most popular and significant new building in
the city for some years. It is the centrepiece of the Jubilee
Street development and the catalyst for regeneration of
Brighton's cultural quarter; it is a highly innovative design
with sustainability at its heart; it is an unusually high-quality
product of the Private Finance Initiative (PFI), delivered on
time and to budget; it has the architectural stature and
ambition of a major public building.

Brighton and Hove's new library is the centrepiece of
a regeneration project that stitches back together the
fragmented streets of the North Laine area near the city
centre.

The masterplan effectively extends the cultural quarter of
Brighton from the Dome northwards to embrace the network
of streets previously cut off by the derelict car park that
was there before the development. To do this, the design
reinstates Jubilee Street to its original alignment, with most
of the new buildings playing a background role in order that
the external spaces predominate. The street level is filled
with shops, cafés and restaurants, with either offices or
residential property above. In the centre of the site, a small
square provides the setting for the new library and a venue
for public art, performance and the Brighton Festival. With
a hotel on its south side and a café on its east, the square
also resolves the unfortunate approach to a 1970s municipal
swimming pool.

In economic terms, the addition of many new properties
is substantial, but it is the mix of building types and the
permeability of the plan that makes this especially significant.

The library itself builds on these themes, with a mixture of
uses that includes a café, a bookshop, a music library, a
children's area, a life-long learning centre, conference rooms
for hire and so on. Access is total, both with respect to
physical disabilities and in relation to legibility and openness.

As with previous buildings by Bennetts Associates, such as PowerGen and Wessex Water, environmental engineering is not only pursued for its own sake but is also the Trojan Horse for structural and spatial expression. The science of sustainability is fundamental to achieving architectural excellence, especially in a context such as PFI, where objective assessment is required at every stage.

The library adopts a formal plan, with activities that require enclosure around the perimeter on three sides and the main reading room/reference library in the centre, where it strikes up a direct relationship with the square outside. The intention was that this should feel like a civic building of importance – a place of repose and presence – as if to demonstrate that modern libraries are not wholly devoted to computers or made obsolete by the Internet.

Concrete and sustainability

Precast concrete planks

Jubilee Library integrates the building structure, fabric and environmental design to create a building whose architecture is a direct reflection of its engineering strategy. The physical form of the new library seeks to minimise the demand on services through a strategy of exposed thermal mass combined with levels of insulation that exceeded Building Regulation requirements and strict airtightness criteria. Architecturally this is expressed in two ways, through the precast concrete plank structure to the building perimeter and the in-situ concrete trees of the central library hall.

The use of the TermoDeck precast concrete plank system

is central to the strategy of an integrated architecture as it provides the structure to the perimeter spaces as well as the basis of the servicing strategy for the whole building. Supported off a steel frame, the prestressed planks provide heating, cooling and ventilation to the building by channelling warmed or cooled fresh air through integral hollow cores, which pass through the centre of each plank. Ductwork, carrying air from the central air-handling units, plugs into these planks, concealed by a perimeter bulkhead detail. A series of diffusers are then located adjacent to the external walls to deliver air into the space below.

Once the tempered air is delivered to the perimeter spaces it is drawn into the three-storey central library hall by the stack effect of the three wind towers, which pulls the air through the building.

The higher demands of different spaces are dealt with by passing the air through a greater number of cores and increasing the number of diffusers to a particular space. Spaces with a particularly high demand, such as the IT suite, were provided with local chiller units to mitigate any peak temperatures. However, the strict contractual arrangement of the PFI project meant that a central chiller was also included to avoid the agreed maximum temperatures being exceeded. To date, this has seldom been used.

The TermoDeck system provides 100 per cent fresh, filtered air, which significantly improves occupant comfort and far exceeds CIBSE minimum fresh air requirements. During the winter months, when the wind towers are closed, heat is reclaimed by being drawn out through high-level vents into the plant room.

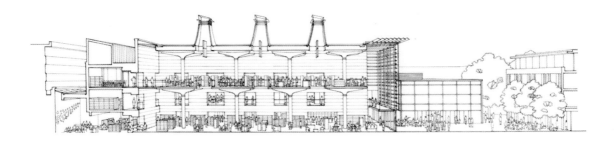

The use of thermal mass in this way is an efficient means of maintaining stable temperatures and occupant comfort inside the building. Because the air passes through the concrete at low velocities it allows passive heat exchange to take place, creating a thermal flywheel effect to the passage of heat which evens out significant external temperature variations. High external daytime temperatures are not therefore reflected internally as the thermal mass and high insulation value of the external fabric delay heat transfer. During unoccupied hours air is pushed through the concrete cores to night-purge the structure and a series of BMS-controlled roof vents and the wind towers remove excess heat from the building. This in turn reduces energy demands for cooling the following day by reducing the cooling load.

In-situ concrete

The main library hall space was designed as a single volume enclosed by a U-shaped strip of supporting ancillary accommodation and offices on three sides, the fourth side bounded only by a glazed façade. Within this enclosure, reinforced in-situ concrete table structures were stacked on top of each other to define the two double-height spaces housing the main library book-stacks and reading areas.

Eight freestanding concrete columns were arranged in pairs, running the length of the central volume. Their height and form were intended to give the space an appropriate civic scale and identity that relates directly to the public square outside.

The tall, cylindrical columns rise from each of the floors and splay out to form column heads, supporting the slab above. At the head of the columns the concrete soffit was articulated and given form by the cantilevered arms that project out beneath the slab. Below this, a recessed band was introduced into the column, forming a collar that integrated the wiring routes and the light fittings used to illuminate the underside of the soffits. The complex tapered and curved shapes of the column heads were cast using

Right
View from the
square looking into
the library at dusk

Below
Plan and sections
of the column
heads

fibreglass moulds. The repetition of similar profiles allowed for multiple usage of each mould.

The square column heads were joined together by a strip of in-situ concrete to form the simple rectangular shape of the floor and roof slabs. The central concrete structure was physically separated from the ancillary spaces around by a void which is crossed at first floor level by a series of bridges providing access from perimeter spaces through the surrounding timber-panelled wall. Lightwells formed around the structure allow natural daylight to enter the hall reading areas and provide paths for air circulation. They have also created good visual connections between the library spaces.

At roof level, three voids within the centre of the slab provide bases for the tall wind towers, which extend above the library roofline. The ventilation system was intended to take advantage of the winds in the coastal location to draw air out of the main hall during warm summer conditions. On the first-floor level the voids are replicated directly below to form lightwells and provide an efficient air path from the ground floor.

Around the perimeter of the roof slab, BMS-controlled lights within the glazed perimeter can be opened to assist natural ventilation of the space and facilitate night-time purging. The roof glazing in conjunction with the glazed south façade also allows natural daylight to enter the library hall and reading spaces.

A high-quality concrete finish was used and the structure exposed to utilise the thermal mass of the material. A white-painted finish was adopted to express the form of the structure while unifying differences in the concrete colouration and reflecting the natural light entering into the reading spaces.

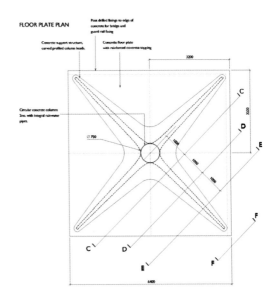

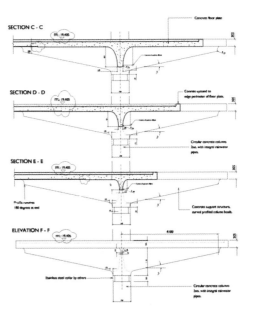

Energy data

Floor area	6,540 m^2

Predicted annual CO_2 emissions	kg $CO_2/m^2/yr$
All regulated emissions from gas and electricity	48
Non-regulated electrical (occupant) emissions	25
Total	73

Project team

Client	Brighton and Hove Council / Mill Group
Structural engineer	SKM Anthony Hunt
Services engineer	Fulcrum
Landscape architect	Land Use
Design build contractor	ROK

Building data

Year completed	2005

Debby Ray, Allford Hall Monaghan Morris

Architecture

Westminster Academy is a new secondary school in West
London, housing 1,175 pupils and 128 staff members. The
sponsor, Exilarch Foundation, and the founding principal,
Alison Banks, had a powerful vision of learning for the school
that embraces the latest thinking in education. Westminster
Academy is a school that sets new standards for educational
buildings, meeting the demands of a highly innovative and
radical educational agenda and creating a place where
pupils, staff and the community as a whole can come to
learn, interact and aspire.

The building is located in a gritty, urban context dominated
by the Westway flyover, 1960s tower blocks and the Harrow
Road. In response to the architectural and environmental
impact of the surroundings, the Academy is a fully sealed,
five-storey building with a separate two-storey sports hall, a
large outdoor area and seven sports pitches.

As the plan developed around a large atrium, the solution
for the structure of the main building was an exposed
in-situ concrete frame with atypical spans varying from
7.5 m to 11 m. It also provided a high level of flexibility in
space planning and adaptability for future change. Another
important feature of the plan was to provide legibility of
the building volume for all users and a high level of passive
surveillance to increase safety and well-being.

The exposed concrete frame is clearly visible within the
building and forms the key palette of materials to the
foreground of the teaching environment. This approach is
cost effective in terms of life-cycle costing, reducing the need
for stuck-on applied finishes and reducing the associated
labour costs at the time of construction. The exposed
concrete is a robust surface for use in a school environment
and, in the long term, will reduce the need for maintenance
and replacement.

A 'market place' on the ground floor physically connects
to all the key communal spaces at this level and visually
connects to the whole school via the full-height atrium,
which has a coloured, sculptural roof. This dramatic central
space embodies the needs of the new learning framework
by operating as the lively hub of the school, and pupils move
between the café, informal working spaces, the library, the
lecture theatre and the dining room on the top floor.

Construction details

A key ambition was to create a new civic landmark in which the pupils, staff and wider community felt a sense of pride and ownership. The façade is boldly stratified into large panels of glazing, vibrantly coloured terracotta tiles and illuminated screens. The use of concrete was driven by a design philosophy to create a building that had an urban presence and reinforced the idea of solidity, durability and longevity.

Due to the air and noise pollution from the nearby Westway, the building form is an efficient sealed box, providing maximum control of the heating and ventilation systems and eliminating costly opening lights. In contrast to the bold colourful exterior, a more restrained approach to materials has been employed internally, using exposed concrete, painted blockwork, timber and acoustic baffles. We worked closely with our structural engineer, Building Design Partnership, to develop the structural solution for the academy.

The additional elements of the scheme, the sports hall and the outdoor playing area, were separated from the main building to allow ease of community use outside of school hours. These different components of the project were connected by the cohesive use of a palette of materials, with the plain finished concrete working in harmony with softer finishes, including timber and wood wool. In particular, concrete is used to create a connection between the interior of the building and the external spaces. The landscaping for the spacious play area between the two buildings is a series of large concrete terraces, which provide robust in-situ steps and benches within an orchard of new trees.

The selection of a concrete frame for the Academy was considered wholly consistent with the architectural expression of the scheme, which was designed to maximise the benefits of the aesthetic and structural qualities of the material. A sense of permanence was important to create a landmark for the community. The toughness of the concrete is balanced by the softer, warmer materials such as solid oak linings, carpet and colourful fabric baffles and furniture throughout.

Within the project, the use of concrete was celebrated within the reception and atrium of the school with a huge, exposed concrete wall onto which the logo of the school was cast. The scale and location of this piece brings a solid, heroic

Above
Main school corridor with baffles and
breakout spaces on either side

Above
Entrance
reception desk

drama to the space, in contrast to the vibrancy, colour and movement of daily school life. Elsewhere within the school, the concrete has formed a canvas for a bold graphic and signage that uses bright colours to contrast with the material. Similarly, a creative lighting strategy transforms the plain concrete walls into a series of art installations.

Sustainability issues

Westminster Academy is designed as a low-energy, sustainable school that strives to meet the environmental comfort and daylight provision set out within the BREEAM Very Good benchmark. Although the project is not formally certified, services engineer Building Design Partnership succeeded in integrating a number of key features that contributed to its low carbon footprint. In addition, green roofs, which make up over 50 per cent of roof spaces, greatly reduce stormwater run-off and enhance biodiversity in the harsh urban environment.

Within the ambition of creating a sustainable school, the use of concrete formed an important part of the environmental and servicing strategy. The robust concrete frame forms the framework for a flexible servicing strategy with ease of access and built-in adaptability. Virtually all 215 mm × 1.0 m columns are carefully integrated flush into the walls with no impact on space planning. Also, the inherent fire resistance and enhanced acoustic properties of the in-situ frame were very beneficial in resolving challenging details for a BB93-regulated, atrium-centred learning environment.

Energy demand is reduced in a number of ways. Green roofs moderate temperature extremes and the thermal mass of the exposed concrete frame absorbs daytime heat and re-radiates it back into the space at night, thereby tempering and controlling heat gain and facilitating night-time cooling. Coupled with these advantages, the enormous amount of natural light in the building significantly reduces the need for artificial lighting. Mechanical ventilation incorporating heat recovery and adiabatic cooling is utilised throughout the Academy through a raised access floor and continuous perimeter heating/ventilation units. This provides passive cooling in the summer and heat recovery in winter, significantly reducing CO_2 emissions.

Right
South terrace
seating area

Below
Study of
elevation

Bottom
Section through
atrium area

The building footprint forms a simple 2:1 rectangular box with its longer edges oriented to the south and north. The efficiency of the box form allowed a significant portion of the façade to be glazed for maximum natural light penetration. Extensive provision of solar shading and glazing treatments minimise solar gain and glare, while maintaining good daylight. This is supplemented by daylight-linked artificial lighting. Glare and overheating is controlled through the use of fixed internal louvres and blinds.

Material selection used natural, recycled or recyclable products such as the terracotta panelled façade, FSC timber linings and roof baffles, low VOC carpet from recycled materials, and locally sourced concrete paviours. The concrete itself was a modest 'plain smooth' finish, which meant it was very cost effective and straightforward to construct. The contractor, Galliford Try, and their concrete subcontractor, Getjar, ensured through early benchmarking that the quality of the concrete was established and maintained throughout. This enabled the use of concrete as a final finish, thus minimising applied finishing materials dramatically and significantly reducing material consumption and building waste.

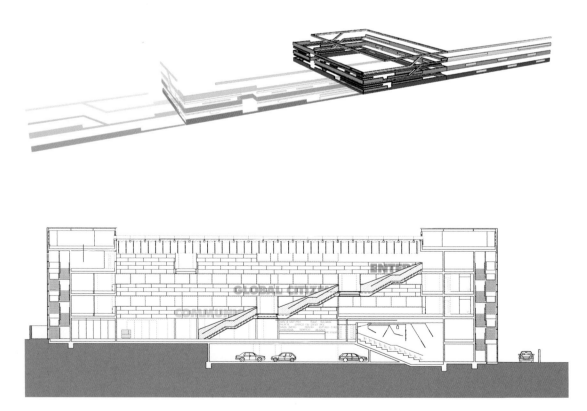

Energy data

Floor area:	
gross	11,100 m²
treated	10,764 m²

Predicted annual energy consumption	*kg CO₂/m²/yr*
Gas space and water heating 1,141.8 MWh	20.15
Regulated electrical usage 247.8 MWh	9.90
Total	30.05*

* Does not include non-regulated energy usage (see notes on page 256)

Description of heating, lighting and energy-saving provision
The thermal mass of the exposed concrete soffits contributes to the building's passive cooling

The building meets the environmental comfort, daylight provision and acoustic performance benchmarks set out in BREEAM sustainability guidelines for a Very Good rating, while significantly reducing CO₂ emissions.

Mechanical ventilation, incorporating heat recovery and adiabatic cooling, provides passive cooling in the summer and heat recovery in winter

Extensive solar shading through cantilevered balconies and glazing treatments minimises solar gain and glare

Exposed concrete structural frame acts as a thermal mass

Green biodiverse roofs and BRE *Green Guide* A-rated materials utilised

Project team

Structural engineer	BDP
Services engineer	BDP
Main contractor	Galliford Try
Concrete frame contractor	Getjar

Building data

Floors	3
Gross internal floor area	13,100 m²
Year completed	2007

Charles Thomson, Rivington Street Studio

York is an historic town. Its location has made it a strategic
centre for centuries, first for the Romans, then the Vikings,
and the defensive walls are still part of the architecture of the
city. It was a major medieval settlement with one of the most
beautiful cathedrals in the country and a preserved centre
which evokes memories of England going back to the 16th
century – dense, intricate and intimate.

York St John University's decision to build on a brownfield
site close to the ancient city walls, within sight of the Minster
and at the junction of three of the city's main roads, was
a great architectural challenge. The chair of the Planning
Committee described the site as the most important in
the city. New building in York has had to contend with a
community which is naturally conservative and nervous of
change. Modern building, with a few notable exceptions, has
done nothing to enhance the architectural quality of the city.

The university was keen to have an exciting contemporary
building and we were determined to design a building which
would respond to the local context, but without pandering to
notions of pastiche or historicism. York is full of architectural
drama, the juxtaposition of the grand and dominant with the
small and intricate. The ancient walls of the city are a great
inspiration: massive masonry walls, curved and roughly hewn
and strikingly beautiful. The narrow streets and alleys, the
mixture of functions and materials contrast dramatically with
the massive architectural drama of the cathedral, but they
are all inextricably part of the same city.

There were certain key functional requirements of the
new building: it had to house more than 100 academic
spaces, ranging from lecture theatres and teaching rooms
to specialised workspaces; it had to sit against a listed
Georgian terrace; and it had to enhance a critical corner site
within the city.

We were keen – perhaps naively keen – to use concrete as
the dominant building material both for the structure and
for the key internal and external walls. Our experience as a
practice of using fair-faced concrete was limited, though we
had used exposed concrete for the structure of our library at
Brunel. Here, we proposed that the curved wall forming the
main street elevation (which was 'defensive' in the sense that
it protected the academic areas from the excessive noise
and pollution of the street) should be concrete.

Top left
Entrance to courtyard between
Georgian flank wall and shuttered
concrete walls to staircase

Top right
Teaching rooms with
simple concrete surfaces

Bottom left
Coloured seats against board-marked
concrete in the lecture theatre

Bottom right
Dark grey compressed board and
western red cedar below roof
overhang at high level in courtyard

We love the quality of concrete: the natural variation of colour, the opportunities for the surface to be smooth or textured and the plasticity of the form. It seemed a natural counterpoint to the historic masonry walls of the city, a material that could be just as beautiful as natural stone. However, we ran into serious resistance as soon as the project went public: public exhibitions and presentations elicited a negative response, not only to the material, but to the massing proposed. The Conservation Officer within the planning department was interested in engaging in an intelligent dialogue about our design approach and our client was heroically supportive, but, with a rapid programme geared to academic need, we had to reconsider our options quickly. It was crucial to develop an approach that would win over at least some of the people we were consulting. We had to lower the building, reduce the overhang of the projections onto the street, 'articulate' the roof and, critically, change the material of the curved wall to something other than concrete.

We decided to retain concrete for the stair cores and for the lift shaft, for the main frame, the floors and the main cross-walls. Wherever possible we wanted the concrete to be exposed. This was partly an emotional response to the material and partly a desire to have surfaces inside and out that would be obviously strong and robust. It was a simple structural decision: reinforced concrete would give us a material that would hold the building up and provide wearing surfaces inside and out. Overlaid on these factors were the environmental aspects: we wanted concrete for thermal mass and for its contribution to the environmental performance of the building and we wanted to ensure good sound insulation between floors and between rooms. We proposed a green roof over the main areas of the building, which would contribute to the insulation, to the local biodiversity and to the management of rainwater outflow. The concrete structure was part of a general strategy to target a BREEAM rating of Very Good.

For the main public façades of the building we changed tack. We sourced a local handmade brick. This looks great with the concrete and, by creating deep window reveals and a relatively small number of random openings, we retained the sense of this being a large, strong and permanent 'city wall'.

In addition, we used timber (both iroko and western red cedar), dark-grey compressed board and dark-grey render for other elevations around the building, with fixed aluminium windows and solid opening panels.

The local conservation groups generally remained very antagonistic towards our proposals, even after we had made the changes to the design, but with the energetic support of the Conservation Officer and the chair of the Planning Committee, the scheme was approved.

We took our clients to see samples of concrete in Bradford and in London. It was a difficult process and the recurring reaction was that the concrete did not represent an 'acceptable' finish, either internally or externally. The texture and blemishes which, for us, represented part of concrete's appeal were typically seen as 'defects'. This was reinforced in a number of the buildings we visited where clients had clearly demanded 'remedial work', which usually involved the concrete being painted.

The client had decided that the project should be procured through a two-stage tender process with a design and build contract (with the design team novated to the contractor). We prepared a detailed set of Work Stage D/E drawings and an outline specification for the tender, but the project was priced at some £1 million over budget and so a rigorous value engineering exercise had to be carried out. One of the first casualties was the concrete finishes specification, which was thrown out entirely, to be replaced by the industry standard concrete specification and a commitment to 'get it right'. The design and build contract has many advantages, but the design team members become employees of the contractor, which removes the design team's traditional authority and detachment. It is critical that a level of respect and trust is established to avoid the design team becoming simply a drawing office resource for a range of cost-related design changes.

During the project there were arguments and compromises, battles and debates, but the contractor and their subcontractor were genuinely committed to doing a good job. Fundamental questions were addressed once the contractor had been appointed:

— Should the external concrete be precast or cast in situ?

— Should the concrete walls be shuttered and poured in a single operation or in two pours?

— How much control could we have over the bolt hole positions?

— How could we control the joint between pours?

— How much variation could we accept in the surface finish and how much 'making good' was productive?

David Bennett was our consultant, advising on the specification and the finish of the concrete. He attended important meetings with the main contractor, Morgan Ashurst, and the concrete subcontractor, Northfield, before and during construction. He was both critical and supportive, providing expertise at vital points in the construction process to the contracting team, the design team and the client.

The external walls were cast in-situ (although we think the subcontractor regretted the decision). They were cast in two pours; however, the joints between pours in the staircases were unsatisfactory. The surface finish was generally fine (with lovely external walls and columns), but deteriorated significantly in the staircases, and making good rarely seemed to make an adequate improvement. Bolt hole positions were sometimes bizarre.

We encountered some classic problems. The shuttering ply was Tulsa MDO, which is absorbent and leached tannins onto the concrete surface. The surface then had to be sanded – it would have been far simpler to have used better plywood. The quality of the joinery used to form the shuttering varied: some was superb, with crisp edges and no movement during pours. Elsewhere we experienced movement and grout loss. Where we had window openings across walls the contractor had to be ingenious to ensure that the concrete was vibrated down and around the openings. Many of the services were cast in, which required careful coordination. Cone holes in some places were beautiful, but in others they were deformed and required patching, which is never as good as getting it right first time. The construction joints in the staircase ended up being filled, which was a great shame. The contractor insisted on bevelling the edges of concrete columns on the basis that right-angled edges might constitute a safety hazard. We generally used flat ply shuttering: only in the lecture theatre

Far left
Curved hand-
made brick wall
with deep reveals
onto Clarence
Street

Left
Bridge link across
De Grey Street

Below
North elevation

did we use rough board shuttering, which is actually more 'forgiving'.

Once the building was finished we really enjoyed the relationship of other finishes with the concrete. It sets off the timber, the brickwork, the Eternit, the render and the plaster beautifully, and those materials add lustre and depth to the concrete itself as it continues to 'mature'.

Concrete contractor's comments

Northfield Construction Limited is the leading reinforced concrete and associated groundworks subcontractor operating throughout the East Midlands and Yorkshire areas and was the concrete subcontractor for the new York St John University building. Northfield specialises in in-situ reinforced concrete structures for commercial, industrial and public sector clients.

The location of the ready-mixed plant is 3.3 miles from the site. Northfield was on site for a period of 30 weeks, with an average of 30 operatives on site for the first 26 weeks, reducing to ten operatives for the remaining four weeks.

Travel by minibus was organised by Northfield for 17 operatives from Leeds. A further five from Hull came together in one car, three travelled by train from Leeds and the remaining five operatives came from Wakefield in two separate cars.

Northfield used approximately 1,000 m^2 of soffit formwork at any one time for the floors, achieving approximately two to three uses per floor. These were then returned to Northfield's depot and reused as groundwork shutters. These usually last for a further five to ten uses in the ground before they are either sent back to the yard or skipped at site to be recycled.

With the benefit of hindsight, we would treat the external exposed wall on the core differently. We would pour the sandwich wall as specified in one thickness, or perhaps precast the external panels on site and post fix them.

Sustainability issues

Sustainability and reducing the need for energy use were guiding themes for this project. The BREEAM bespoke methodology was used to benchmark performance and ensure that all the various aspects of environmental sustainability were addressed, with the project achieving a Very Good rating. To reduce the need for energy, a number of passive design strategies were used in conjunction with high-efficiency mechanical and electrical plant. The very high thermal performance of fabric elements, combined with the use of exposed thermal mass for night-time cooling, helped to significantly reduce heating and cooling requirements throughout the year. This, in conjunction with high-efficiency plant, resulted in a 27.6 per cent improvement over 2006 Building Regulations CO_2 emissions levels.

Energy data

Floor area:

gross	4,403 m² (new building only)
treated	4,403 m²

Predicted annual energy consumption	*kg CO_2/m²/yr*
Gas space and water heating 92.73 MWh	4.00
Electrical usage 135.86 MWh	13.27
Total	17.27*

* Does not include non-regulated energy usage (see notes on page 256)

Part L 2006 target CO_2 emission rate	24.56 kg CO_2/m²/yr
Predicted building CO_2 emission rate	17.27 kg CO_2/m²/yr

Description of heating, lighting and energy-saving provision

Heating requirements minimised through the very high thermal performance of fabric elements and the use of very high efficiency, very low NOx emission boilers (30 mg/kWh)

Cooling requirements minimised through the use of exposed thermal mass for night cooling, solar shading and, where cooling was required, very high efficiency chillers were combined with passive chilled beams

Artificial lighting requirements minimised through the efficient lighting fittings zoned and controlled for efficiency using both time switches and photoelectric cells

Fitting out completed with energy-efficient white goods with an A+ rating under the EU Energy Efficiency Labelling Scheme

Sustainable materials

Wide use of *Green Guide to Specification* 'A-Rated' materials and 100 per cent use of FSC-certified timber

Low GWP and zero ODP insulating materials utilised

Occupant comfort and well-being:

occupant-controllable glare control system in all occupied spaces

thermal comfort enhanced through extensive design-stage analysis

excellent acoustic reverberation times achieved in teaching areas

Low water use:
WCs with low (4.5 litre) flush volumes

solenoid valves controlled by PIR detection in toilet areas

Performance rating
BREEAM Bespoke 2006 Very Good

Energy Performance Certificate CO_2 index score of 51 (C rating)

The engineer who validated the above figures was Nigel Banks of Faber Maunsell

Project team

Structural engineer	Robinson Consulting
Services engineer	Faber Maunsell
Main contractor	Morgan Ashurst
Concrete subcontractor	Northfield Construction

Building data

Number of floors	ground floor + 3 (4 storeys) at the north of the site ground floor + 2 (3 storeys) for the remainder, except adjacent to the listed building where 2 storeys
Building dimensions	4,800 m² (gross) of accommodation including listed building (around 400 m²)
Year completed	2008

Left
Slot window
into teaching
room

Simon Henley, Buschow Henley

Architecture overview

The brief sought two new halls – one for assemblies, the other for examinations – a new chapel, a music school and modern languages department, sickbay and visitor and pupil entrances.

The school is set in the Victorian and Edwardian suburb of Ealing, in West London, and its site is dominated by the presence of Ealing Abbey, which was founded by monks from Downside in 1897. Like many private schools, this one, founded in 1902 as the priory school, had grown over the years by colonising a number of houses, and putting up new buildings as and when the need arose and funds allowed. And, in a sense, this new building is no different, it is just another piece in the jigsaw, although for now it is the one that completes the puzzle.

An early design decision was to plan the new building like Russian dolls, with one hall inside the other. The inner two-storey examination hall is framed by a cage of columns and doors, which, when open, doubles the area to create enough space for assemblies. The physical form and plan of the halls invokes the image of a cloister at the very centre of the school, reflecting the culture of the Benedictines.

A new stair and lift are set in a foyer between the new hall and the dining hall, linking the new pupil entrance to the west with the new visitor entrance to the east. Inside, the cloister is used to organise both new facilities and the school estate as a whole, and addresses changes of level as great as 1.8 m.

Materially, the main concrete spaces are akin to those of a monastery. The atmosphere of the attic storey is a softer environment, with engineered timber interiors provided for the music school, which frames the chapel and garden in which it stands. The new chapel, dedicated to the Sacred Heart of Jesus, is a simple space. The plan seeks to represent a progression from external contingent realities to the autonomous idealised form of the institution. Some elements carry meaning (the halls, visitor entrance, chapel), others are abstract and functional – the symbolic elements of the school come in and out of focus.

Top right
The new visitor
entrance

Far right
External fibreC
cladding

Bottom right
The cloisters

Since the opening, the hall has been used for drama classes, play rehearsals and performances, exhibitions, receptions, concerts and fencing practice. On completion the new building was christened 'the Cloisters' by the school.

Construction details

The new structure at St Benedict's School is very simple. An in-situ cast reinforced concrete frame, with floor, columns and roof grid, is inserted between a grouping of existing school buildings. A top storey of cellular accommodation is formed of cross-laminated timber construction.

The two materials share simplicity of detailing, and their proximity in this project allowed us to compare their structural effectiveness and sustainability. Concrete has some disadvantages – high embodied energy due to its cement content, and its reuse is limited to recycling as aggregate – but these are mitigated by using low embodied energy cement replacement and recycled concrete aggregates. The carbon footprint of the material is adequately compensated by the reduction in energy demand achieved by using concrete's thermal mass.

For reinforced concrete to be plausible as a sustainable building material, it must offer more than just framing, and in this project it provides the 'total form'. The emissivity of the exposed surfaces is exploited to moderate the environment. The top-lighting to the main hall is modulated by the deep baffles of the roof grid. Columns shade into walls and vertical planes. The 'as struck' surfaces required no finishing trades. They are also robust and will weather well with continued use.

The timber superstructure, a composition of prefabricated panels forming a cross-wall structure, was assembled by lifting units directly from lorries into place and securing with screws only. The assembly could be readily demounted and reused at some later date. This dialectic between site and factory construction is not quite as clear cut as it might at first appear. The solid lumber is carbon positive, even after it has been brought by road from the forests of Eastern

Europe. It is produced in a safe factory environment and site work is all dry and limited to battery-powered hand tools.

The rain screen cladding is a 13-mm thick glassfibre reinforced panel, called fibreC, which is manufactured by an Austrian company, Reider. It is ivory in colour. The panel is largely made of cement and sand with layers of glassfibre ribbons. It is given an IBO Certificate (Austrian Environmental Label) which recognises products that meet strict biological and ecological criteria. It is also accredited with ISO 9001.

Sustainability issues

The scheme design is passive and does not depend on active systems, which would require maintenance and, ultimately, would need to be replaced. The building employs night-time cooling, engineered timber construction, a sedum roof, solar hot water collectors and strong links between inside and outside space (courts and garden courtyards). No cooling is provided as the building fabric has a high thermal mass, which assists in minimising overheating during the summer. Heating is provided for winter use, served by condensing boilers and variable volume pumping. Solar panels provide domestic hot water for the kitchen.

Where the previous building crowded the neighbouring ones, the new building steps back from the original house immediately to the east of the Cloisters, to create a two-storey courtyard garden which provides daylight to both the new building and the old at both levels. This courtyard is also integral to the natural ventilation strategy. At low level in the courtyard, louvres with integral dampers supply fresh air to a hypocaust (an approximately 1 m diameter drainage pipe) that runs beneath the central hall around its perimeter. There, the supply air is heated before it enters the hall through perimeter floor grilles. The air can be exhausted through the nine opening skylights or either of two flues that rise within the north end of the chapel overhead. One relies on stack effect; the other incorporates a fan to extract the air when the air pressure, wind and temperature conditions are less favourable. In this way, the inner hall can be fully enclosed with doors but remain naturally ventilated.

Good environmental comfort is integrated into the building fabric. The exposed heavy mass of the concrete allows the building to absorb solar gain, mitigating detrimental summer overheating. In spring, autumn and winter the thermal mass enables the building to capitalise on any beneficial solar gain, storing the heat that may gradually be released into the spaces. At night, the rooflights and flues above the main hall allow the hot, stale air that accumulates during the summer days to be flushed out and cool fresh air to be brought in at low level, readying the building for the next day's cycle.

The green sedum roof at second floor level further helps to provide thermal mass. This has a strong visual impact at second-floor level.

Overall, the impact of the new building extends far beyond its original remit.

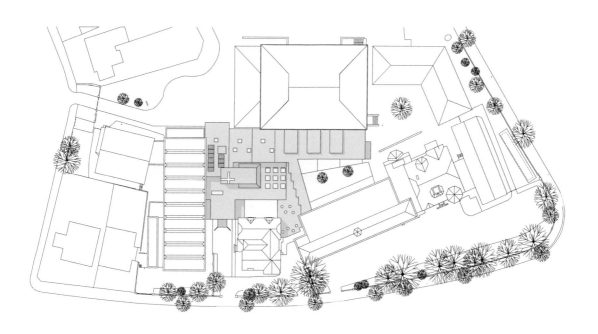

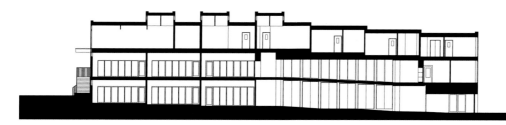

Energy data

Floor area:

gross	2,197 m²
treated	2,197 m²

Predicted annual energy consumption	*kg CO₂/m²/yr*
Space and water heating 115.2 MWh	12.94
Electrical usage 77.6 MWh	14.66
Total	27.60*

* Does not include non-regulated energy usage (see notes on page 256)

Description of heating and cooling provision

Renewable energy	solar water heating

Project team

Client	St Benedict's School
Structural engineer	Techniker
Services engineer	Furness Green
Quantity surveyor	Gleeds
Project manager	Gleeds
Main contractor	Jerram Falkus
Concrete subcontractor	O'Halloran & O'Brien Ltd

Building data

Number of floors	3
Building plan dimensions	height 11 m, length 51 m, width 28 m
Year completed	2008

Left
Cast in-situ roof

ST MARYLEBONE SCHOOL, LONDON

Philip Gumuchdjian, Gumuchdjian Architects

Architecture overview

St Marylebone School is an inner-city voluntary-aided secondary school specialising in the performing arts. The school operates on a cramped site with very little open space and had no dedicated facilities for its specialised subjects. The brief required a new gymnasium and dance studios, and a new music and art department. Without these facilities it was doubtful that the school could continue to operate in its central location and cater for its 900 students.

The school's skyward development was constrained due to its position in a conservation area, while its proximity to listed buildings and the exorbitant land values in the area prevented it from purchasing any neighbouring sites. So the new facility was built on the existing footprint as a five-storey structure with three floors below ground and two above which interlock with two open spaces at ground and basement levels. The new build creates a sense of identity for the school by transforming its unkempt public open spaces into a coherent 'collegiate' campus, linked visually to the neighbouring pocket parks.

The gymnasium, located under the new playground, is naturally ventilated and lit. One entire façade of the gymnasium is enclosed by a transparent and retractable polycarbonate wall, which opens directly onto a large open courtyard. Above ground, the new arts and music building and the existing Grade II listed buildings enclose the new playground. The building façade and the lift shaft are clad in Corten steel to echo the red brick and orange faience of the surrounding buildings.

The centrepiece of the new garden is an 18th-century stone obelisk dedicated to Charles Wesley (d.1788). The obelisk is set on the boundary of the garden and the schoolyard, and is balanced on a platform which projects high above a deep sunken courtyard that admits light to the glazed façade of the school's new subterranean gymnasium. Vines and climbers – including Virginia creeper, purple grape, crimson glory vine, honeysuckle and jasmine – planted in the adjacent beds eventually cascade over the edge of the garden walls and railings to form a green blanket on the concrete walls of the sunken courtyard. The new garden complements the existing small courtyard gardens that surround the school.

The new playground was previously an important 18th-century cemetery containing the remains of notables such as Charles Wesley, James Gibbs and George Stubbs. This greatly increased the complexity of the project, which involved Home Office approvals, archaeological investigations of over 20 per cent of the site, Church of England and English Heritage approvals for below- and above-ground works, Conservation Officer approvals, consultations with local community groups, etc. A monumental restraining structure had to be built to prop the surrounding buildings during the excavation work and the archaeological dig.

The design makes use of the costly civil engineering structure and transforms it into a coherent 'architectural' language. The detailed design, the considerate construction and the craft skills employed in the execution of the work is apparent wherever you look. The project showcases both the structure and the building fabric, which comprises in-situ concrete, solid timber and Corten steel. The choice of simple building forms, strong urban relationships and the use of weathered materials set the building firmly within its environment.

Construction details

The completed building exploits the properties of concrete – in structural terms, it provides basement retaining walls and, above ground, a structural frame. In energy terms, the thermal mass of concrete provides (especially below ground) the solid-state heart of the energy-saving system. In acoustic terms, concrete dampens and isolates activities. In aesthetic terms, the beauty of the fair-faced concrete with all its natural variations is exposed, giving the project a quality far beyond that expected in a state school project.

While the roof and floor slab of the gymnasium are insulated, the concrete retaining walls are not. The retaining walls form an integral part of the cooling strategy for the gymnasium and dance studios. Steady-state ground temperature 'charges' the thermal mass of the concrete retaining wall, helping to stabilise the internal temperature in the gymnasium. In the summer, operable windows and mechanical ventilation to the dance studios provide overnight cooling to the thermal mass of the concrete. Fresh air supply

comes from the lower courtyard, which itself is passively precooled by the cooler conditions within the courtyard.

The 'column and beam' structure starts at a massive scale below ground. The 18-m span beams incorporate threaded couplers instead of standard rebar splices, to minimise the width and depth of beams. The gable elevations of the above-ground building act as sheer walls and are expressed as the continuation of the beam and column frame in the basement. The rooftop concrete beams of the arts building mirror the gymnasium elevation and support a lightweight timber roof. Corten steel cladding was used to link the building visually with its red-brick context and to contrast with the bright orange and green colours of doors and steel staircase that signal the public areas.

Sustainability issues

The building is divided into two parts: the above-ground arts and music building and the below-ground sports and drama gymnasium. This generates an emphasis on cooling below ground and heating above. The building makes use of solar orientation, the 'coolth' of the concrete retaining structure below ground and the thermal mass of the floors above it.

The below-ground spaces rely on the thermal mass of the exposed concrete retaining structures to provide an even-tempered environment which avoids the seasonal peaks and troughs of the outside temperature. The main gymnasium requires a temperate rather than a heated environment. It is naturally ventilated from the large courtyard area, by adjustable clerestory windows and large glazed garage doors. Mechanical air extraction is limited to the changing rooms and toilets.

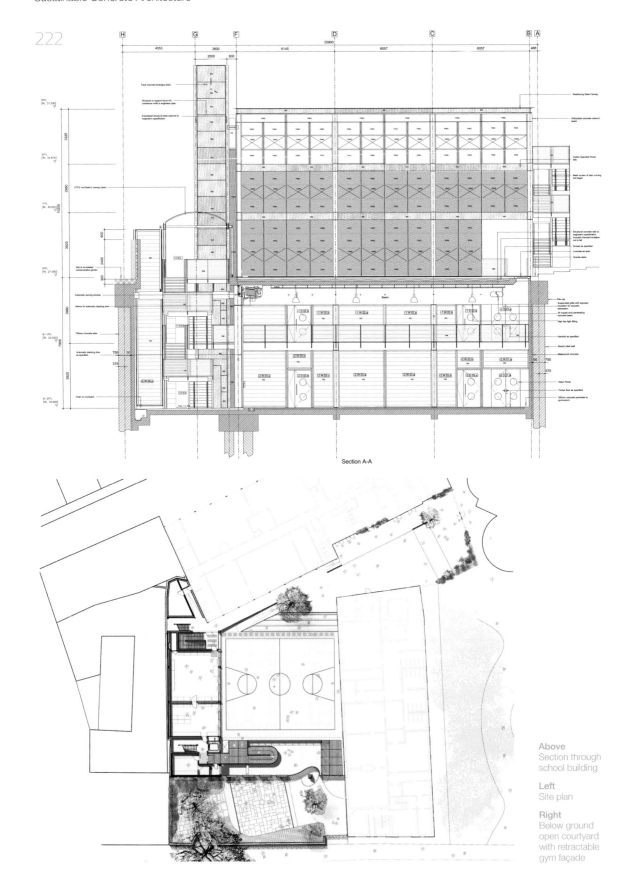

Section A-A

Above
Section through
school building

Left
Site plan

Right
Below ground
open courtyard
with retractable
gym façade

Project team

Client	St Marylebone School
Structural engineer	Alan Consibee and Associates
Services engineer	Industrial Design Associates
Quantity surveyor	Sawyer and Fisher
Main contractor	Mansell Construction Services
Concrete subcontractor	Mitchellson

Building data

Number of floors	5
Footprint of building	31 × 25 m
Total floor area of building	2,340 m²
Height of building above ground	10.2 m
Height of building below ground	7.9 m
Year completed	2007

THE POTTERROW DEVELOPMENT, EDINBURGH

John Miller, Bennetts Associates

Forty years after the curtailment of the Basil Spence scheme for Edinburgh University's city-centre campus, the first phase of a substantial new development has been completed in an area that was cleared for development in the 1960s. It is the major component of the university's new masterplan for the George Square and Bristo Square area, replacing a windswept car park with a rich mix of buildings, courtyards and reinstated street-lines.

Bennetts Associates was appointed in 2003 by the University of Edinburgh to design several new academic buildings on the city-centre site at Potterrow, Edinburgh. The appointment followed an OJEU process, which culminated in a design competition between six architects.

The brief for Potterrow was to design academic accommodation that could be constructed in phases. It is noteworthy that the university also had the foresight to build a major CHP plant to serve new buildings in the George Square area. The brief set a range of objectives, including the pursuit of BREEAM Excellent rating, creation of student- and pedestrian-friendly precincts, encouraging the area to become a central hub for the city's annual festival, and the creation of an 'atrium' type space, providing a focal point for the building and a place for large gatherings.

Planning approval was obtained in May 2005 and, to date, two-thirds of the total development has been built. This comprises the Informatics Forum for the School of Informatics and the Dugald Stewart Building for the School of Philosophy, Psychology and Language Science. The remaining phase of construction for the College of Humanities and Social Science will follow when funding is in place.

In broad terms, each of the two primary building volumes is planned round an atrium, facing each other across a shared courtyard. Their form allows them to overlap on the street edges and to vary in storey height from three floors to eight. From the inside, the buildings are rational and simple; from the outside they appear far more complex and responsive to their surroundings.

The academic space is relatively uniform and, unlike much of the university's estate, readily adaptable to potential future uses. Much of the accommodation is cellular, so the floor plates have been laid out to ensure that circulation routes engage with a variety of viewing points, open-plan break-out spaces and double-height volumes.

Construction

The construction reflects the simplicity of the plan, with a low-energy strategy based on exposed concrete slabs and air supplied from the floor and supplemented by opening windows.

Externally, the elevations play on the distinction between the stone-faced streets of Edinburgh and the need for more light-reflective surfaces to the courtyard. Different types of stone cladding and contrasting ratios of solid face to voided spaces are used to highlight the hierarchy of the different façades. Charles Street, being the major thoroughfare, has the greatest need for surface animation and articulation, while Potterrow is more regular and calming. A similar pattern of storey-height precast panels is used in the courtyard spaces; the polished white marble concrete providing a tone and atmosphere more suited to external spaces in a northern climate.

The building achieved a BREEAM Excellent rating with a score of 72 points. It was one of the first projects in Scotland to monitor BREEAM during construction. Post-completion, the building has retained the Excellent rating.

The cost of the Phase 1 buildings is £40.6 million. The cost per square metre is less than £2,600, representing very good value for money for a stone-clad, highly cellular city-centre building.

Concrete

Concrete was chosen for a number of reasons. Thermal mass was a significant benefit. At the time of tendering, the concrete superstructure was competitive on price when compared with a steel frame. It was also a straightforward solution to the problem of supporting precast concrete façade panels weighing 3–4 tonnes. The panels were fabricated in Belgium and shipped to Edinburgh. A precast solution was adopted because it provided factory control of quality and the panels could be craned directly onto the concrete frame, avoiding the use of scaffolding. The panels are supported on cast-in fixings and faced in either natural stone or polished concrete. Windows were designed to be fixed from inside the building.

The superstructure is predominantly of 275 mm deep in-situ concrete slabs supported on precast columns. The column grid is generally at 6 m centres, but this is altered to 3 m centres at the perimeter, so that the slim façade columns do not intrude on the perimeter rooms. The main columns, with an average dimension of 600 × 600 mm, would have reduced flexibility and been more intrusive. All of the columns have a fair-faced finish, whereas the soffits are painted. The grey concrete columns provide a contrast to the white walls and ceilings. Fair-faced concrete walls are also exposed in the cores and the contrast in colour and texture differentiates between the permanent nature of the cores and the lightweight partitions that form the rooms. This helps with orientation around the building.

Sustainability issues

The strategy for sustainability focuses sequentially on reducing heating loads, utilising passive design theory and using renewable energy. This is in contrast to most local authority guidelines, which primarily focus on renewable energy.

The external façade proportions the solid and glazed areas to maximise daylight but minimise solar gain. Daylight optimisation took account of the quality of natural light rather than just its quantity. The tall, high windows reflect the Georgian nature of much of Edinburgh's historic architecture, giving varied levels of daylight across the cellular rooms that users occupy. An efficient glazing ratio of 60 per cent was arrived at and a high-performance glass specified where necessary, with additional solar shading on south and west façades.

A plan width of 13.5 m with high floor-to-ceiling heights of 2.87 m helps with the application of passive design principles. The atrium volume is used both as a thermal buffer and a return air path, without the need for return air fans and ductwork.

Right
View from the
roof terrace

Below left
Section through
the Forum

Below right
Charles Street
elevation

The exposed reinforced concrete slab soffits provide significant thermal mass and free cooling of the building. This has been fully exploited by the use of night-time ventilation. The other advantage that exposed thermal mass offers is generally higher floor-to-soffit heights for the same floor-to-floor dimension. This has resulted in lighter, airier and more flexible spaces, which also avoid the undifferentiated sameness of suspended ceilings.

Both precast and in-situ post-tensioned and reinforced floor slab options were considered. In the completed building, a combination of precast columns and in-situ flat slabs was chosen because the high quality of finish of the columns, combined with the cost-effective simplicity of the slabs. Proprietary metal falsework was used for constructing the in-situ slabs and wall cores. The contact face was shuttered using phenolic film-faced plywood.

A post-tensioned concrete flat slab had been considered, but the potential saving in overall slab depth was not sufficient to justify the extra cost. Typical floor slabs were conventionally reinforced, except for the large spans over the meeting rooms which were designed as post-tensioned coffered slabs.

Displacement ventilation was installed throughout with thermal recovery at rooftop plant-room level. Air is supplied at temperatures close to normal conditions throughout the year. Opening windows also supplement ventilation and provide enhanced user control.

Initially, natural ventilation was to be relied upon for the perimeter offices. However, this was re-evaluated post RIBA Work Stage C, when it was decided to employ the same system for all offices. The advantages of this are reliability, future-proofing and simplification of both controls and façade detailing for airtightness.

WC flushing utilises rainwater, which is stored in basement storage tanks. Low-flush toilets, spray taps and leak detection in areas of cold-water services are all employed to further reduce water usage. Energy use by artificial lighting is digitally controlled and managed. Daylight levels are sensed to allow automatic dimming and PIR is utilised to provide an auto shut-off facility within user-programmable constraints.

Low-carbon technology

The building was designed in advance of the local authority's requirements for on-site renewables for this size of development. However, from the outset the building was able to make use of the installation of high-efficiency, low-CO_2, low-NO_x boilers within the campus-wide CHP plant provided by the university. The building itself therefore has no boilers, and radiators are fed directly from the neighbouring CHP plant. In the summer, this same facility provides a cheap and efficient source of chilled water that the building also utilises for 'coolth' on the hottest days. The CHP system has been estimated to reduce CO_2 emissions by a further 30 per cent over and above the passive and active measures.

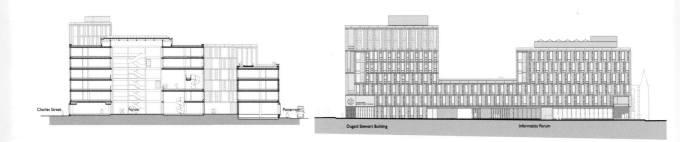

Energy data

Floor area:

gross	16,528 m²
treated	12,940 m²

Predicted annual CO$_2$ emissions	*kg CO$_2$/m²/yr*
Space and water heating (gas)	16.8
Regulated electrical usage	18.6
Unregulated electrical usage	14.0
IT/special electrical usage	14.0
Renewables	−13.0
Total	50.4

Description of heating and cooling provision

Passive and active – gas-fired shared CHP plant provides both heat to the radiators and chilled water

Ventilation – mixed mode, with displacement ventilation within the floor void supplemented by opening windows

Solar shading – small percentage of external fixed shading and low-emissivity glass as the building is shaded by a neighbouring tall building to the south

Airtight construction – airtightness testing and thermal imaging was carried out. Phase 1 achieved 6.5 m³/h/m² at 50 Pa

Project team

Client	University of Edinburgh
Structural engineer	Buro Happold
Services engineer	Buro Happold
Quantity surveyor	Turner and Townsend Cost Management
Main contractor	Balfour Beatty Construction Limited
Precast columns/stairs	Creagh Concrete Products Ltd
Precast cladding	Loveld

Building data

Number of floors	3–8
Building dimensions:	
plan depth	13.5 and 12.0 m
column grid	6 × 6 m
floor-to-floor height	3.6 m
Year completed	2008

NATURUM HÖGA KUSTEN, SWEDEN

Ulla Antonsson, White Architects

Architecture overview

Naturum is a concept for a series of visitor centres connected to nature reserves, World Heritage Sites or National Parks throughout Sweden.

The earth's bedrock contains a strong residual force that is very slowly raising the land out of the sea. This force was created when the earth's crust was pressed down by the colossal weight of glaciers during the last ice age. The rate of uplift at Höga Kusten (the High Coast) in the north of Sweden is the largest in the world, which is why it was selected by UNESCO as a World Heritage Site. This is also the reason behind the decision to open a Naturum in this area.

The vision of the building is to create a direct understanding of the special features of the rock. Alongside the majestic mountain Skuleberget there is a cut into the land's surface. The top section is lifted off to reveal the innards of the mountain. The remaining space becomes the building, in which answers to the site's mysteries can be found.

The effects of the inland glaciers and presence of the bedrock are the key visual elements on the site. These elements are reflected in the choice of the main building materials: the natural rock in the concrete of the roof, and the ice in the glass façade. The mountain itself is the horizon alongside the E4 motorway. The glade between road and mountain forms the site. The open surface is a kind of meadowland, with neatly cut paths and signposts signalling the site's infrastructure.

The building is a simple rectangular box, nestling into the ground with just one long façade visible. The interior of the building is an open space where large, freestanding volumes are placed like erratic blocks in a landscape. These blocks break through the roof and create a distinct silhouette against the backdrop of forest and mountain.

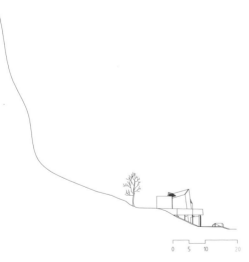

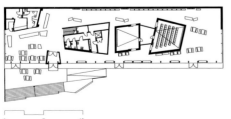

The entrance, with reception and restaurant, is the social heart of the building, leading straight into the exhibition room or via steps to the roof and then up onto the mountain. The interior of the building is characterised by its two long sides, the inner darker gallery with a back wall in prefabricated concrete and the outer long façade made completely of glass.

Along the glass façade, which provides excellent scenic views, is the social space where visitors can eat, shop or study. The permanent exhibition is staged in the inner gallery, where the light can be controlled more easily. The exhibition area can be expanded or contracted as desired. Temporary exhibitions and the auditorium are placed in the freestanding volumes.

The building and its fittings match the grey tones of the rock and mountain; the exhibition, however, is in complete contrast. Like a well-stocked sweet shop, the exhibition offers a mixture of all the clearest nuances in the colour

Left
Dramatic
illumination of the
roof structures

spectrum. The exhibition displays the 13,000-year history of Höga Kusten and the land uplift, which at this moment is 273 m and rising!

Construction details

Concrete can be seen as a modern interpretation of rock and stone. Various applications of concrete are used in Naturum, corresponding to different aesthetic considerations as well as economic and technical needs.

The floor consists of cast in-situ concrete, which has been waxed to give it a smooth finish. Rough, prefabricated concrete has been used for the visible back wall and the hidden roof construction. The ceiling consists of cement boards, with large sheets of wood-wool cement boards functioning as acoustic dampers. The load-bearing pillars along the building's front are made of precast concrete. They are pulled back slightly from the glass façade to allow a seamless mantle of glass.

The walls of the freestanding volumes are clad in cement boards, which continue through the roof. The seams between the boards form a pattern inspired by the natural fissures and cracks in the rock. On the inside of the volumes, the walls and floors are clad in natural wood panels, to give a soft impression as a contrast to the hard surfaces in the rest of the building. The roof is a transparent glass construction that provides a stunning view towards the top of the mountain.

All technical installations are hidden within the walls and floor slabs.

Sustainability issues

The project has a strong focus on sustainability, led by an environmental manager during the design and construction phase. A specific environmental programme has been performed, with targets for sustainable building materials, healthy indoor climate and low energy use.

The region has a cold climate during winter and is warm in summer. The situation of the building, in the lea of the mountain, combined with the thermal mass of the concrete makes it possible to create a steady indoor climate all year round, decreasing the need for energy for heating. The large glass façade faces east, which makes it possible to benefit from the solar energy that can be stored within the massive concrete construction.

The energy for any heating and hot water is produced by renewables, using two biofuel pellet boilers and a solar panel. The solar panel has a unique design and function, as it produces both hot water and electricity. During the summer, the solar panel will cover the hot water and heating requirements, with no need for the boiler to be used. The heating distribution system consists of radiant underfloor heating and, because renewable energy is used for heating, the CO_2 emissions are very low.

The ventilation is provided by a mechanical ventilation system with heat recovery. The skylights in the roof allow natural daylight into the interior of the building. The light is also efficiently reflected by the surface of the concrete. All artificial lighting consists of low-energy fittings and T5 fluorescent lamps. Daylight adjustment and presence detectors keep the electricity use low.

The building has been built with a relatively limited range of materials, which decreases the use of natural resources. The materials are mainly stone, concrete, tiles and wood, which have low environmental impact and long-term durability.

To reduce the natural impact on the landscape the existing ground vegetation has been grown to cover the roof, keeping alive the biodiversity in the area.

Right
Interior gallery
space

Energy data

Gross floor area	825 m²
Predicted annual energy consumption	*kWh/m²/yr*
Heating building	71
Electricity usage	24
Energy production solar panels	–9
Lighting	<10

Project team

Client	West Norrland County Administrative Board
Architect	White Architects
Structural engineer	Stiba
Services engineers	Bengt Dahlgren, Oveko Elkonsult
Project manager	West Norrland County Administrative Board
Main contractor	PEAB

Building data

Number of floors	1
Year completed	2007

Helen Newman, Glenn Howells Architects

Architecture

The design for the Theatre and Arts Centre in Armagh, aka 'The Market Place', was the result of an international competition which the practice won in 1996. The design was chosen from 70 competition entries. The building was officially opened by the Prince of Wales in a Millennium ceremony in April 2000.

The new arts complex replaced the old one, which had been destroyed in a terrorist attack in the 1980s. The project had the potential to bring together different communities and create a 'living room' for Armagh and for the region surrounding it, where anybody could go, day or night, to socialise with other people. The key elements of the brief included a 400-seat main auditorium, a 120-seat studio theatre, two art studios and an art gallery, meeting rooms, offices, dressing rooms and café-bar.

From an urban design perspective, the site provided the potential to create an active edge to the steeply sloping Market Square leading up to St Patrick's cathedral and to link with the nearby St Patrick's Trian Visitor Centre. There is also a historic precedent for specifying the local limestone to clad public buildings in Armagh. Armagh is recognised as one of the finest Georgian cities in the British Isles, largely due to Archbishop Richard Robinson's vision to transform the city into an ecclesiastical capital.

Rather than competing for prominence with St Patrick's cathedral, the new building is tucked into the hillside, with the large volume of the main auditorium located at the lowest point of the site. The impact of this extensive element was further reduced by utilising a stage loft rather than a fly tower to ensure that the views of the cathedral were maintained.

The space requirements within the building fall into two distinct categories – highly serviced inward-looking spaces, such as auditoria and gallery spaces, and outward-looking spaces such as the entrance foyer and café-bar. The inward-looking spaces are treated as solid 'boxes' that are separated by lighter translucent glazed elements. The 'boxes' are arranged around a central street that links the Market Square and St Patrick's Trian Visitor Centre.

Right
Foyer interior

Bottom left
Entrance canopy

Bottom right
Theatre foyer café
space

The site's level changes are used to advantage in the scheme to create dramatic public spaces over three floors with a generous double-height entrance canopy and colonnade to the Market Square entrance.

The choice of building material was a key early decision that would inform the detail design at every level and communicate the building concept. This concept of solid boxes linked by a glazed street led to an in-depth investigation of the local Armagh limestone and architecture. We worked with Robert McKinstrey, a leading Ulster architect, to undertake this research. The quality of the local limestone and precise detailing of narrow joints in architect Frank Johnston's buildings was particularly impressive. These buildings had been taken to a level of detail where the fireplace and chimneys were lost in the depth of the walls.

Precast concrete or modern cast stone was investigated and samples developed with suppliers to demonstrate its ability to be finished in a variety of colours and textures to emulate the local limestone. Precast concrete offered many advantages to the scheme, both in terms of flexibility, to be used internally and externally, and to provide thermal mass to reduce energy usage. The structural and planning grid of the building as it developed was coordinated to precast panel sizes. The floor-to-floor heights of the internal central concourse were therefore exactly six panels high. The precast cladding panels generate a horizontal module of 1.2 m to produce a structural grid of 7.2 × 3.6 m.

The qualities of the colour and texture of the local limestone, with its slight heather tone and sparkle, were not easy to match. Samples were collected from many suppliers all over Europe to test for quality, performance and weathering. The final mix of coarse Derby limestone and Spanish 'dolomite fines' was carefully tested against the Armagh limestone. The smooth, precast ashlar walls with 5-mm thick joints express this planar geometry really well. Both from the internal street and externally, these stone 'boxes' are clearly legible.

The visibility of the roof elements of the scheme from above and below was an important consideration in achieving a high-quality building that did not appear overscaled. The roof had a number of functions to perform in addition to providing a simple covering. These included permitting indirect daylight into the foyer and internal street due to the constraints of the steeply sloping site, the integration of artificial lighting and carrying the drainage and services within a shallow depth.

We worked closely with our precast concrete supplier, Histon Concrete, to develop the solution for the roof. A thorough design process using mock-ups, models, computer visualisations and sun-path models and 57 roofing panel prototypes led to the final result – a polished precast panel 7.2 m × 3.6 m × 350 mm deep, with the same mix as the walls. This ensured a building with a continuous surface of material between wall and roof, visually unbroken between inside and out.

The panels integrate with downlighters, wall washers, stainless steel rainwater disposal systems and fire detectors. The integral louvres provide solar shading to the double-glazed rooflights, but reflect indirect light into the foyer below.

The precast panels are supported on 350 mm diameter cast stone columns, each up to 8.1 m long with four steel dowels on each column supporting the corners of four slabs. To obtain the quality of finish, a floor polisher fitted with diamond abrasive pads was used for the soffit and a handheld electric polisher accessed smaller areas. To obtain a progressively smoother polished finish, coarse abrasive pads followed by finer pads were used.

Heating and cooling provision

The building makes use of passive low-energy design principles in terms of enhanced fabric performance and thermal mass, and incorporates a fully engineered heating and cooling solution, using the TermoDeck ventilation and environmental control system.

The building incorporates high levels of thermal insulation (the fabric is designed to a U-value of 0.2 W/m²K) and achieves low air permeability. The TermoDeck system utilises mechanical ventilation to draw air through the building structure, which is composed of standard hollow-core concrete planks. This maintains the internal comfort conditions in the main spaces (auditorium, studio theatre and galleries), making use of the thermal mass of the fabric and, in so doing, avoiding the need for a conventional wet heating or cooling distribution system.

Right
Underside of
external canopy

Below left
View from the
Market Square

Below right
Plan sketch

The building has, in effect, two systems. The first uses the physical exposure of the thermal mass of the concrete walls and roof to stabilise temperature fluctuations.

The use of thermal mass to aid environmental comfort is well documented. The principle is to use the large thermal capacity of the exposed heavyweight materials to moderate the internal climate. The index adopted by CIBSE for thermal environments is the dry resultant temperature. The dry resultant temperature in a space has both radiant and convective components. Even though the air temperature in a space (the convective component) may rise, the actual comfort conditions are also dependent on the mean radiant temperature, and if this remains low (because the thermally massive walls and floors have a long time lag before warming up), then the space will remain comfortable.

The second system uses fan-assisted fresh air that is cooled as it passes through the hollow precast concrete floor planks. On a hot day, with a temperature of 25 °C outside, the air will have cooled to approximately 19 °C by the time it is delivered to beneath the seats in the auditorium.

In the summer, the precast planks are precooled by night-time purging of the system, when the external air temperature drops. This allows 'coolth' to be stored in the concrete structure for use the next day. The principle for integrating precast concrete planks with the environmental system was originally developed by Loa Andersson in Sweden. At an early stage, The Market Place design team saw the opportunity to apply this innovative technique to the project. It was the first project to adopt this technology in Northern Ireland at the time. The coordination process was made easier by the fact the design team had already used this technology on another theatre project, in Hereford.

The mechanically operated fan is the only running cost in the system. The whole system is managed by a BMS, which monitors and controls the internal temperatures.

Sustainability issues

At The Market Place, energy metering has not been installed to monitor or verify the energy consumption of the environmental systems specified. However, we know from similar projects that the TermoDeck solution can be very energy efficient and typically consumes substantially less energy (and therefore generates lower CO_2 emissions) compared with conventional systems. With hindsight, dedicated metering could have been installed to monitor the environmental systems in order to give the client and design team specific feedback data.

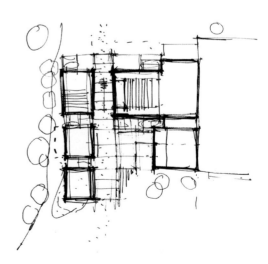

Energy data

Gross floor area	4,500 m²

Predicted annual energy consumption	*kg CO$_2$/m²/yr*
Space and water heating 330 MWh	14.06
Electrical usage 270 MWh	25.80
Total	39.86*

* Does not include non-regulated energy usage (see notes on page 256)

Project team

Client	Armagh City and District Council
Structural engineer	Dewhurst McFarlane
Services engineer	Fulcrum Consulting
Acoustic consultant	John Wyckham Associates
Landscape architect	Nicholas Pearson Associates
Main contractor	Gilbert-Ash
Precast walls and roof	Histon Concrete
Precast slabs	Breton Precast

Building data

Floors	5
Total floor area	4,020 m²
Year completed	2000

THE NEW HERBARIUM AND LIBRARY WING, ROYAL BOTANIC GARDENS, KEW

Lara Michael, Edward Cullinan Architects

The Royal Botanic Gardens at Kew hold one of the world's largest and most important collections of samples of plant diversity. However, many are stored in overcrowded and unsuitable accommodation, which poses a threat to their continued survival. It is for these reasons that Kew wished to build a new wing as an extension to the herbarium.

The new herbarium building is a large repository for the national archive of dried and preserved plant and seed specimens. For more than a hundred years the ever-growing collection has been housed in period buildings with natural ventilation and widely fluctuating temperature and humidity. Key aspects of the brief were to introduce stability into the environmental conditions, to ensure temperature levels that would resist animal infestation and to provide secure fire-resistant containment, with a design life to match the existing buildings. These requirements led the team very quickly to the conclusion that concrete would really be the only sustainable long-term solution to meet these objectives.

The new wing to the herbarium and library provides 5,000 m² of increased storage space in controlled climatic environments, a state-of-the-art pest decontamination unit with walk-in freezer rooms chilled to temperatures of minus 40 °C, north-lit study spaces for viewing and illustrating the collection and space to provide reading rooms and further study spaces. In addition, the new facility provides better access for large groups to gather and to be taken on tours without disturbing the scientists at work, and it meets all the design criteria of respecting and maintaining Kew Gardens' World Heritage Site status while protecting the TROBI champion trees on the site.

The design

The core of the new wing is a four-storey, brick-clad, concrete frame treasure-box containing the precious specimens, which are stored within ceiling-high, purpose-made mobile shelves. These archive rooms are kept at a constant 15 °C – a temperature that is cool enough to prevent any herb pests from reproducing. As the contents are best examined in daylight, these areas are located on the perimeter of each floor and screened by an undulating timber façade on one side, brickwork on another and trellised with greenery that clings to the concrete treasure-box.

Right
Shadows cast by the *brise soleil* move across the south-facing offices on sunny days

Far right
Study bays are provided in the undulating corridor to the west of the archives, which are within the brick-clad treasure-box

Below
View towards the north elevation of the drum. The timber rainscreen cladding undulates with the wavy corridor along the west elevation

The main workspace for graphics, editing and computer staff is located on the top floor, within the large open-plan concrete vaulted roof.

The circular drum entrance and staircase link the new building to the existing herbarium, and provide orientation and reception facilities for the herbarium, library, arts and archives building as a whole. The public places, such as the reading room, the open-plan botanist room and training room, are gathered in the drum. The finely cast concrete main staircase to the rear of the drum curves up and around the fair-faced lift shaft walls to enjoy the warmth from south-facing glazing, while the collection is protected from direct sunlight.

The in-situ concrete structure was chosen to support the heavy rolling loads from the shelving racks, and the floor soffits stabilise the temperature fluctuations while the thermal mass helps to maintain the internal temperature at 15 °C. Natural materials, such as carpets and timber, are ideal breeding grounds for pests, so choosing clean hard finishes, such as a concrete topping to the floors and fair-faced concrete walls, exposed soffits and fair-faced blockwork walls finished with a dust sealer, became an obvious choice. The concrete topping also allowed us to exploit its thermal mass by incorporating heating pipes within its build-up to heat the naturally ventilated spaces.

We wanted the fair-faced concrete to be of an excellent quality and invited David Bennett to join the design team to produce the visual concrete specification and to oversee all the site work. This specification focused on the concrete mix, the formwork and all aspects of concrete workmanship.

The site is within a conservation area and is a World Heritage Site. The listed buildings of the existing herbarium, along with the positioning of the new drum, now frame a southern courtyard with an existing hornbeam tree in the centre. Colours in the original bricks on these buildings are picked up in the new wing, with the colour of Kew Palace influencing the choice of the striking red brick, laid in Flemish bond.

We originally wanted a green roof and to collect the rainwater but the client was not keen on the maintenance involved. A high priority in the client's brief was for a robust roof

with absolutely no possibility of leaks. With a precedent of zinc on the roof to part of the existing herbarium, we specified Rheinzink. We used SpectraPlan for the waterproof membrane on roof areas and Ruberoid at ground areas because of their guarantees.

One of our aims was to try to source materials locally and so we used locally grown western red cedar for our cladding. By lifting the timber cladding one floor off the ground, and with careful detailing to ensure adequate ventilation and to allow rainwater to run off, and providing end-grain protection in terms of preservatives to the trellis and zinc caps to the cladding, we anticipate that the timber cladding will have a life of at least 50 years, as TRADA experts suggest.

As the building is primarily climate-controlled, most areas of the building are sealed, so logically we relished the idea of floor-to-ceiling glass. We wanted to minimise the number of joints, which carry the possibility of failure, and found that the Schüco system provided us with what we wanted without having to design bespoke mullions. We have tried to make the most of the views of the beautiful trees and the river beyond. The wavy corridor accommodating study spaces undulates around the TROBI champion trees to the north of the drum. Botanists and other researchers are now able to work with views out through the leaves of these trees.

The interiors are minimal. We have used Sto acoustic recycled-glass suspended ceiling boards with a trowel-finish in the flat ceiling areas and a sprayed-finish on the suspended curved acoustic panels in the vaulted space. Where access is required, we have opted for ceiling planks that have a similar texture to the Sto boards. In the circulation spaces we have chosen to use a polished plaster finish which is tough so that decorating maintenance is reduced. In keeping with our pallet of natural colours, we have opted for warmer metals, such as bronze, and the dark chocolate brown and bronze metals of the interior are a clean contrast to the pale umber of the exterior mullion caps.

Externally, we were fortunate to have the ideal client to choose a selection of plants to climb up the trellis, and consideration is being given to displaying the collection of ivy on Ferry Lane wall, opposite the large ground-floor window to the east.

The building fabric

For almost any building the construction of the building fabric and the design of the façade have a much more profound effect on the internal environment and energy efficiency than the design of any of the engineering systems it contains. Although it is possible to design heating plant (or air-conditioning systems) to deal with high heat losses in winter (or high solar gains in summer), the comfort levels are rarely as good as those that are achieved when the building fabric has been designed to shield the occupants from these two extremes.

The objective in winter is to maintain a warm, condensation-free environment with minimal consumption of energy for heating and lighting. In order to achieve this, the building fabric must be designed to minimise heat losses, to exploit passive solar gain and to maximise the use of available daylight.

The parameters having the most effect on the winter performance of a building are:

— insulation levels – measured by the U-value

— thermal mass – achieved by exposing the concrete frame

— infiltration levels – determined by the airtightness of the building construction

— fenestration and solar control – useful for providing passive gain and natural daylight, but with a heat loss penalty which must be minimised.

Implementing the lower U-values can reduce the fabric heat loss by almost one-third. Improving the airtightness of the building can also make a significant difference to the heat loss.

Construction

Long-term reductions in terms of CO_2 emissions were addressed during the consideration of the design approach. Reducing CO_2 emissions in the short term was achieved by reducing embodied CO_2 through recycling formwork, minimising waste and reducing the delivery transport emissions by sourcing materials locally.

Reuse of formwork

The design consists of straight fair-faced walls and soffits and curved walls and a vaulted roof. The formwork shutters for the basement walls were reused seven to eight times. The columns and sheer walls had between ten and fifteen reuses and were refaced where required. The flat soffits were less efficient as there are a number of deep down-stand beams and the bolt hole layouts meant that cut pieces of plywood could not be reused once they had been drilled. New plywood was brought in for the fair-faced vaulted soffit on the third floor, but generally the soffit sheets were reused between three and four times.

Prior to starting on site, our structural engineer, Buro Happold, reviewed whether the floor slabs could be post-tensioned to assist in the speed and safety of the construction by trying to eliminate all of the down-stand beams, but this proved not to be practical.

The birch ply shutters for the curved wall at stair 3 were reused three times, and the lift-shaft shutters were used four times, i.e. reused at each floor level.

There were two sets of birch ply shutters for the main stair beam/balustrade, and these were used three times each. They were sanded and resealed after each use. New top and bottom shutters had to be cut for each pour because each beam is slightly different in geometry since the floor-to-floor levels were not regularised as the drum floor levels were tying-in to the existing building.

All timber and plywood used was FSC-certified. However, the timber came from Scandinavia and the plywood from Latvia, all supplied by Laver Timberworld, based in Reading, Bucks. At the end of the project all reusable timber and plywood was transferred to other projects for use in ground beams by the concrete subcontractor, Toureen Mangan. Unusable pieces were placed in dedicated timber skips for removal from site by the main contractor, Willmott Dixon.

The requirement for back screwing the wall shutters to achieve a fair-faced concrete surface free of nail and screw heads meant that twice as many plywood sheets were required for each formwork panel. This added to labour time and costs for the initial shutter construction, but this contingency was considered at the preconstruction stage

Left
The southern stair follows the same design principles as
the concrete stair within the drum – precast treads are
cantilevered off the curved in-situ concrete wall

Middle
Finely cast concrete detail, where the top of the balustrade
meets the lift shaft of the stair within the drum – the bronze
handrail contrasts with the concrete balustrade

Bottom
Main staircase leading from the ground floor inside the drum

and built into the plan. The wall construction would have
been quicker without the precise tie bolt layouts, enabling
the use of proprietary panel systems with preformed tie
holes; however, this would have resulted in a greater amount
of remedial work, the infilling of unwanted bolt holes and
extra cost.

The concrete materials were sourced as follows:

— cement from Rugby, Warwickshire (overnight by road)

— limestone aggregate from Shepton Mallet, Somerset (rail
transport)

— sand from Dagenham, Kent (by road).

Ready-mixed concrete was delivered from London Concrete,
which is based two miles from the site at Kew.

Mechanical and electrical services design

The cellular design of the building allows for different control
regimes for temperature and humidity to accommodate the
different types of material that are being stored – from plant
specimens to rare books and illustrations – and each archive
has a separate control system in the form of a closed control
unit.

The building is air-conditioned using a ground source heat
pump system linked to open loop boreholes in the grounds
of the building, which provide a source for heating and
cooling throughout the year. A key requirement of the project
was that the archive rooms should have a high degree
of thermal mass to provide stability and control and to
minimise peak loads during the occasional periods when the
herbarium or library archive rooms are heavily used.

The use of concrete allowed us to minimise the size of the
air-conditioning systems, which control both temperature
and humidity, as the thermal mass absorbs fluctuations
in heat gain and prevents the temperature from swinging
too rapidly as loads are imposed or removed. The
hygroscopic (water absorbing) nature of the material also
helps to attenuate fluctuations in humidity, once the initial
construction moisture has been released.

Further, the high thermal mass allowed us to incorporate less redundancy into the plant and equipment than would otherwise have been required. It is envisaged that, in a situation where an individual climate control unit within an archive store malfunctioned, the store area would be isolated for access temporarily by restricting entry and the lighting turned off to minimise heat gains. In this situation the high levels of insulation and the high thermal mass of the store will maintain adequate conditions within the structure for a period of one or two days while the equipment is repaired.

This characteristic of concrete, its ability to absorb heat gains, although not immediately appearing to be 'sustainable', is therefore very much a key factor in allowing us to reduce the size of the plant, the operating hours of the plant and the duplication of systems, and allows us to use considerably fewer resources in both the construction and the operation of the building.

By any definition, a building that does more with less is more sustainable than an alternative solution. There is clearly some penalty to be paid for the embodied CO_2 in the concrete itself; however, it was felt that the combination of the environmental benefits and the benefits in terms of fire suppression and security for this very important archive, and from the reduction in resources and energy use, more than compensated for the decision to use concrete throughout the building.

Sustainability issues

The building design achieves a 23 per cent improvement on the target emissions rates based on the 2006 Building Regulations Part L, which has lower targets than the 2002 Part L which was current at the time of design. This result was due partly to the client's BREEAM rating targets to improve U-values by 15 per cent, and partly to the use of the ground source cooling installation. Edward Cullinan Architects' design of the building fabric allowed the U-value improvement to range between 10 and 50 per cent improvement, depending on which element was considered; the drum roof, the insulated rendered soffits and the timber rainscreen cladding scored the best improvements.

Airtightness

To comply with Building Regulations, the 'On-Site Whole Building Air Tightness Test' to CIBSE TM 23 needs to achieve a minimum of 10 m³/h per m² at a test pressure of 50 Pa. However, to achieve the client's BREEAM targets, this figure needed to be improved by 25 per cent. Attention to designing the detail between the cladding materials and the junctions with the roof, soffits and floor focused on an airtight construction. The details are bespoke, so achieving good results in the post-construction airtightness test also relied on the contractor's ability to build the details well.

The on-site tests achieved 5.07 m³/h per m², which is a 50 per cent improvement on Building Regulations and a 25 per cent improvement on the design's target figure.

Energy data

Gross and treated floor area	5,000 m²

Predicted annual CO_2 emissions	*kg CO_2/m²/yr*
Space and water heating	3.12
Regulated electrical usage	8.85
Total	11.97*

* Does not include non-regulated energy usage (see notes on page 256)

Our services consultant, Atelier Ten, carried out as-built calculations and the building is consuming 15 per cent less energy annually than our aim. The target annual CO_2 emission was 14.10 kg/m²; however, the building is achieving 11.95 kg/m².

Description of heating and cooling provision
Improving the U-values over and above Building Regulations, using the concrete's thermal mass, orientating the rooflight to the north, and orientating the windows using careful solar studies and by providing fixed *brise soleil* to the south-facing glazing, have passively contributed to reducing energy consumption and CO_2 emissions.

Providing night-time cooling and natural ventilation to the ground floor and third floor spaces, where pest control is not as high a priority as it is for other areas in the brief, are among the active measures to reduce energy consumption. The heating and cooling is provided by GSHPs and both air-handling units are fitted with a thermal wheel for heat recovery, and the unit controlling humidity is also fitted with a moisture-recovery wheel (or entropy wheel). These features have also actively contributed to reducing energy consumption and CO_2 emissions.

Project team

Client	Royal Botanic Gardens, Kew
Structural engineer	Buro Happold
Service engineer	Atelier Ten
Quantity surveyor	Fanshawes
Landscape architect	Chris Blandford Associates
Concrete consultant	David Bennett
Main contractor	Willmott Dixon
Concrete subcontractor	Toureen Mangan

Building data

New wing	5 floors
Dimensions	width 14 m, length 45 m
Year completed	2009

DARWIN CENTRE, NATURAL HISTORY MUSEUM, LONDON

Anna Maria Indrio, C. F. Møller Architects

Architecture overview

C. F. Møller Architects was chosen for the commission to design the second phase of the Darwin Centre in 2001 after an international competition. The brief called for responses to the need to preserve the collection and provide laboratory space while offering unprecedented access to the public. We responded by providing a compelling and strong architectural identity for the largest extension ever undertaken by the Natural History Museum.

The 'cocoon' we devised clearly symbolises the world-class collection of specimens set within a protective shell that not only contains, but also represents the vast entomological and botanical collections of the Natural History Museum. While providing essential laboratory, administration and storage facilities, the second phase of the Darwin Centre also completes the western section of the Natural History Museum estate, linking the existing buildings and enhancing and clarifying the circulation patterns within the museum for both staff and visitors.

The Darwin Centre improves and transforms the existing buildings into something more than the sum of its parts. The new building creates a dialogue between the existing and new buildings, forming a set of dynamic, spatial experiences that bridge the past, present and future for the museum.

The project is intended to manage the difference in scale and architectural approach between the original landmark Alfred Waterhouse museum building and the more contemporary addition of the first phase of the Darwin Centre. It also serves as a landmark building in its own right, with the 30 m glass curtain wall partially veiling the solid mass of the cocoon within an extraordinary atrium space.

Public access to the scientific core of the second phase of the Darwin Centre takes the form of a visitor route up and through the cocoon, overlooking the science laboratories across the atrium and the adjacent collection areas within the cocoon, while not compromising the building's core activities of protection, preservation and research.

At the top of the cocoon, the visitor enters a cavernous space where the boundaries between the inner and outer worlds of scientific research are blurred. The visitor can experience the Darwin Centre as a compelling and interactive learning space, observing the scientific and research activities without interrupting scientific work in progress.

The scale of the cocoon form is such that it cannot be seen in its entirety from any one position. This emphasises the endless nature of the continually expanding collection, giving the visitor a tangible understanding of the vastness of the collections contained within.

Perhaps most importantly, we wished to create an inherently sustainable building, through the quality of its construction and detail, that will not only prove useful, but also hopefully be loved and cherished well beyond its 60 year design life.

Construction details

The irregular geometry of the cocoon shape is derived by minimising the footprint to increase the public areas at the lower public levels and expanding higher up to accommodate the collection, while providing enough clearance for cleaning and maintenance of the cocoon surface and atrium glazing. Sprayed concrete proved to be a cost-effective solution to create this complex form, whose continuous construction avoided inaccessible areas for cleaning, as required by the rigorous pest management regime set out by the museum.

Sprayed concrete gave the team considerable freedom to create an amorphous shape that achieved the desired form. The structural steel or conventionally formed concrete wall options were limited by the need for modularity and repetition. While the form is complex, the construction is simple, with an orthogonal arrangement of reinforcement bars that were bent to shape on site.

The continuous sprayed reinforced concrete shell is used as a load-bearing structure and, as such, is the largest of its kind above ground. Meanwhile, its thermal mass maintains temperatures within the collection area environments, while ensuring flexibility of services distribution.

The shell is typically 250 mm thick and thickens at the base due to higher loading and increased curvature of the surface.

As the floor slabs are conventionally cast, the reinforcement at the perimeter is turned up and down to meet an orthogonal cage of steel bars.

By using a simple system of scaffold tubes, survey points could be taken from the Rhino 3D model and transcribed on site approximately every metre to set out the precise form. Expanded metal mesh was then fitted to the steel rebar framework and a 250 mm thick layer of concrete was sprayed by subcontractor Shotcrete to create a 3,500 m² raw concrete surface.

Deviations in the surface were highlighted with survey data fed back into the Rhino model. Any areas falling outside the agreed tolerances were addressed with a final render coat. To this was applied 50 mm of rigid insulation using adhesive and over 16,000 insulation fasteners. This, in turn, was covered with a layer of reinforcing mesh bedded into a render basecoat ready to accept the polished plaster finish.

With such a large surface area and with variations in temperature within the vast atrium, the polished plaster has to be allowed to expand and contract. A solution was devised of intersecting 'silk threads' that wrap the surface, which were set out onto the 3D model by using the parameters derived from the openings and niches, maximum field areas of plaster and minimum angle of intersections. The 'threads' were then transcribed onto the surface using data from an 'as built' Rhino model. A custom cutting machine was devised by Armourcoat Ltd, which could then cut an accurate slot to accept a total of 5.6 km of customised metal extrusion to create the individual panels which make up the cocoon surface. The result is a vast, endless canvas that changes with the shifting light of the day, helping to create an extraordinarily dynamic spatial experience for visitors to a reinvigorated museum.

Sustainability issues

The collection spaces within the cocoon required particular internal environmental conditions of 17 °C and 45 per cent relative humidity. The sprayed concrete shell and reinforced concrete floor slabs created an inherently stable environment by the exposing of thermal mass to the internal environment. This dramatically minimised the energy loading for the building and thereby greatly reduced CO_2 emissions.

Right
The new and the
old

Below left
Interior sketch

Below right
Section through
cocoon

The cocoon is insulated at its outer surface, thereby enabling the internally facing structure to remain at a relatively constant condition. Internal environments are created by air-conditioned ventilation systems, which closely control temperature and humidity levels in the collections. Once the structure is at room temperature, the absorbed energy surrounds the collection; even if the ventilation system is switched off the collection will remain at a stable storage temperature for many hours.

To achieve the desired collection conditions within the building, the museum's estate-wide district heating and cooling systems were utilised. The museum has tri-generation central CCHP system. The design team worked closely with the museum's engineers in the development of suitable energy sources for the building that would maximise CO_2 reduction benefits by deploying desiccant drying in summer and adiabatic humidification in winter.

The contractors enthusiastically engaged with the museum and design teams' environmental considerations with a rigorous waste policy. Material take-back schemes were specified and all waste was segregated for recycling and recovery by the contractors. Water run-off on site was closely controlled because of the site's proximity to the museum's wildlife garden.

To overcome the inherent difficulties of the west-facing atrium, the space is considered an 'outside space' for air permeability purposes. The internal atrium glazing and cocoon shell therefore become the external envelope and had to achieve a leakage rate of 5 m³/h per m² at an internal to external pressure difference of 50 Pa. Additionally, the IPM requirements particular to this scheme demanded that collections areas and key science areas be tested on a room-by-room basis. This required the contractors to work to close tolerances and demanded excellent workmanship.

Energy data

Gross floor area	16,000 m^2

Predicted annual energy consumption	kg CO_2/m^2/yr
Thermal usage: space and water heating 880 MWh	10.5
Regulated electrical usage 1,465 MWh	39.4
Total	49.9*

* Does not include non-regulated energy usage (see notes on page 256)

Project team

Client	Natural History Museum
Structural engineer	Arup
Services engineer	Fulcrum Consulting
Quantity surveyor	Turner and Townsend
Project manager	Manly Development Services
Main contractor	BAM Construct UK
Concrete subcontractor	Shotcrete (sprayed concrete), Getjar (RC frame)

Building data

Area	16,000 m^2 arranged across 8 floors
Development cost	£78 million
Construction period	110 weeks (main contract)
Year completed	2009

EXPLANATORY NOTES TO THE CASE STUDIES

Regulated and non-regulated energy

The consumption of energy from mains gas and electricity as regulated by Part L of the Building Regulations is defined as the 'regulated energy' usage. This includes energy used for building services, space heating and cooling, lighting, water heating and ventilation. An estimate for the occupant energy consumption, for example for the provision of restaurants and IT services, is termed the 'non-regulated energy' usage. For the most part, the building services provision in the design has little or no influence over the occupant energy consumption, although this figure may be quite large and difficult to predict.

Where no provision has been included for non-regulated energy consumption, this has been indicated in the energy data tables.

Energy consumption data

All the energy data shown in the case studies is based on predicted or estimated values, which is common practice at present. The benefits of an efficient, low-energy design building may possibly be negated if the end-user simply ignores the low-energy systems provided. Post-occupancy evaluation of end-user energy usage is vital, and will be essential for better long-term energy management.

Conversion factors

Gas	kWh to kg CO_2	× 0.19
Electricity	kWh to kg CO_2	× 0.43

ABBREVIATIONS

AECB	Association for Environment Conscious Building, the Sustainable Building Association
BMS	building management system
BRE	Building Research Establishment
BREEAM	Building Research Establishment Environmental Assessment Method
BSA	blastfurnace slag aggregate
BSRIA	Building Services Research and Information Association
CCC	Centre for Cement and Concrete (University of Sheffield)
CCHP	combined cooling, heat and power
CHP	combined heat and power
CIBSE	Chartered Institution of Building Services Engineers
CSR	corporate social responsibility
Defra	Department for Environment, Food and Rural Affairs
EAF	electric arc furnace
FES	fabric energy storage
FSC	Forest Stewardship Council
GGBS	ground granulated blastfurnace slag
GHG	greenhouse gas
GIFA	gross internal floor area
GLA	Greater London Authority
GPS	global positioning system

GRC	glass-reinforced concrete
GRP	glass-reinforced plastic
GSHP	ground source heat pump
GWP	global warming potential
ICF	insulating concrete formwork
IES	IES thermal modelling software
IMechE	Institution of Mechanical Engineers
IPM	integrated pest management
LOI	loss on ignition
M&E	mechanical and electrical
MIT	Massachusetts Institute of Technology
MVHR	mechanical ventilation with heat recovery
ODP	ozone depletion potential
OJEU	Official Journal of the European Union
OPC	ordinary Portland cement
PFA	pulverised fuel ash
PFI	Private Finance Initiative
PIR	passive infrared
RCA	recycled concrete aggregate
SAP	Standard Assessment Procedure
SBEM	simplified building energy model
SSSI	Site of Special Scientific Interest
TAS	TAS thermal modelling software
TRADA	Timber Research and Development Association
TROBI	Tree Register of the British Isles
VOC	volatile organic compound

BIBLIOGRAPHY

Useful publications

Anderson J. and Shiers D., *The Green Guide to Specification* (4th edition), Wiley-Blackwell, 2009.

Barnard N., *Dynamic Energy Storage in the Building Fabric*, Technical Report TR9/94, BSRIA, 1995.

Berge B., *The Ecology of Building Materials* (2nd edition), Architectural Press, 2009.

BRE, *Recycled Aggregates*, BRE Digest 433, BRE Press, 1998.

BRE, *Standard U-values*, BRE Digest 108 (Revised 1991), BRE Press, 1991.

BSRIA, *Air Tightness Testing*, Technical Note TN 19/2001, BSRIA, 2003.

BSRIA, *Environmental Rules of Thumb*, Technical Note TN 12/99, BSRIA, 2000.

BSRIA, *Environmental Code of Practice for Buildings and their Services*, Code of Practice 6/99, BSRIA, 1999.

The Carbon Trust, *Energy and Carbon Conversions*, Fact sheet CTL018. 2008 Update, London: Carbon Trust, 2008.

The Carbon Trust, *Energy Use in Offices*, Energy Consumption Guide 19 (ECG 19), Carbon Trust, 2003.

CIBSE, *Testing Buildings for Air Leakage* (TM23), CIBSE, 2000.

CIBSE, *Guide A – Environmental Design*, CIBSE, 1999.

CIRIA, *Concrete Pressure on Formwork*, CIRIA Report 108, London: CIRIA, 1985.

The Concrete Centre, *Thermal Mass Explained*, TCC, 2009.

The Concrete Centre, *Energy and CO_2: Achieving targets with concrete and masonry*, TCC, 2006.

The Concrete Centre, *Thermal Mass: A concrete solution for the changing climate*, TCC, 2005.

DFES, *Acoustic Design of Schools – A design guide*, Building Bulletin 93 (BB93), The Stationery Office, 2003.

Dunster B., Simmons C. and Gilbert B., *The ZED Book*, Taylor and Francis, 2008.

Feilden Clegg Bradley Studios, *The Environmental Handbook*, Right Angle Publishing, 2007.

Hall K. (ed.), *Green Building Bible*, volume 1, Green Building Press, 2007.

Hammond G. and Jones C., *Inventory of Carbon and Energy*. University of Bath, 2008.

Orton A., *The Way We Build Now: Form, scale and technique*, Taylor and Francis, 1987.

Smith P.F. *Architecture in a Climate of Change*. Oxford: Architectural Press, 2006

Woolley T., Kimmins S., Harrison P. and Harrison R., *Green Building Handbook*, E&FN Spon, 1997.

Standards

BES 6001. *Responsible Sourcing of Construction Products* (BRE Environmental and Sustainability Standard).

BS 882:1992. *Specification for Aggregates from Natural Sources for Concrete* [see BN EN 12620].

BS 4027:1996. *Specification for Sulfate-Resisting Portland Cement*.

BS 3892-1:1997. *Pulverized-fuel Ash. Specification for Pulverized-fuel Ash for Use with Portland Cement* [see BS EN 450-1:2005+A1:2007].

BS 4449:2005+A2:2009. *Steel for the Reinforcement of Concrete. Weldable Reinforcing Steel. Bar, coil and decoiled product. Specification*.

BS 6566:1985 [see BS EN 636:2003].

BS 8110-1:1997. *Structural Use of Concrete. Code of Practice for Design and Construction* [see BS EN 1992-1-1:2004].

BS 8500-1:2006. *Concrete. Complementary British Standard to BS EN 206-1. Method of Specifying and Guidance for the Specifier*.

BS EN 197 Series:2000. *Cement. Composition, Specifications and Conformity Criteria for Common Cements*.

BS EN 313-2:2000. *Plywood. Classification and Terminology. Terminology*.

BS EN 314-2:1993. *Plywood. Bonding Quality Requirements.*

BS EN 413-1:2004. *Masonry Cement. Composition, Specifications and Conformity Criteria.*

BS EN 450-1:2005+A1:2007. *Fly Ash for Concrete. Definition, Specifications and Conformity Criteria.*

BS EN 635-1:1995. *Plywood. Classification by Surface Appearance. General.*

BS EN 636:2003. *Plywood. Specifications.*

BS EN 1992-1-1:2004 (Eurocode 2). *Design of Concrete Structures. General Rules and Rules for Buildings.*

BS EN 12620:2002+A1:2008. *Aggregates for Concrete.*

BE EN 15167-1:2006. *Ground Granulated Blast Furnace Slag for Use in Concrete, Mortar and Grout. Definitions, Specifications and Conformity Criteria.*

BS EN ISO 6946:2007. *Building Components and Building Elements. Thermal Resistance and Thermal Transmittance. Calculation method.*

BS EN ISO 9001:2008. *Quality Management Systems. Requirements.*

PICTURE CREDITS

Preface Nigel Rigden
Introduction Sarah Blee
Part I: Technology
Amos Goldreich/Feilden Clegg Bradley Studios, page 80 (left)
BRC, page 31
Castle Cement, pages 5, 6, 7, 8 (top)
Celsa, pages 29, 30
Charcon Precast Products, pages 24, 42
Chris Brink, page 78 (bottom)
Civil and Marine, pages 8 (bottom), 9, 10
Consolis Group, pages 44 (left), 46 (left)
David Barbour/BDP, page 4
David Bennett, page 46 (right)
Edward Cullinan Architects, page 62
Foggo Associates, page 76
Lignacite, page 22
Lindon Sear (UKQAA), page 11
London Concrete, page 40
MJP Architects, page 79 (top, bottom)
Natasja Jovic, page 44 (right)
Outinord, page 80 (right)
Patrick Gartman, page 82 (bottom)
Patrick Phillipaj, page 82 (top)
Rod Dorling, page 77
Tarmac, page 43 (top)
The Concrete Centre, pages 43 (bottom), 52, 53, 64, 67, 73, 74, 75, 79 (middle)
UPM-Kymmene, pages 34, 36, 37
Urban Splash, page 78 (top)

Part II: Case studies
Drawings and plans are reproduced with the kind permission of the architectural practices.
House in Highgate Cemetery / Eldridge Smerin, pages 94-101: Lyndon Douglas
Abito apartments / BDP, pages 102-107: Martine Hamilton Knight, 102; David Barbour/BDP, 105-107
Arabianvillat / Ark House, pages 108-113: Jussi Tiainen
Jesuit Residence / Elder and Cannon, pages 114-119: Keith Hunter
Clay Fields / Riches Hawley Mikhail Architects, pages 120-123: Nick Kane
'New Forest House' / Perring Architecture & Design, pages 124-133: Nigel Rigden, 124, 127, 128, 132 (top left and right), 133; Darren Bray, 130 (left); Wendy Perring, 130 (right); PAD, 132 (bottom)

House by a lake / Clancy Moore Architects, pages 134-139: Alice Clancy
106 Tooley Street / Allford Hall Monaghan Morris, pages 140-147: Tim Soar/Allford Hall Monaghan Morris
The Katsan Building / White Architects, pages 148-153: Natasja Jovic, 148, 150 (top), 153; Åke E:son Lindman, 150 (bottom)
11 Ducie Street / BDP, pages 154-161: Martine Hamilton Knight, 154, 156 (right), 157; David Barbour/BDP, 156 (left), 158, 160, 161
Heelis / Feilden Clegg Bradley Studios, pages 162-169: Simon Doling/Feilden Clegg Bradley Studios
The Yellow Building / Allford Hall Monaghan Morris, pages 170-175: Tim Soar/Allford Hall Monaghan Morris
New Street Square / Bennetts Associates, pages 176-183: Peter Cook, 176, 179, 180; Bennetts Associates, 182; Edmund Sumner, 183
One Coleman Street / Swanke Hayden Connell, pages 184-189: Stanhope plc
Jubilee Library / Bennetts Associates, pages 190-195: Peter Cook, 190, 195; James Brittain, 193 (left); LCE Architects, 193 (right)
Westminster Academy / Allford Hall Monaghan Morris, pages 196-201: Tim Soar/Allford Hall Monaghan Morris, 196, 198, 199 (left); Matt Chisnall/Allford Hall Monaghan Morris, 199 (right); Rob Parrish/Allford Hall Monaghan Morris, 201
York St John University / Rivington Street Studio, pages 202-209: Sarah Blee
St Benedict's School / Buschow Henley, pages 210-217: David Grandorge
St Marylebone School / Gumuchdjian Architects, pages 218-223: Ben Blossom, 218; Morley von Sternberg, 221 (top, bottom right); Richard Davies, 221 (bottom left), 223
The Potterrow development / Bennetts Associates, pages 224-229: Keith Hunter, 224, 227 (top, bottom right), 229; Bennetts Associates, 227 (bottom left)
Naturum Höga Kusten / White Architects, pages 230-235: Johan Fowelin
The Market Place Theatre / Glenn Howells Architects, pages 236-241: Chris Hill
The new herbarium and library wing / Edward Cullinan Architects, pages 242-249: Edward Cullinan Architects
Darwin Centre / C.F. Møller Architects, pages 250-255: Torben Eskerod, 250, 253, 255; C.F. Møller Architects, 254

INDEX